Classic
Spirits
of the world

A COMPREHENSIVE GUIDE

GORDON BROWN

Classic
Spirits
of the world

A COMPREHENSIVE GUIDE

GORDON BROWN

Abbeville Press Publisher
New York London Paris

First published in the United States of America in 1996 by
Abbeville Press

First published in 1995 in the United Kingdom by
Prion Books Limited,
Imperial Works, Perren Street,
London NW5 3ED

Text copyright © 1995 Gordon Brown
Copyright © Multimedia Books Limited 1995

Printed and bound in Singapore

First edition
2 4 6 8 10 9 7 5 3

ISBN 0-7892-0165-8
D.L.TO: 1243–1995

Contents

Publisher's Foreword

When Gordon Brown died in November 1994, he had just completed the manuscript of *Classic Spirits of the World*. Gordon felt passionately about this book and had devoted more than a year to the task of documenting the best-known spirits and tracking down little-known but worthwhile drinks. Prion wishes to thank all the writers, manufacturers and individuals who helped Gordon in his quest for information and pictures. We also wish to thank Jim Murray and Andy Henderson for their assistance with the captions to the pictures.

Preface

Spirits have benefited enormously from the dramatic increase in interest in wines worldwide in the past couple of decades. In a non-wine-producing country like the UK this has had a profound educational and cultural effect. Once consumers were locked reflexively into the received wisdom that, whatever you chose from a wine list, it had better be French; now they have been exposed to an increasing number of delicious, well-made and, mostly, fairly priced wines from countries like Italy, Spain, New Zealand and, more recently, Chile, South Africa and Australia.

It taught us that, after all, we did not know all there was to know about these things and the hunt was on for information about what we liked and others that we might like. Specialist magazines were established and every newspaper took on a wine writer. We learned about wines, became curious about them and, most importantly, learned how to appraise them.

What has been clear for a number of years now is that we are following a similar path with regard to spirits. Those specialist wine magazines now carry many articles on spirits, popular and obscure, and, unprecedentedly, there are spirits columns in several national newspapers, including my own in *The Guardian*. Having got the hang of wine, our curiosity and capacity to judge spirits are already in place; we now need the information. Part of the problem is the greater extent to which with spirits it comes down to brands, as opposed to types, and globally distributed brands at that. When your brand sells five million cases a year and you want to sell six million, the important thing becomes your name and not what your product is. Many (but by no means all) large brand owners would not mind if you thought their cognac were a whisky as long as you kept on buying the brand name.

Since the ultimate choice is always our own, this does not really matter, except that when it comes to information it tends to be about the brands and it can be difficult to get details of the product-category.

With *Classic Spirits of the World*, I have set out to supply some of this information: what the products are, how they differ from those alongside, what the best-known brands (and some of the worthwhile unknowns) are, and so on. Can you tell a French Napoleon brandy from a cognac? A real Russian vodka from one that merely sounds Russian? Pernod from Ricard? I have sought to answer these little queries that perennially drum at our minds and also to tell the stories behind the brands large and small.

Gordon L. Brown

Introduction

What are spirits?

When an organic substance ferments, it produces alcohol and when the alcohol is boiled, so that the vapour is collected and condensed, the alcohol is further concentrated. This, baldly, is what distillation is — concentration, or increasing, of alcoholic strength. A wine of 8% alcohol by volume condenses into distillate of 20% vol after being boiled off in a pot still; if it is boiled a second time the strength goes up to about 60% vol. Take the wholesome middle-cut of that run, missing out the poisonous first part and the watery final part, as distillers learned to do, and you have grape spirit, eau de vie, brandy of about 70% vol. The volume of the liquid reduces substantially too; a litre of brandy is the distillation of nine litres of wine.

Spirits at this kind of strength carry many of the aromas and flavours of the original plant or fruit from which they were obtained, but they also acquire an identity of their own. The appeal of spirits lies in their delivery of fruit and plant flavours but differently rendered with more complexity and intensity — and alcohol. High-strength alcohol loses its particularity but gains in smoothness of texture, hence the modern use of neutral alcohol in mixing drinks; add spirit and your fruit juice becomes zesty and silky.

The first-ever distillations may well have taken place as long ago as the third millennium BC in Mesopotamia when perfume-makers had a technique for isolating the scented oils of flowers and plants. Indeed there may well have been a dozen or more locations where widely different processes included elements of distillation. Two thousand years ago in Greece rudimentary oil distillates were produced by spreading a piece of leather across a vat bubbling over a fire and, as the contents condensed on the leather's underside, it was intermittently wrung out into a separate container.

Such distillation yielded solvents, unguents and so on for everyday life and had nothing to do with drinks. A fourth-century scientist named Zozimus wrote of a retort he had seen in Memphis, Egypt, that he described as a 'pelican', suggesting an ovoid body with the head and long beak indicating a dome and descending condenser pipe.

Irish whiskey in its most prototypical form not only could have been in existence by the sixth century AD but the clerics in the Irish monasteries may well have had a hand in the subsequent dissemination of distillation skills around Europe. There are indications that during the Dark Ages, from the sixth to the ninth centuries, the Irish monasteries were the repositories of the elements of civilisation swept away by marauding barbarians: reading and writing, the word of God, scientific study and with it, perhaps, the secrets of distillation.

From 1,000 AD when it was safe to travel again, Irish missionary monks went out into Europe to proselytise, founding more than 110 monasteries across the continent. They would have taken with them their capacity to make 'strong water 'and it is likely that whiskey-making crossed over into the south-west of Scotland at this time. Because of this early Celtic involvement in distillation and since Latin was the European *lingua franca* of science and scholarship, the universal Latin term *aqua vitae* is probably a translation from the Gaelic *uisce* (or *uisge*) *beatha* rather than vice versa as has long been

Barley is classified by the number of rows in each ear. The most common, two rows, is the variety favoured for malt whisky.

This harvest of Normandy apples is the inspiration for the local Calvados.

Dressed for an Australian winter; methodically pruning the vines in preparation for another season and a new vintage.

assumed. Soldiers of the English king Henry II's army encountered this *uisce* when they campaigned in Ireland in 1171 just as their counterparts were introduced to Dutch genever in Holland 400 years later.

The Arabs studied distillation and took their techniques with them on their military campaigns. When they conquered Sicily in the ninth century they distilled the grapes that grew there to make lamp-fuel and disinfectant for wounds. It was the Sicilians themselves who steeped fennel in it and made *tutone*, the first recorded anise-flavoured spirit-drink. The Arabs took distillation into the southern part of what is now Spain when they overran it. Over the centuries following the reconquest of Spain between 1164 and 1492, knowledge of distillation moved slowly northwards. The people of Armagnac on the other side of the Pyrenees were making spirits from the 12th century through contacts with the south and were trading in eaux-de-vie with Dutch merchants by the start of the 1400s.

Farther north on the other side of the Gironde estuary, the wine growers around La Rochelle also traded with the merchants from northern Europe. In the 1500s the Dutch designed what would go on to become the classic cognac pot still, so that the French could distil the wine *in situ* prior to the merchants' visits. This meant a ten-fold increase in the *brandewijn* — the burnt wine — that could be taken back to Holland on each trip.

As is explained in more detail elsewhere in the book, alcohol was more medicinal potion in medieval times than leisure drink. Therapeutic herbal infusions in badly made alcohol tasted dreadful and, despite the conviction people often have that the nastier the medicine tastes, the better it is probably for them, additives were steadily introduced to make draughts more palatable. Even when leisure drinking of spirits became fully fledged, fruit and spice flavourings were usually added to mask the off aromas and tastes of bad alcohol.

By the 16th century, distillation was generally known in Europe as far north as Scandinavia and as far east as Russia. In the 1600s, emigrants to America took distilling skills with them and produced brandy from local fruits and rum from molasses bartered from the sugar plantations in the Caribbean.

For a long time single distillation would have been the rule until it occurred to someone to see what happened if the process were repeated. Credit for this innovation, at least in the context of cognac, is given to the Chevalier de la Croix Marron, who had the idea in the mid-1500s of a second purifying boiling of his distillates.

Stills

The standard still at the time was the pot still, which was basically an enclosed kettle which narrowed towards the top to collect vapour driven off by boiling the contents. A downward pipe from the head of the still carried the vapour through cold water which caused it to condense and run into a receiving container. Copper was — and is — the best material because it scavenges certain impurities out of the alcohol. Improvements had been made since the earliest days of the crude alembics and pots, but it was still a laborious procedure loading up, boiling off, emptying dregs and recharging for the next run. Pot stills can only distil one batch at a time.

It was not until the late 1820s that a new form of still was invented which produced spirit in a continuous stream for as long as wine, beer or some such mildly alcoholic wash was fed into it. It was called the continuous, or column, or patent, or, latterly, Coffey still and consisted of two columns, one of which had steam rising and wash descending through successive 'storeys' inside. The steam stripped out the alcohol from the wash and carried it over to the second column where it circulated until it could condense at the required strength.

The benefits of the continuous still were cheaper and purer spirit, the latter due to the higher distillation strengths that were possible using it. The continuous still was invented by Robert Stein, a relative of the Scotch whisky Haigs (qv), and first went into commercial production in Cameronbridge distillery in Fife, Scotland. Aeneas Coffey, a Dublin Excise officer who had attended a demonstration of the new still, took the idea and developed it further. It was Coffey's version of the continuous still that eventually caught on worldwide, although ironically he never received a single order from any of the Irish distillers who regarded him as a mountebank for compromising the craft of whiskey distilling.

From this point on, the alternatives open to distillers were to use the labour-intensive pot still which carried the fragrances and flavours of the raw materials, or the faster, cheaper continuous still with its potential for high-strength, pure but tasteless spirit.

This old alambique from Périgueux in the Dordogne comes from the days when *bouilleurs* (itinerant distillers) travelled from site to site with portable stills.

Below: This German brandy still, from 1892, has feet depicting various 'guardian' animals, no doubt to banish evil spirits.

Range of spirits

Above: Preparing the botanicals for Bombay Gin

Top: 'Turning the grain', in the drying sheds of Glenfiddich, prevents the little germinating rootlets knotting. The use of the wooden shiel avoids bruising.

Whisk(e)y, vodka, genever, gin, some schnapps and akvavit derive mainly from grain and it is a kind of beer or ale which is made for distillation into spirit. Specific grains are sometimes important. Malt whisky (Scotch and Japanese) and genever are made from malted barley; best vodka and certain Canadian blending whiskies from rye; Finnish vodka comes from wheat, and German schnapps mostly from corn; Japanese shochu from rice. Some Polish and Russian vodkas come from potatoes. The English styles of gin depend on juniper and other botanicals that flavour it. Since these are macerated and then redistilled, all that is required initially is clean, neutral spirit irrespective of the base from which it has been made.

Most people regard brandy as referring to grape brandy and as such it is distilled from wine, in turn usually taken to mean grape wine.

Rum and cane-spirit, including the Brazilian cachaça, are made mostly from sugar- or beet-molasses, with a small proportion of rum being produced direct from cane juice.

There is no mystery regarding the source materials from which fruit brandies are made, other than the fact that many are named in different languages. These unsweetened distillates of fermented juices or liquors from the myriad fruits that grow on the planet tend to bear the name appropriate in the countries where the best examples of their kind were produced. Kirsch, framboise and slivovitz, respectively from cherries, raspberries and plums, are examples of names that have become generic to the appropriate fruit spirits irrespective of where they are distilled.

Proof and alcohol by volume

The term 'proof' as an indicator of alcoholic strength derived from the early use of gunpowder in testing spirits. With no prior knowledge of the possible strength of a given distillate, an operator would mix the spirit with gunpowder and attempt to light it. If the mixture did not ignite, the spirit was underproof; if it lit and burned steadily this was 'proof' of a recognised level of alcoholic strength. However, if it exploded the operator (or his next-of-kin) could report the distillate as overproof and recommend further dilution with water.

Both the USA and the UK have used so-called proof systems of expressing alcoholic strength but it did not help that they were different from each other; 100% proof in the USA is only 87.7% British proof. US proof was at least related to strength by volume, being exactly double the latter but British proof was based on an abstruse calculation based on the relative volumes of alcohol and water at a temperature of 51° Fahrenheit (as opposed to Celsius, which the outside world might more easily have understood). The Gay-Lussac system expressed alcohol as a percentage of content in a liquid and happily this means of measurement is fast becoming universal. Note, however, that the Germans and Russians occasionally like to throw in the occasional expression of percentage by weight.

In these health-conscious days the spirits category plunges low down the strength-scale to include light schnapps and liqueurs of often only 17% and 18% vol alcohol. For this book I have listed only the best-known brands. I have given alcoholic strengths in percentage volume where available and/or proof. Most whiskies/whiskeys are 40% or 43% vol, although high strength is a quality-indicator with bourbons; most controlled-appellation cognacs, armagnacs and brandies are 40% vol, as is the classic Moscow-style of vodka; Polish vodkas and Caribbean rums vary quite widely, some of them very strong; and Western high-volume mixer vodkas tend to be 37.5% vol.

Above: The first trickle of eau de vie is a crystal clear liquid, nearly double the strength of the finished, aged and bottled cognac.

Left: Torres was the first to introduce the quality factor of cold fermentation in stainless steel to Spain.

In countries like Russia and Poland over the past 50 years and more, there have been no brand names in the Western sense. The state has been the brand and the main label terms have been product descriptions. Nonetheless, I have used these latter terms as brand names to differentiate the wide range of vodkas produced in these countries.

Whiskey

WHISKEY IS RELATED TO VODKA, AKVAVIT AND A NUMBER OF OTHER SPIRITS in that it is made from grain but an important distinguishing feature of whiskey is that it is aged, often for very long periods, in barrels, usually made of oak. The barrels endow much of the distinctive aroma, flavour and the smooth texture of whiskey. Beyond these common aspects, other details of whiskey styles depend on where and how they are made. (On the matter of spelling, by convention 'whisky' indicates Scotch and Canadian, and 'whiskey' most other things, including generic references. See Factfile for further details.)

In the world at large, whiskey tends to be associated with Scotland, although the spirit probably originated in Ireland and the first whiskey to have a presence in countries around the globe was Irish. However, when cognac succumbed to phylloxera in the 1870s and vanished from the world's tables and bars, Scotch was able to make a grand entrance and it has stayed centre stage ever since. There are, in fact, other countries which make national styles of whiskey but which allow for regional variation and individuality of house style by the manufacturers.

The original Scotch whisky is malt, produced from malted barley which is dried over peat-fuelled fires giving it a smoky, peaty finish. Quieter grain whisky is produced for blending with the malts to make the famous brands like Ballantine's and Chivas Regal, which have become household names everywhere.

Ireland, too, has a range of both malt and blended styles but Irish malts are dried in sealed kilns away from any peat influences. This means the prevailing whiskey style is malty but, unlike Scotch, non-smoky. It is also that little bit smoother in texture from a third distillation.

Canadian whisky had its beginnings in the early distilling efforts of Scots and other immigrants but it evolved its own distinctive light, subtle and often sweet-edged national style from sophisticated blending techniques which make the best of the prevalent rye and other grains used.

Kentucky and Tennessee whiskeys in the USA are made from Indian corn and have a full-blooded, distinctive wood, toffee and vanilla style partly fostered by the law that requires barrels for ageing the whiskey to be used only once. Even the very best bourbons and Tennessee whiskeys have these exuberant characteristics, the latter showing a touch more silkiness in their finish due to a detail of their production.

Japanese whisky is perhaps still evolving but it is already showing its own elegant and well-thought-out adjustments away from the Scottish style that was the foundation of its national industry in the 1920s. Long dependent on imports of bulk malt from Scotland to lend gravitas to its whiskies, Japanese blenders have come to show flair and acumen in understanding their own products and the particularity they can offer.

Other countries produce whiskeys, some of them, like India, in considerable volume, others, like New Zealand, Turkey, Germany and suchlike, in ones and twos. Or a brand may stand alone and so enjoy an element of novelty value, like the colourless 'white' whiskey made in the Isle of Man, off the west coast of England.

Whiskey no longer needs to be Scotch or Scotch-styled to achieve credibility in consumers' eyes. Non-Scotch whiskey styles have been increasing their market share in numerous countries for some time now and look like continuing to do so in the future.

The finest whisky-making barley is grown in fields close to Elgin in Scotland's Speyside, although Scottish distillers also import this sturdy grain from mainland Europe and Ireland.

Scotland

Inverary Castle, complete with Disneyesque turrets, is one of the more dramatic sites in the wild and rugged western Highlands. It is the home of the Clan Campbell who, inevitably, have a blended whisky named after them.

IN SCOTLAND, WHISKY HAS ITS ORIGINS IN THE HEATHER ALE BREWED IN PREHISTORIC TIMES. Archæologists on an island off the west coast found dregs in a pottery shard from 2,000 BC and, after analysing them, scientists made a fresh brew. It was all a bit grassy, so when simple distillation techniques came along (probably from Ireland) a long-term flavour-improvement programme began.

Whisky has been intrinsic to Gaelic life over the centuries and homesteads had primitive stills in place just as we have coffee pots in the kitchen today. Whisky was made in the *ad hoc* quantities that were needed by households, and farmers made it on a part-time basis, some of it for sale. For long it was rudimentary and to make high-quality spirit would often need four distillations.

From 1707, when Scotland was first governed from London, continued insensitivity in fixing excise duties for whisky (as opposed to English gin) enabled illicit distillation to flourish. The problem was never going to be easily resolved because the smugglers, who lived amid the finest raw materials, made very good whisky and the licensed distillers, who had to cut so many corners in order to pay the crippling duties, did not. In the late 18th century there were eight licensed distilleries in Edinburgh and 400 unlicensed stills.

The Excise Act of 1823 was the common-sense watershed that enabled the industry to take shape. Distilleries were built, Robert Stein invented the continuous still (which was faster and cheaper — but not better — than the traditional pot still) and the first efforts in blending malts and grains were all introduced in the following decades. Bottle sales made whisky more easily accessible, and then, in the 1870s, when phylloxera destroyed the Cognac vineyards, demand for Scotch boomed. Blends were more finely honed, with foreign consumers in mind, to be milder and consistent, and brands like Johnnie Walker, Buchanan's and others came into being. There was no challenge from the Irish, who refused to recognise grain spirit as whiskey until after the 1909 Royal Commission's decision that both pot and continuous stills were eligible to produce whisk(e)y.

The character of Scotch whisky has been determined historically by the aromas and flavours drawn from the barley that grew in the fields, the peat fuel used in smoky fires to stop the germination, and the yeasts that fermented the beer. It is only in the past 200 years that studying still shapes and cask types has enabled finessing of the spirits. In turn, the merit, distinctiveness and renown of Scotch whisky today derive from its rich and varied pot-still malt spirit.

Malt whisky production in Scotland is divided into the following four geographic areas: Highland, Lowland, Islay and Campbeltown.

Highland malts from the northern half of the country are mostly elegant and well flavoured but this is a large category and there are a number of sub-groups. The main ones are Speyside malts, which have an extra dimension of rich, sweet complexity, and the smoky, spicy and concentrated Island malts.

Lowland malts produced in the southern part of the mainland are light, soft, sweetish and understated.

Islay is an island off the west coast whose traditional style of malt is pungent, smoky, medicinal and intense in flavour. Three of the island's seven working distilleries, however — Bunnahabhain, Bruichladdich and Bowmore — now produce malt in gentle, subtle styles.

Campbeltown in the south west, which has only two remaining distilleries, yields salty, spicy, full-flavoured malts.

Grain whiskies are not divided into zones since their place of origin has no influence on their character. The principal role of grain spirit (made in continuous stills) is in the making of blended whiskies where they smooth off and complement the more vivid malts. There are two branded grain self-whiskies.

To make malt whisky, barley is soaked and left to germinate. At a critical point, when the starch has turned to sugar, the germination is stopped by drying the barley, traditionally with a peat-fuelled fire which imbues it with smoky fragrance. Modern maltsters dry with neutral heat and introduce measured amounts of peat smoke to aromatise the barley to the customer's requirement. Up to five parts per million represents light peating, more than 30 parts makes for a heavy classically phenolic Islay peating. Since the smokiness in the barley passes over in the distillation to the final spirit, the degree of peating — or peat reek — is an important stylistic decision.

The dried barley, peated or not, is called malt and is milled and mashed with hot water. The resulting sugary wort ferments to make a beer which is distilled twice in copper pot stills. Distilleries usually install pairs of stills, the larger wash still being used for the first distillation, the spirit still for the second and final distillate. As the condensate runs off the still the heart or centre cut is collected, rejecting the first part (foreshots), which is volatile and unpleasant, and the tail end (feints), which is practically water.

The eerie Cuillin Hills on the Isle of Skye are often mist-shrouded and make an imposing sight from the shores of Lock Slapin. Just beyond them is the revered Talisker distillery.

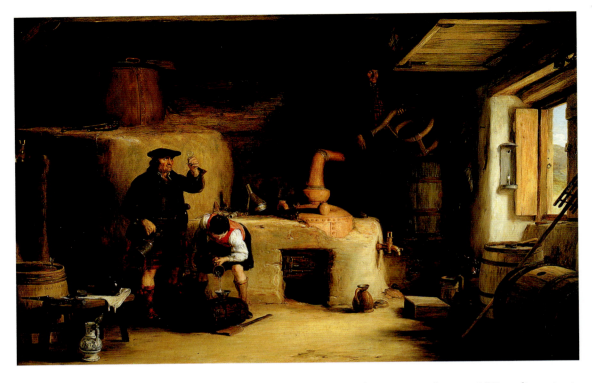

Above: Many 19th century oil paintings of both illicit and legal distillation were in the romantic style, although the truth was often different. This one, *The Whisky Still at Lochgilphead* (1819) was the creation of Sir David Wilkie (1785-1841).

Right: There are eight distilleries on Islay, seven of them working. There are, however, a lot more sheep than people.

Whisky must be aged in oak for at least three years but most matures for much longer. Casks which have previously held bourbon whiskey or oloroso sherry are widely used for ageing malts. Ex-bourbon oak endows woody characteristics, which allow a whisky's subtleties to show through, while ex-sherry wood puts a rich, sweet overlay of sherrywine flavour and aroma on to the existing oak and whisky elements . Both types of wood create complexity in a mature whisky, but sherrywood adds body and texture. There is much fine-tuning in wood management since casks may be used up to three times, each re-use making for subtler influences. Sherrywood can be used to 'finish' a whisky, *ie* a bourbon-matured malt is put into a sherry cask for the final ageing.

Grain whiskies offer less to build upon, so although they are fully aged in oak, there is little variation in their wood treatment. Any age statement made on a label must be that of the youngest whisky in the blend and in a good blend any age stated will be that of a grain whisky, since they need much less ageing than malts. It usually also means that the average age of the malts in the bottle is that much higher.

A good 'standard' blend has 30 to 40 malt and grain whiskies in it and up to 40% malt content; 45%, such as in Teacher's, is a high malt count. Standard blends do not have an age statement although, in 1994, Bell's was upgraded to an eight-year-old. Most de luxe blends have an age statement — 12 years old is typical — but both unknown brands with blends too young to merit description as de luxe, and long-established brands with magnificently mellow blends, often do not. To distinguish between them, be guided by the names you know and the prices asked.

Aberlour • Highland (Speyside) single malt and distillery. Aberlour was built in 1826, just a dozen years after the village itself, which was a planned community. The distillery was part of the construction bonanza that followed the Excise Act of 1823, making distilling viable as a business. The water supply had long been celebrated and was well known as having been used a thousand years ago for baptisms by a local cleric who was subsequently canonised as St Drostan. Today, spring water from nearby Ben Rinnes mountain is used for the whisky making. The business did well but the distillery burned down on two occasions; it happened once in the middle of the night but still the people of the village arrived at the gates to roll the barrels away from the flames. There are two pairs of stills dating from 1973.

Available aged in both sherry and bourbon oak, the whisky has a rich, sweetish elegance. Usually 10 years old. Recent special editions go back to 1964 and a series of millennium hogsheads is due for release in the year 2000. Aberlour is used in Clan Campbell blends (*qv*).

An Cnoc • Highland single malt formerly known by its distillery name of Knockdhu (*qv*) and re-named by its new owners, Inver House (*qv*).

Argyll • Brand which belongs to the Duke of Argyll and which is marketed in prestige locations, including duty-free outlets around the world as well as at his splendid seat, Inverary Castle. Argyll began as the 'house' whisky on the Queen Elizabeth II liner with Springbank single malt from Campbeltown (the Duke is chief of the Clan Campbell) in the pre-malt-boom days. Nowadays the Duke uses whiskies such as Aberlour from the House of Campbell group (of which he is a director) for his range. Available as 12-, 15- and 17-year-old single malts, standard and 12-year-old de luxe blends.

Auchentoshan • Lowland single malt and sister distillery to Bowmore and Glen Garioch (*qv*). It is set on the north bank of the Firth of Clyde, near Glasgow, and although a Lowland malt, Auchentoshan is made with Highland water from the Kilpatrick Hills to the north. The distillery has been in intermittent production since 1800, but recently Morrison Bowmore, a specialist whisky-broking and distilling firm, has revitalised the brand. The malt is lightly peated and the spirit triple distilled so there is a single set of three stills which vary in age from three to 30 years.

The whisky is soft and smooth as would be expected of a triple-distilled spirit and has its own fresh, floral and fruity character. Firm and slightly spicy. Usually available at 10 and 21 years old; used in the Rob Roy blends.

Auchroisk • Highland (Speyside) distillery that produces The Singleton single malt. In the 1960s, a Justerini and Brooks executive chanced upon a spring in a secluded ravine near Aberlour, so the company paid £5 million for it and the surrounding land; in 1975, construction of the new distillery of Auchroisk was completed on the site. Auchroisk (pronounced 'Ah-thrusk') produces lightly peated blending whisky for the J & B brand, but it was eventually discovered that the spirit was also a fine self-whisky, a bonus that could never have been planned in advance. The Singleton of Auchroisk is that whisky and it has already won a number of trophies.

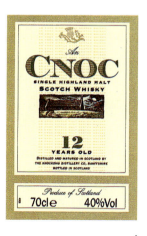

The Singleton is medium in weight, fruity and malty with some smoke and a fine mellow-texture. It is aged in bourbon wood with a sherry finish. Usually 10-12 years old from a single year of distillation, which is stated on the label.

Ballantine's • One of the world's biggest-selling Scotch whiskies, selling at two bottles every second. It had its origins in a modest licensed grocer's shop established in Edinburgh in the 1820s, and in 1895, the firm obtained the Royal Warrant to supply its whisky to Queen Victoria. After World War I new owners tackled the export market and all through the Prohibition period in the USA, James Barclay worked covertly and often in considerable danger to build sales contacts. As a result, after repeal, an enormous distribution network for Ballantine's whisky was already in place; aspiring Hollywood actor David Niven was on the staff at the time, subsequently to be remembered as the US agent's 'first and worst salesman'.

The whisky is blended at Dumbuck on the Firth of Clyde, near where former Formula One world motor-racing champion Jackie Stewart grew up. The security system for the great maturation warehouses containing 1.5 million casks is entrusted to flocks of highly territorial Chinese geese — the 'Scotch Watch' — which cut loose with the most appalling din at the slightest intrusion from the outside world. Ballantine employs a full-time gooseman to look after them. A large consignment of Ballantine's was on board the *SS Politician* when it ran aground on the island of Eriskay off Scotland *en voyage* to New Orleans in 1941, the incident on which the famous movie, *Whisky Galore* (*Tight Little Island* in the USA), was based. Miltonduff and Balblair distilleries contribute much of the Ballantine house style. Available as standard and de luxe up to (very rare) 30 years old.

Balvenie • Highland (Speyside) single malt and sister distillery to Glenfiddich (*qv*). In 1892, William Grant built his second distillery into the abandoned shell of New Balvenie Castle, designed by the Adam brothers. It was just four years after his first successful whisky-making venture on the Fiddich Burn, and Grant made use of old stills from Glen Albyn and Lagavulin distilleries he had acquired. Floor malting is still carried out at Balvenie (very rare indeed now on the Scottish mainland) supplying about 15% of the distillery's malt requirements. The peat used is hand cut locally, dried and seasoned before being used to fuel the malt kiln. Balvenie has four pairs of stills which are taller than those at Glenfiddich, so the whisky is different in style despite its being next door. Balvenie is big, sweet, rich and malty.

Available as a range of three: 10-year-old Founder's Reserve, 12-year-old Doublewood from bourbon and sherrywood casks, and 15-year-old from a single barrel.

Right: Balvenie Castle — although Balvenie distillery is built into the remains of a castle, the ancient building from which it takes its name stands detached and aloof.

Below: Many malts star in the make up of Ballantine's but the biggest star to sell it was David Niven.

John Begg • Blend established by the owner of Royal Lochnagar (*qv*), now a minor United Distillers brand, other than in Germany and the island of Madeira. Its advertising slogan, 'Take a peg o' John Begg', gave the brand a high profile for many years. Available as a standard blend.

Bell's • The brand-leading blended Scotch in the UK (but not Scotland), and number four brand in the world. In 1837, Arthur Bell began work as a travelling salesman for Thomas Sandeman's wine and spirits shop in Perth and, in 1851, he became a partner. Experiments in blending malt and grain whiskies were getting under way at the time and, in 1860, a change in the law allowed blending in bond. This prompted Bell to spend the next two years visiting as many distilleries as he could to taste their whiskies; as a result, his first blends went on sale in 1863. Malt whisky from Blair Athol distillery (*qv*) in Pitlochry is the heart of Bell's and its nutty, spicy characteristics come through in the final blend. There are 35 constituent whiskies in the Bell's make-up and, until recently, the malts were aged from five to 12 years.

In 1994, however, Bell's boosted the quality of their 'standard' blend to minimum eight years old and put an age statement on the label — the first time any whisky firm had done so. The move was to try to revitalise their own blended Scotch sales as well as those of the sector which has been losing market share to bourbon and whiskeys from other countries. The rest of the Scotch trade was left trying to decide how they were going to respond.

Ben Nevis • Highland single malt and distillery. It was long associated with 'Long John' McDonald, who built it in 1825 in the lee of Britain's highest mountain, Ben Nevis. He was a very tall man and, although the whisky he produced was called 'Dew of Ben Nevis', his own nickname was later used as a famous brand-name for the distillery's blended whisky. Ben Nevis was owned in the 1950s by Joseph Hobbs, who came to Scotland from Canada, became a distilling entrepreneur and set up a cattle ranch, complete with cowboys on horseback, in the glen near the distillery.

Ben Nevis is now owned by the Japanese whisky firm Nikka (*qv* Japan). There are two pairs of stills. A bottle of 63-year-old Ben Nevis recently changed hands for £2,000 and a 26-year-old has recently been available. Dew of Ben Nevis blend is available at four to 21 years old and occasional single malt vintages are bottled at cask strength, the broad style being light in peat and sweetish, with a grassy/spicy tone.

Ben Nevis distillery is found amid Scotland's most dramatic landscape and, in winter at Loch Eil, one of the most beautiful.

Black & White • James Buchanan's famous blended brand that featured the two Scots terriers, one black, one white, in its advertising. However, his first brand, blended for mildness and smoothness and already with an eye to attracting interest abroad, carried his own name — The Buchanan Blend. It had a plain black bottle with a white label and, after noticing that people were asking for the 'black-and-white whisky' he changed the name to Black & White, complete with the cute dogs. After several years selling Mackinlay's whisky by the barrel, Buchanan had opened his own first office in London in 1884 and, just a year later, secured a prestigious contract to supply the House of Commons of the UK Parliament. The blend he called, predictably, 'House of Commons', and the Buchanan arm of United Distillers continues to supply it to the MPs' bar to this day.

As whisky barons thrived, their empires included palaces to be proudly displayed. Sometimes, though, advertisements could be a little more subtle, even whimsical.

In 1899, he gained the Royal Warrant to supply Queen Victoria and in 1907 the Emperor of Japan granted a similar privilege. Buchanan was innovative in his publicity, having his whisky orders delivered to London customers by liveried draymen on smartly painted wagons pulled by splendid shire horses, and being among the earliest advertisers in newspapers. The brand has remained popular and today is one of the top dozen in the world. Available as a standard blend.

Black Bottle • Full-flavoured, slightly quirky blend with growing following in Scotland and elsewhere. The brand began in 1897 as the hobby of the Graham brothers in Aberdeen, who were tea-blenders. When friends asked to buy their creation it became a business but served only the local clientele in and around Aberdeen until recently, when ownership by Allied Distillers expanded its distribution potential. The brand's quality was tweaked upwards not long ago. Its core malt is Laphroaig (*qv*) and the bottle's shape is based on that of a pot still which smugglers used to call 'black pots'.

Bladnoch • Lowland single malt and distillery. Scotland's southern-most, set in the delightful south-western corner of the country. It was the last of a dozen or so distilleries which used to operate in the district and has itself now stopped production, although there is talk of it reopening as a working museum. Bladnoch dates from 1817 and stayed in the same family until 1938, when the distillery closed down. It passed into Northern Irish, then American, hands before being bought by United Distillers. Bladnoch is lightly peated. It is light and subtle in aroma and fills out to a degree on flavour, with a 'cut-grass' finish. Available, but stocks dwindling, at 10 years old.

Blair Athol • Highland single malt and distillery in Pitlochry, a pretty town where Robert Louis Stevenson wrote some of his short stories. It is one of today's few surviving distilleries from the 18th century, in this case 1798. The malt is lightly peat-smoked and is used in Bell's (*qv*), the UK's top-selling blend. The single pair of stills was supplemented by a second pair in 1973. Only spirit intended for sale as a self-whisky is matured in Blair Athol's old-fashioned traditional warehouses; the rest is sold on or stored elsewhere. Fresh and gently peaty with resonant aroma and flavour. Recently increased in age from eight to 12 years old.

cast-iron vat and a riveted still, remain in use. In 1938, Bruichladdich was bought by a group of North Americans keen to cater for the post-Prohibition market in the USA. They included Joseph Hobbs, a Scots Canadian who went on to own other Scottish distilleries and also established a cattle ranch beside the Caledonian Canal in the central Highlands.

A whispery, gentle malt with scarcely a trace of peat. Usually 10 years old but older versions are also available.

Bowmore • Single malt and distillery on the island of Islay off the west coast of Scotland. It was built in 1779, making it one of the oldest distilleries still in production in Scotland and it recently became the first Islay distillery to become wholly Japanese owned. At Bowmore close attention is paid to traditional production values, among which is the continued use of its own floor maltings, now very rare in Scotland. Manager James MacEwan brings other perspectives to the job; he has also been a whisky blender and a cooper in his time.

One of Bowmore's grain lofts served as a Coastal Command operations room during the last war, coordinating the movements of flying boats which flew U-boat-spotting patrols in the Atlantic. Queen Victoria liked the whisky and used to have supplies sent to Windsor Castle.

The whisky distilled in the four stills has attracted considerable fame and praise in the hands of the present owners, Morrison Bowmore, and has won a number of competition trophies. It does not have the full famous Islay pungency, tailoring its peatiness to a more accessible but still rich elegance. Usually available at 10 and 17 years old.

Bruichladdich • Single malt and distillery on the island of Islay. Bruichladdich is the lightest and least typical of the Islay whiskies famous for their medicinal pungency and concentration. The distillery was built in 1881, at a time when demand was heavy for component whiskies to make blended Scotch. Much of the original equipment, including a

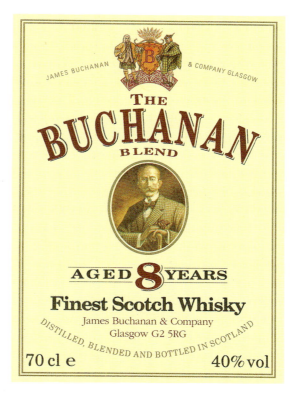

Top left: Once, whisky-making was a labour-intensive industry as this old line drawing of Bowmore distillery shows. But it is only in relatively recent years that directly firing the stills has been phased out.

Buchanan's • The original 'black and white' blended whisky — black bottle, white label — being sold by James Buchanan when he set up his sales office in London in 1884. 'The Buchanan Blend' eventually became 'Black & White' (*qv*) but the Buchanan name coexisted peacefully with it, carving out its own loyal markets abroad and contributing fully to the successful growth of the company. The brand does particularly well in Central and South America. The distillery especially associated with Buchanan's is Dalwhinnie (*qv*), once the highest above sea level in Scotland. Available as a 12-year-old de luxe.

Bunnahabhain • Islay single malt and distillery. Even today, Bunnahabhain's position on the north-east coast of the island of Islay off the Scottish mainland is isolated. It was a brand-new, self-contained community that was set up in 1881 when the distillery was founded. The whisky company had to build its own road to the site, and shops, houses and a school were all provided for members of staff and their families. It can be a wild spot; a rusting ship's hulk has lain on the rocks below the cliff since 1974.

Bunnahabhain (pronounced 'Boona-hav'n') is one of Islay's gentle malts, avoiding the powerful pungency associated with the island by collecting its water at source so that it does not pass through peat beds. An unusual aspect is that the water used is hard — just like another of Scotland's fine, subtle malts, Glenmorangie (*qv*). Both bourbon and sherry casks are used for maturation but the latter is carefully controlled to avoid masking the malt's natural delicacy. Ageing at the edge of the Atlantic inserts a certain marine saltiness into the final character. Available at 12 years old.

Burn Stewart • Brand name of a de luxe blend and a 'new' company in the Scotch whisky firmament. Formed in 1988 by a combination of experience, zeal and the right amount of venture capital, the company comprises an accomplished team already succeeding as independent whisky distillers with awards for business acumen and export achievement. Their core brand is Scottish Leader but they have also bought Deanston (*qv*) and Ledaig (*qv*) distilleries, a clutch of previously cobwebby whisky brands and new brands (like Burberry's 12-year-old blend) which are now being vigorously groomed for stardom. A particular asset is the broad-based inventory of mature whiskies they have acquired. Available at 12 years old.

Cameron Brig • Single grain from Cameronbridge distillery, which was the scene of a great leap forward in whisky making in the early years of last century. The first distillery on the site was built by the Haig family (*qv*) in 1813, but it was superseded by another in 1824 which produced Lowland malts from a single pair of pot stills. In 1827, however, a relative, Robert Stein, invented a continuous still and two were installed at Cameronbridge. They yielded lighter-flavoured but cheaper and more easily produced spirit and when Stein's design was improved upon by Aeneas Coffey, two more stills were added, this time of the latter type. Cameronbridge was thus able to produce a wide range of whisky styles, from highly flavoured malt to practically silent grain. (Most Irish whiskey today is similarly made at a single distillery — Midleton [*qv* Ireland], near Cork — by combining distilled fractions from different still-types.)

The distillery had its own gasworks to provide power for coppersmiths, engineers, joiners, a brass foundry, a sawmill and a cooperage. One of the Haig daughters held the community's Sunday School in one of the distillery granaries; it was dubbed the 'Kirk Loft', kirk being a Scottish term for church. Cameronbridge now solely produces grain whisky from Coffey stills. The pot stills were removed in the early years of this century and Stein-still production was discontinued in 1929. One of only two grain self-whiskies (the other is Invergordon, *qv*), Cameron Brig is light, sweet, smooth and muskily aromatic.

luck in whisky making over in the Fiddich Glen.) Cardhu had been supplying blenders John Walker of Kilmarnock with spirit for some time and the distillery was sold to them shortly before the Johnnie Walker blended brands were launched so successfully.

The whisky has floral, nutty aromas and spicy, gently smoky flavours; a suave, shapely malt. Available at 12 years old.

Chequers • Standard blend from United Distillers which is particularly popular in South America.

Chieftain Choice • Range of malts and blends from an independent broking and blending firm. There is a clutch of very old single malts which varies according to each bottling but which recently ranged from 21-year-old Speyside to 30-year-old Lowland.

Chivas Regal • Prestigious de luxe blend which consistently retains its perceived value as a gift or as a sophisticated, fine whisky. The Chivas brothers never owned a distillery and, although the brand is now safe in the arms of Seagram, the special merit of Chivas, *ie* excellence in blending, has remained the same as it was in the Aberdeen grocery shop where the business began. When Queen Victoria began

Below: Strathisla distillery, Keith — always one of Scotland's most glorious distilleries, it has just undergone a major upgrading programme to show visitors that this is the spiritual home of Chivas Regal.

Cardhu • Highland (Speyside) single malt and distillery. Cardhu is the malt at the heart of Johnnie Walker blends and began as an illicit whisky made by a tenant farmer to make ends meet. John Cumming leased Cardhu farm in 1811 and, as a skilled distiller, produced spirit on a part-time basis. He was convicted many times and some of the court judgments now hang framed on the wall of the distillery manager's office. His wife, Helen, was bright and capable and could always disguise the fermentation and mashing as bread-making if the excise officers called unexpectedly. Her acumen built up the business when it was eventually licensed and the Cummings' daughter-in-law, Elizabeth, kept up the momentum, eventually rebuilding the distillery. (The old worn-out stills she sold for £120 to a Mr Grant, who was about to try his

spending summers at Balmoral in the 1840s, it was the Chivas shop which regularly provisioned the estate and the Royal Warrant was granted in 1843. The Chivas shop offered a Harrods-like range of high-quality goods and services and among these was whisky-blending and supply in gallon-jars. Their own blend first appeared in the 1870s and sold all over Europe to a very classy clientele. Other blends followed; all were successful and included Chivas Regal which was introduced in 1891 and not long after was being exported to North America.

The core malt of Chivas Regal is from Strathisla distillery (*qv*) in Keith which, besides being outrageously beautiful, yields full-bodied, rich spirit; Glenlivet, Glen Grant (*qqv*) and Longmorn also play their part. There are 30-plus whiskies in the blend. Seagram has owned Chivas since 1949 and, in terms of all Scotch whisky, with sales of over three million cases a year, it is the fifth-top-selling brand in the world — ahead of many so-called volume brands — and the top de luxe. Available as 12- and 15-year-olds.

Clan Campbell • Blended range from the Pernod Ricard group, which owns the Aberlour (*qv*) and Edradour (*qv*) malt distilleries. The blending house of Campbell had been around since 1879 but the quality of the blends had fallen off by the time Pernod Ricard came along. When the Duke of Argyll, who is chief of the Clan Campbell, suggested to them that 'they were doing the impossible — making a poor Scotch whisky', and that their advertising lacked respect, they invited him on to the board to help relaunch the brand. Clan Campbell is now approaching the million-cases-a-year mark and could well be the fastest-growing Scotch blend in Europe. Available as standard and 12- and 21-year-old de luxes.

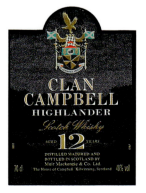

Claymore • Blend now owned by Whyte & Mackay but which was introduced in the late 1970s by its then-owners, Distillers Co. Ltd., as a 'cheapie'. These were brands specially created to sell at very cheap prices in order to drain some of the whisky lake overstock that lapped the Scotch industry's feet at the time. Some of the whisky used was really excellent, since it had matured for much longer than would have been

customary. Margins were cut to the bone and stockist customers who paid the fastest got the best prices. Claymore was one of the best known of those UK 'subsidiary' brands and, even after the industry overstock and the brands associated with it had disappeared, demand for Claymore held up. Whyte & Mackay have nurtured further growth, including some export development, and the brand is now in the UK top six.

Available as a standard.

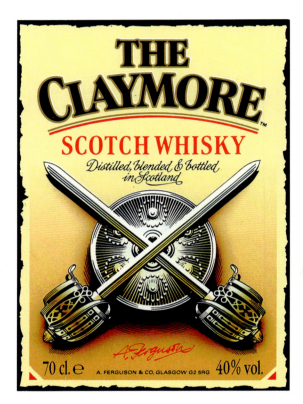

Cragganmore • Highland (Speyside) single malt and distillery. Cragganmore whisky is one of the Classic Malts range marketed by United Distillers and the distillery was built in 1869 by one of the ablest distillers of the day. John Smith had managed Macallan, Glenfarclas and Glenlivet distilleries (*qqv*) in his time but this was his own business where he gave free rein to his own ideas. Smith sold all the spirit he made and the product has continued to be prized as a blending malt; it is only in recent years that bottled Cragganmore has been available other than at the distillery door.

The whisky is aristocratic and even a little austere. Drier than most Speysides, complex but subtle in delivery. Available at 12 years old.

Crawford Three Star • Blend that has long been held in high regard in Scotland and, although it is widely exported now, was never groomed for international stardom by its owners, Whyte and Mackay. There used to be an excellent Five Star de luxe partner brand, but it is not presently in production.

Cutty Sark • International blend, more than half of its volume selling in the European Community and most of the rest in the USA. Like J & B, Cutty Sark is light in colour, due to the non-addition of caramel, and light in style. This 'new' whisky was created in the 1920s when Berry Brothers and Rudd, the London wine merchants, added it to their list of traditional whiskies. The Scottish-built sailing clipper *Ferreira* had just returned to British waters and, in reclaiming its original name, *Cutty Sark*, the ship suggested a topical and essentially Scottish name; the couplet from Robert Burns's narrative poem *Tam O'Shanter* — 'Whene'r to drink you are inclined/Or Cutty Sarks run in your mind…' — seemed to decide the matter.

The famous yellow label was a printer's error but when Berry's realised its greater visibility over the demure shade of cream that had been originally requested, they kept it. Cutty Sark was one of the 'Real McCoy' products supplied to Rum Row off New Jersey during Prohibition by Captain Bill McCoy

(*qv* Bacardi rum). This led to a visit by gangster Legs Diamond to Berry's shop in London in the late 1920s. He bought a consignment of Cutty Sark and took it away there and then in a fleet of taxis.

The blend is light in style but the whiskies used spend four to 10 years in American oak, most of which has held sherry. Available as standard and 12- and 18-year-old de luxes; also some special editions.

Dallas Dhu • Highland single malt, now rare, and former distillery now a museum. Dallas Dhu is a perfect Highland distillery preserved to show how the work was done and still has dwindling quantities of its whisky available for sale. It is an Ancient Monument, or rather, semi-ancient, since it was built in 1899. Dallas Dhu survived the Whisky Crash (in the year of its birth), two wars, the depression and a 1939 fire, but eventually succumbed to a limited water supply.

Below: Dallas Dhu is now a government-owned museum. Connoisseurs still lament the loss of a magnificent malt.

The whisky has good body and a silky, glyceral texture with botanical, slightly spicy zest. Last distillations were in 1983 and batches are still appearing intermittently, such as the recent 18-year-old and 1978 vintage.

*D*almore • Highland single malt and distillery. In 1839, Alexander Matheson, partner in the Jardine Matheson trading company in Hong Kong, bought Ardross farm, north of Inverness, had a still built and put in a tenant to make whisky from it. The Mackenzie family, who worked on Matheson's estate, took over the running of the distillery and eventually bought it. As early as the 1870s, the Mackenzies recognised the benefits of ageing the whisky in sherry casks and these were used for maturing their superior quality. Whyte & Mackay own Dalmore today but the Clan Mackenzie stag's-head emblem on the label remembers the family who fostered the business for almost a century. Dalmore is a major constituent of the Whyte & Mackay blends.

About a third of the whisky today is still finished in sherrywood prior to bottling, lending a sweet edge to its natural smoky, dry flavour and silky texture. Available at 12 years old.

*D*alwhinnie • Highland single malt and distillery. The whisky is one of the Classic Malts range from United Distillers and reveals how soft and fine whiskies can be despite (or because of) their deriving from the wildest and most exposed locations. Staff have been known to climb out of first-floor windows to get to work when snow drifts are deep in hard winters. Dalwhinnie stands at 1,073 feet / 327 metres above sea level, on droving routes from the north and west Highlands that used to take cattle to the markets in the Lowlands. Bonnie Prince Charlie and his men passed through in 1745 and the distillery lies on the line of General Wade's military road north.

The distillery was originally called Strathspey, and was built in 1898 high on the road through the Drumochter Pass in order to get as close as possible to the pure water in a small loch there. Due to the Whisky Crash of the time, the company went into liquidation and the distillery was eventually bought to produce spirit for Buchanan's Black & White brand (*qv*), hence the buildings' black-and-white colour scheme. The distillery is also an official weather station. Available as a fragrant, gently smoky 15-year-old.

*D*eanston • Highland single malt and distillery just outside Doune in Perthshire. The town is renowned for its 14th century castle (where the movie *Monty Python and the Holy Grail* was filmed) and 17th century pistol-making craftsmanship. The distillery is a former textile mill designed by Richard Arkwright, inventor of the spinning frame, and built on a bank of the Teith, still a fine salmon river, in 1785. Conversion to distilling took place in the 1960s and the water that had previously powered water turbines for the mill is now used for whisky making. Burn Stewart (*qv*), the present owners, acquired it in 1991.

The whisky is today unpeated and, in its bottled form, almost wine-like in its appearance and benignity of aroma and flavour which is soft, fruity and malty. Available at 12, 17 and 25 years old, these current whiskies were the work of the previous owner; it remains to be seen whether the Burn Stewart house style will evolve or alter in any way in the future.

The WHISKY of HIS ANCESTORS

ever made for a commercial product. It featured wild, grinning kilted figures stepping out of a portrait and dancing a jig; not terribly sophisticated but immensely attention-getting (and expensive) in its day. In 1895, a New York office had been opened. Both brothers became Members of Parliament — for different political parties. John was a Liberal (and later became Lord Forteviot), while Tom was a Conservative (and was later knighted).

The Dewar house style is distinctive and has a rich, full-bodied flavour. Available as standard (White Label) and 12-year-old de luxe (Ancestor).

Dewar • Dewar's White Label is the top-selling blend of Scotch in the USA and the sixth bestseller in the world. John Dewar was first to bottle quality Scotch with his own name as a guarantee of merit. He was a carpenter by trade but set up as a wine and spirit merchant in Perth in 1846. Whisky was customarily sold in kegs or stoneware jars but in the 1860s he began putting his blend into bottles. This brought down the unit cost and, at least to begin with, he picked up all the in-bottle repeat trade. The business prospered and grew. After Dewar died in 1880, his two sons, Thomas and John, took over and, in 1892, the former set off on a two-year business trip round the world during which he signed up new agents in the 26 countries he visited.

The brothers gained the Royal Warrant to supply Queen Victoria and built Aberfeldy distillery; since 1898, when it began production, the distillery's make became the heart of Dewar whiskies and remains so today. In the same year, Dewar's hired Thomas Edison to shoot the first moving-picture advertisement

Dimple • The famous dimpled bottle — Dimple in Europe and Pinch in America — contains de luxe blended whisky from the Haig company. The dimple bottle made its first appearance at the turn of the century as Dimple Scots and immediately attracted a lot of attention. Haig was involved in a continuing stream of prosecutions against imitators of the bottle which was supposed to be a protected design. It had been officially registered in 1919, only the second bottle after that of Coca-Cola to have such registration. Even perfume-manufacturers had to be pursued for using miniature dimple bottles for their fragrances. Eventually in 1952 the concept of exclusivity to Haig was awarded by the Scottish Court of Session. Labelling was always a problem due to the dimples and only finally solved with the recent introduction of silkscreen-printing the label direct on to the bottle. The wire netting around the bottle, always hand-applied, was originally to prevent the cork coming off if the whisky spent any time on board ship. Whisky from the Lowland malt distillery of Glenkinchie (*qv*) features strongly in the Dimple blend. Available as 12- and 15-year-old.

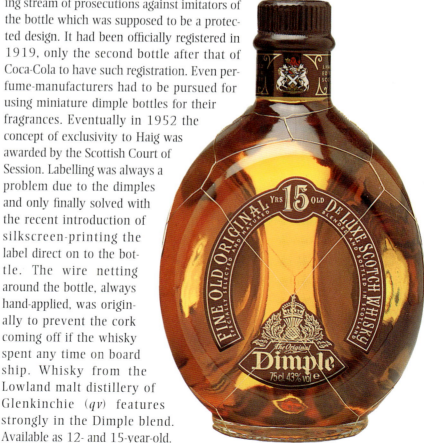

Dewars developed a distinctive line of advertising. Dimple relied on the distinction of their bottle to do the talking.

Dunhill • Fastest-growing super-premium Scotch in the world, created and marketed for this international luxury-goods brand which is applied to clothing, jewellery, tobacco and so on. Dunhill's core blend since 1981 was rich and round Old Master, but it was complemented in 1993 with a more robust and peaty Speyside style called Gentleman's Blend — perhaps the only Scotch whisky to describe itself as, 'distinctively British in character'. 1993 was the 100th year since Alfred Dunhill founded his business, so the Centenary Cask was issued — a blend based on 30-year-old Strathmill with a further 15 malts between 15 and 30 years old, each from distilleries that had been operating a century before. Each cask yields 30 cases of Scotch and costs £43,000, although included in the price are two first-class tickets from anywhere in the world to enable purchasers to fly to Strathmill to inspect their casks. About half of the 100 casks were sold in the first six months.

Available as Gentleman's Blend.

Edradour • Highland single malt and distillery, the smallest in Scotland. Edradour, near Pitlochry, is very pretty — all whitewashed buildings, picket fences, wooden bridges and a stream running through the middle. It has a production staff of three and, at 12 casks of 70% vol spirit a week, it takes Edradour a year to produce what a standard Scotch whisky distillery yields in a week. At 40 gallons, the stills are the smallest permissible by the Excise and just 2,000 cases are available each year.

The distillery licence dates from 1825, before which it produced illicit spirit, and it is the last of the Perthshire farm distilleries. It was originally called Glenforres, a name now used for a vatted malt brand in the House of Campbell portfolio. Edradour has a rich, spicy style with some smoke, toffee and fruit. Available as a 10-year-old.

Famous Grouse • Excellent blend from Gloag's that is the top seller in its native Scotland, number two in the UK (and still growing), and number nine in the world. Matthew Gloag was a butler in early 19th century Perth, Scotland, and his wife, in service to a local aristocrat, took over a wine and spirit shop in the town in 1825. Gloag did not join her full time until 1835. He supplied wines and spirits to the local aristocracy and catered for the banquet on Queen Victoria's first visit to Perth. A nephew — also Matthew — took the business into whisky specialisation, founding the first brand, Bridge of Perth, in 1896. Just a year later, Famous Grouse, a seven-year-old, was introduced and widely advertised. Exports to the USA began in 1908. Military messes during World War I ordered heavily, prompted by former customers who were now officers in the services.

Gloag's were always blenders, never owning a distillery, but now, as part of Highland Distilleries (since 1970), they are closely associated with Highland Park, Bunnahabhain (*qqv*) and other distilleries, all of whose whiskies figure in the Grouse make-up, especially Tamdhu, whose malt's rich sweetness makes a significant contribution to the blend's style. Reputed for using older whiskies in its standard blend, the brand's quality is pitched somewhere between customary standards and de luxes; when first 'exported' to England it was listed as a de luxe product and priced above all other standard competition. It is a favourite brand of Princess Margaret.

Available as standard and stated-age de luxes.

Bunnahabhain is the least smoky of all Islay's whiskies; here another of its casks is destined to become part of the Famous Grouse.

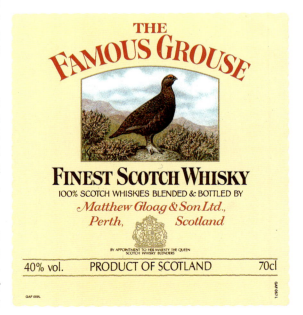

THE FAMOUS GROUSE
FINEST SCOTCH WHISKY
100% SCOTCH WHISKIES BLENDED & BOTTLED BY
Matthew Gloag & Son Ltd.,
Perth, Scotland
BY APPOINTMENT TO HER MAJESTY THE QUEEN
SCOTCH WHISKY BLENDERS
40% vol. PRODUCT OF SCOTLAND 70cl

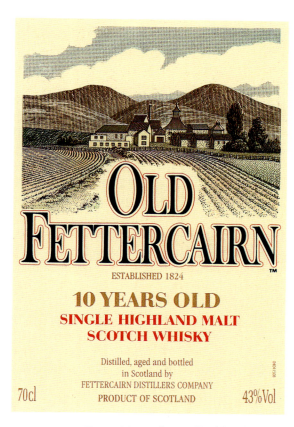

money malt, has excellent supermarket distribution in France and elsewhere in Europe. Available at five, eight and 12 years.

Glendeveron • Highland single malt distilled at the Macduff distillery (*qv*).

Glendronach • Highland single malt and distillery. Glendronach remains a very traditional distillery, carrying out the entire whisky-making process on the spot. This includes floor malting local barley, kilning malt and coopering casks. The fermentation vessels are made of wood, the stills are coal fired and the maturation warehouses have moisture-retaining, beaten-earth floors. The buildings are spick and span but have changed little structurally since the distillery was founded by a group of farmers in 1826. The spirit is used in Teacher's blends.

There used to be two Glendronach whisky styles, one 100% sherrywood, the other from plain and sherry casks. Now the definitive Traditional is a lighter sherry style which lets other facets of the spirit show through. Big texture, good balance of smoke, vanilla and toasty toffee. Available at 12 years old.

Glenfarclas • Highland (Speyside) single malt and distillery. The whisky used to be available in both sherry- and plain-wood versions but the company took tighter control of cask sales so that a uniform 100% sherrywood style could prevail. The distillery was built in 1836 and it has been in the Grant family since 1865. The Whisky Crash of 1899 hit the Grants particularly hard because Pattison's, whose failure caused the collapse, were the family's partners in the distillery. Eventually all creditors were paid and the distillery was secured. The casks used for ageing include second-fill wood, which gives an extra element of finesse to the spirit.

Glenfarclas is rich, fragrant and mellow with good body and texture. It 'goes down singing hymns', as one taster most eloquently put it. Available at several ages from eight to 25 years old, including a cask-strength version.

Fettercairn • Highland single malt and distillery. Fettercairn was originally a cornmill, and converted to a distillery in 1824 as part of the new wave of whisky making following the previous year's Excise Act. It was located on the Fasque estate in Kincardineshire, bought by the family of William Gladstone, later to be prime minister, and the whisky came to be used in famous blends like Buchanan's and Johnnie Walker. Between the wars it was silent and was close to being dismantled before a buyer was finally found, Joseph Hobbs of Ben Nevis fame (*qv*).

Now owned by Whyte & Mackay (*qv*), Fettercairn is prominent in the make-up of that firm's blends. It is lightly peated but made from peaty water so there is good smoke and spice as well as nut, fruit and creamy maltiness. Available at 10 years old.

Glen Blair • Vatted malt from Burn Stewart (*qv*), owners of Deanston and Ledaig distilleries (*qqv*), a top-ten seller in France. Glen Blair shows some Speyside robustness with Islay peatiness and, as a value-for-

Right: Glengoyne — a pretty, unobtrusive distillery through which the Highland-Lowland whisky line runs its course.

smokiness and dryish, spare delivery. Older bottlings show greater body, sherry and silkiness. Available as Special Reserve (about eight years old) and numerous stated ages up to 50 years old.

Glen Garioch • Highland single malt and distillery. One of Scotland's oldest distilleries, Glen Garioch (pronounced 'glen gheery') was built in 1797, in the Aberdeenshire village of Old Meldrum, and it still makes its own malt on the original floor maltings. The distillery has won awards for its energy-conservation policy, using waste heat to produce tomatoes in greenhouses an acre in area, the atmosphere of which is enriched by carbon dioxide from the whisky-making processes. The stills are heated by natural gas from the North Sea.

Glen Garioch is a full-bodied malt with a fruity core and dry, smoky finish. Available as a range of four ages from eight to 21 years old.

Glengoyne • Highland single malt and distillery associated with Lang's blends (*qv*). Glengoyne is the southernmost Highland distillery in Scotland and has some of the gentle characteristics of the Lowland malts to the south. Its origins go back to the illicit distilling days in the glen — once the haunt of Rob Roy and his cattle rustlers — when girls would make the day-long walk to Glasgow with whisky under their skirts. The distillery was built in 1833 and Lang Brothers bought it in 1876.

Glenfiddich • Highland (Speyside) single malt — the world's bestseller — and distillery. William Grant's (*qv*) re-introduced malt whisky to the world, yet it was only in 1963 that they decided to 'export' to England. Into what were universally blended Scotch markets, Glenfiddich was introduced as a different product, one that was the traditional unblended whisky of Scotland, a Scotch whose taste and personality revealed its origin like a château-bottled wine.

Founder William Grant worked for 20 years at Mortlach distillery, leaving to build his own distillery, Glenfiddich, in 1887. He bought second-hand patched stills from Cardhu distillery and began distilling on Christmas Day. His daughters brought in the peat and his sons watched over the equipment, their anatomy and maths primers propped up in corners as they also studied for entrance to Aberdeen University.

Balvenie distillery (*qv*) followed in 1892 and, nearly a century later, Kininvie distillery was built. The Grant family still run the show and the entire traditional whisky-production process, 'from barley to bottle', can be seen at the three-distillery complex — floor malting, peat drying the malt, coopering, coal firing the stills and, unusually, bottling.

The whisky is light and subtle with a gentle

Glengoyne is unusual in Scotland in that its malt is dried without peat so that the flavour has no smoky overlay. It is an elegant, clean, malty whisky with good fruit and dry close. Available at 10, 12 and 17 years old plus limited-volume special editions.

Glen Grant • Highland (Speyside) single malt and distillery. Glen Grant was built at Rothes in 1840 by the Grant brothers who were former smugglers, a circumstance James did not find inconsistent with his also being a lawyer. When a second distilling unit (later designated a separate distillery, Caperdonich) was built across the road in 1898, whisky flowed freely, but out of reach, running above the villagers' heads in a pipe that linked the two sides.

Besides release as a single malt, Glen Grant is in the make-up of many prestige blends, including Chivas Regal and Royal Salute (*qqv*). Much of Glen Grant as a self-whisky is drunk young (five years old), particularly in Italy, where the zesty, fresh and nutty character of the malt is massively popular. There is also some grassy sweetness to it. Other available ages start at 10 years old and vintages go back to the 1930s.

Glenkinchie • Lowland single malt and distillery. Scotland was in the forefront of European agricultural research in the 19th century and the barley produced in the Lowlands near Edinburgh was of superb quality. Glenkinchie began as a part-time function to exploit the fine crops in the surrounding fields and the distillery was built in 1825. It became one of the more distinctive Lowland malts, with an untypical dryness. It is one of the Classic Malts range from United Distillers. A museum of Scotch whisky, with a collection of implements formerly used in the industry, now takes up the old maltings. The whisky is light, sweetish, soft and quite rounded. Some smoke and spicy edge. Available at 10 years old.

Glenlivet • Highland (Speyside) single malt and distillery. Illicit distiller George Smith was one of 79 applicants for distilling licences under the new Excise Act in 1823 and he happened to be first in the frame with the Glenlivet name for his distillery. This was important because the illicit whisky from the glen had long been highly prized and the until-then generic name was a beacon of quality and was even regularly supplied, wholly illegally, to King George IV.

Several distilleries were burnt down by grudging smugglers in the unrest of the transition but Smith survived, partly thanks to a pair of pistols that had been presented to him by the Laird of Aberlour and which he kept in his belt for several years. Smith moved to the present site in 1858 and, in 1880, the company went to court to protect its registered 'Glenlivet' name, which was being used by other distillers. Smith's whisky was established by law to be 'The Glenlivet' and other firms in or near the Livet glen or river could hyphenate 'Glenlivet' onto their own names. Nowadays most choose not to do so.

Part of Glenlivet's complexity comes from a combination of lightly and heavily peated malt as

Pistol-packing George Smith, one of the first Highland distillers to go legal. In so doing he created a name, The Glenlivet, synonymous with truly exceptional single malt.

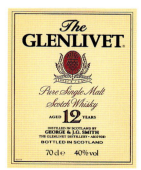

well as both soft and hard water. The whisky is succulent, sherried, spicy and medium-smoky. Available at 12 to 21 years, with numerous old vintages and ages from independent bottlers.

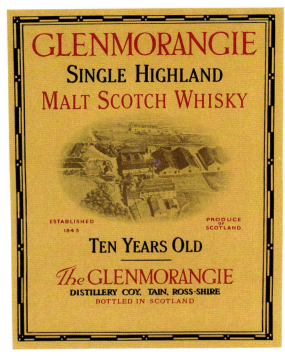

Glenmorangie • Highland single malt — the world's second-bestseller — and distillery. Distilling at the old Morangie farmhouse goes back to the 1730s and, in its time, it was a brewery and a lemonade factory; licensed whisky making began in 1843. Water takes 100 years to filter through the rock and emerge in the distillery's springs; unusually for Scotland, it is hard water and in the old days boilers had to be regularly chipped free of limescale. The stills are the tallest in Scotland and each has a 'boil-pot', a bulge in the neck. The combination of these factors helps to deliver only the finest of vapours to the condensers.

Glenmorangie is a delicate but intricate malt with floral and often teasing nutty complexity. The company use only ex-bourbon wood in ageing, carefully avoiding sherrywood for fear of masking the malt's gentle harmonies (a Parisian *parfumier* detected 26 distinct aromas in its bouquet). Certain special editions are, however, finished in sherry casks when the spirit is older and fuller than the usual 10-year-old

bottling age. Under a maturation comparison programme organised with Maker's Mark distillery in Kentucky, USA, a cask of Maker's Mark bourbon (*qv*) is under study at Glenmorangie to see how it develops away from home; an equivalent case of Glenmorangie is maturing in new oak in Kentucky.

Glen Moray • Highland (Speyside) single malt and distillery. This is the sister distillery to Glenmorangie (*qv*) and sits below the gallows hill on the old road to Elgin. An early 19th century brewery was converted for distilling in 1897 and became Glen Moray, just in time for the Whisky Crash in 1899. Glenmorangie's owners were so impressed with the distillery's spirit quality that they turned down an opportunity to buy Aberlour (*qv*) in 1923 in favour of Glen Moray.

The whisky ages in ex-bourbon casks which introduce a vanilla element to the spirit's own fruit, spice and sweet richness. Usually 12 years old but older editions and a number of vintages also available.

Glen Scotia • Campbeltown single malt and distillery. One of the only two remaining distilleries of what used to be a thriving category in south-west Scotland. Glen Scotia was founded in 1832 and remained in the hands of the original licensees and an associated follow-on company until 1919. It closed in the 1920s, following the drop in Campbeltown's reputation at the time and again, more recently, in the 1980s, following an extensive refit. Now owned by Glen Catrine Distillers, the future of the distillery is again open. Lightly smoky, salty and a delicate overall structure but well flavoured. Available at eight years old.

Glentromie • Vatted malt, *ie* a blend of malts from more than one distillery, from a family firm which has worked towards producing its own whisky over the past 40 years. In 1955, George Christie bought land near Kingussie in the Highlands, close by the Speyside distillery which had failed in 1911. Work on building the distillery on a bank of the River Tromie began in 1969; it was to be stone-built and operations were directed by a local drystone wall-

maker. It was 1985 before the building was complete, and 1990 before distilling got under way. Meantime, Glentromie has been making inroads in Japan and America, and there is also the Speyside (*qv*) range of blends. Available as 12- and 17-year-olds.

Glenturret • Highland single malt and distillery. Whisky making at this pretty spot in the Highlands goes back to 1717, when the stills used were illicit. With buildings at the present Glenturret going back to 1775, it may fairly be regarded as the oldest distillery in Scotland, although distilling on the site has not been continuous.

The present operation is one of the most dynamic in the industry, small, innovative and enthusiastic. Many different versions of the malt are bottled (including a liqueur), the visitors' centre is one of the best in the country and the whiskies have won many competition trophies in recent years.

Back in 1957, James Fairlie revived the distillery, which had been dismantled in 1920. At a time when malt whisky was almost a secret known only to a few enthusiasts within a small radius of each distillery, he wanted to establish an integrated artisanal operation that would display the traditional Scottish distilling skills in context. He made an excellent whisky into the bargain.

Glenturret is at core full flavoured and aromatic with nutty/malty length but the woods, ages and other finishing used make it a multiple-personality malt. Usually available at eight to 25 years old.

Grant's • Range of blends from the distillers of Glenfiddich (*qv*), the world's top-selling single malt, and Balvenie (*qv*). William Grant began distilling for himself in 1887 and his intention was to supply the blending trade, which was flourishing at the time. When Pattison's, the cornerstone company of the blending industry, collapsed in 1898, Grant was left with no outlet for his stocks and the continuing production of his two distilleries. The Grants had to create their own blend and market it, areas in which they had no experience. Their salesman, a son-in-law, made over 500 calls to firms in Glasgow before the first sale was made — for a single case. Things gradually got better and the bottled blend was named 'Standfast', in honour of the family's solidarity in working together through the crisis.

Throughout the 1900s, business was built up in England and family members travelled to North America and the Far East to build distribution facilities. The distinctive triangular bottle was adopted to attract attention, a notably successful marketing move. Kininvie (est. 1992) distillery is now in production as case sales go over the three million mark; Grant's is said to be the fastest-growing blended Scotch in the world.

The Standfast name recently gave way to Family Reserve for the standard quality; the de luxe range goes up to 21-year-old and includes high-strength and decanter-packed versions.

Haig • Blend from one of the great distilling dynasties. The Haig family goes back to the Normans, who settled the British Isles in the wake of the Conquest in 1066. An early event in the family's distilling pedigree was in 1655, when Robert Haig, a farmer in Stirling, was publicly reprimanded by the local church authorities for distilling on the Sabbath. In the late 18th century, the Haigs began building distilleries, of which Cameronbridge (*qv*) in Fife is still in production. The Haigs were related through marriage to the Stein family, also distillers. Robert Stein (not Aeneas Coffey, as is generally believed) invented the continuous still in the 1820s, after carrying out experimental work at Port Ellen distillery on Islay.

Together with the Steins, the Haigs became very powerful in the early years of the 19th century. They began supplying the English market and went to great lengths to protect this important business. They once put a Fife competitor out of business by buying a mill upstream of his distillery and cutting off his water supply. In the 1850s, Haig began to lean towards blending and the creation of brands; Dimple/Pinch (*qv*) has been successful since its introduction at the end of last century and Haig was the top-selling brand in Britain between the wars. Available as standard and de luxe.

Hankey Bannister • Blend from Inver House. Hankey Bannister were London wine and spirit merchants to the gentry in the 18th century and towards the end of last century, when whisky was a boom industry, they began producing their own blend. Having latterly come to specialise in military and diplomatic sales, the brand has grown considerably since it came under its present ownership. It sells well in Europe, South Africa and in international duty-free outlets. Available as standard and 12-year-old de luxe.

Highland Park • Highland (Island) single malt and the northern-most distillery in Britain. Highland Park comes from Kirkwall in the Orkney Islands off the north coast of Scotland, a fascinating nook of civilisation on the fringe of Europe. The distillery was built in 1798 on the site of a smuggler's still, the owner of which was also a church official who hid full casks under false funeral coffins and his church's pulpit to keep them out of the hands of the Excise officers. A highly traditional distillery, Highland Park still has its own floor malting and peating operations, uses local peat and has old-fashioned but highly efficient beaten-earth floors in the warehouses where the casks are aged. Highland Park is smoky and full-flavoured, with a salty edge from the moist Atlantic winds. Available at 12 years old, with occasional vintages and other special editions.

Highland Queen • De luxe blend from the owners of the Glenmorangie distillery (*qv*).

The company is based at Leith, the port of Edinburgh, where Mary Queen of Scots landed from France in 1561 to try to claim her rightful throne in an increasingly divided country. Highland Queen, dating from the 1890s, commemorates the event and the owners used it to tackle some of the less obvious export markets of the time, such as Central and South America, the Far East and Egypt. Available as 15- and 21-year-old.

House of Lords • Blend from the owners of Aberlour and Edradour distilleries (*qqv*). William Whiteley established the brand — an excellent blend and a counterpart to Buchanan's House of Commons — in the 1920s, with every intention of exploiting the lofty associations elsewhere. It was the Prohibition era in the USA and Whiteley adopted many stratagems to get his whisky exports through to his customers. Torpedoes were adapted to be fired on to Long Island beaches full of cases of whisky; a submarine was used to get inshore undetected by the coastguards; and distribution was by garbage scow, roadsweeper's trolley and baskets of dirty laundry. Such ruses had an excellent pedigree — that of the pre-1823 smugglers in the Highlands. Whiteley had a special bottle made to withstand the rigours of delivery to clients; it was square and, although light, also tough.

House of Lords was regarded as worth the trouble because it was a particularly fine blend, and one that Whiteley himself thought could not be bettered. He

Below right: Low-beamed, gravel-floored warehouses are considered to be ideal for maturing malt. Here at Highland Park, the casks lap up the clammy atmosphere.

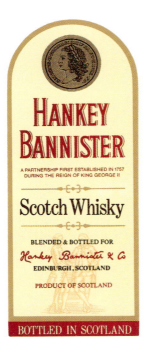

had a good palate, too. On days he was due to taste, he had himself driven to the office so as to avoid smoky train compartments, and he sipped spring water on the way. He also refused to advertise the brand, deeming it undignified to do so. Another of Whiteley's brands, King's Ransom, was for a time the world's most expensive whisky. It was on the dinner table at the Potsdam Conference in 1945 and was regularly served at the White House. Quite a quantity of it was redistributed in the cottage thatch, under the beds and behind the peat stacks of the islanders of Eriskay when the *SS Politician* (*qv*) ran aground on its rocks in 1941. The story is told in the much-loved movie, *Whisky Galore* (*Tight Little Island* in the USA).

Available as eight- and 12-year-old.

100 Pipers • Popular blend from the owners of Chivas Regal and Glenlivet and Glen Grant malt distilleries (*qqv*). Available as standard.

Immortal Memory • High-quality blend from specialist whisky blenders and stockists Gordon & MacPhail, located on Speyside. Awarded trophy for 'Best Blended Whisky in the World' at the 1991 International Wine & Spirit Competition in London. Available as eight-year-old.

Invergordon • Highland single grain and distillery. Invergordon is the only grain distillery in the Highlands and is very large and modern. Deep within its bowels lies Ben Wyvis, a little malt distillery that has been silent since 1977. Most of Invergordon's production is for the open blending market but the elegant single-grain, distillery-bottled whisky — one of only two in Scotland, the other being Cameron Brig (*qv*) — was an inspired creation. The whisky has a deliciously fruit-and-spice flavour, pleasing smoothness, succulent cereal aroma and the extra nip of 43% vol. Available at 10 years old.

Inver House Green Plaid • Export blend from owners of Speyburn and Knockdhu distilleries (*qqv*). Inver House Distillers has thrived since a man-

agement buy-out in 1988, winning the Queen's Award for Export Achievement just four years after going independent. The malt whisky pot still at Glen Flagler is no more but stocks are still used in blending and vatting. Green Plaid has the lightness of style and appearance of J&B and Cutty Sark (*qqv*) and does well in southern Europe, Central America and duty-free outlets. Available as standard, and 12- and 17-year-old de luxes.

Islander • Blend from the producers of Bell's (*qv*). This brand offers an exclusively 'island' style with its combination malts from Orkney, Skye and Islay. Available as a standard.

Islay Mist • Vatted malt. The brand has been around since the 1920s, having been created as a local commemorative issue. Originally produced by the then-owners of Laphroaig distillery (*qv*), it combines the power and concentration of Islay with the lighter elegance of Speyside malt and Caledonian grain. The brand was acquired by recently formed independent MacDuff International, who are in the throes of building it up in export and duty-free markets. Available as standard and 17-year-old.

A scene from the black and white movie classic, Whisky Galore. Here a jealous landlord plots heart-breaking revenge.

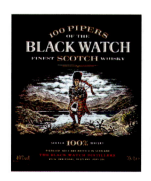

*I*sle of Arran • Distillery and single malt Scotch whisky, neither of which exists yet, other than in the mind of ex-Chivas Brothers managing director, Harold Currie. His courageous family project to build a new private distillery on Arran, off the west coast of Scotland, is just getting started. Lochranza will be the blended partner brand. Distillation was due to start by 1995 and sales, after compulsory maturation, by 1998.

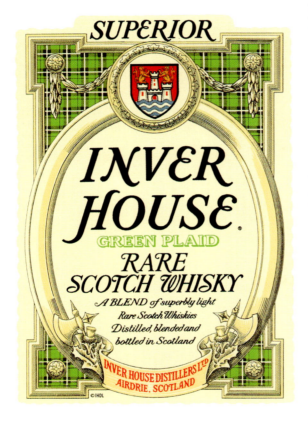

*I*sle of Jura • Single Highland malt and distillery, the only one on the island. Jura lies off the west coast of Scotland, a short ferry ride from Islay, and more deer than people live peacefully on it. George Orwell wrote *1984* in a cottage in the north of the island in 1948, simply reversing the year's final digits to obtain his title.

Jura whisky used to be a smoky, heavy malt in the style of near-neighbour, Islay, but when the distillery was rebuilt in the 1960s after years of derelic-

tion, the stills were designed to produce the elegant Highland type of spirit which is associated with the name today. Between 1775 and 1831, distilling at Craighouse, where there was a mill and a drying kiln, progressed from illicit production in caves to the first indoor licensed operation. A demanding laird caused the distillery to be abandoned in 1901 and there was no legal production on Jura until the 1963 operation began. The distillery has two water systems: one direct from the Market Loch for making the whisky; the other, occasionally showing its chlorine content, being the 'town' supply. Gentle, silky, subtly peaty and mellow. Available at 10 years and occasionally as 26-year-old Stillman's Dram.

J& B • International blend from the owners of Knockando and Singleton of Auchroisk (*qqv*). J & B's heritage goes back as far as the wine merchanting partnership of Italian Giacomo Justerini and Londoner George Johnson, set up just three years after the Battle of Culloden ended the last Jacobite Rebellion. The business thrived, and when wealthy Mr Brooks (the gardens of his London house were big enough to support a snipe shoot) bought out the Johnson family in 1831, the modern title of the firm was formed.

In the 1880s, they began buying mature whisky supplies from Scotland and produced their own blend, called Club. It was the time when cognac had all but disappeared from merchants' shelves because phylloxera had wiped out the vineyards in the Charente. Immediately after Prohibition ended, J&B was heavily promoted in the USA. It was at this stage that the J&B Rare brand's house style was fixed upon, in keeping with Americans' perceived preference for lighter Scotch. By 1962, it was a million-case seller; today sales are about five million cases and it is the world's second-top-selling Scotch.

Speyside malt is predominant in the J&B blends, J&B Jet having been specially formulated for the Asian Pacific and duty-free markets. There are more than 40 different whiskies in the blends which, after assembling, go back into wood for six months' marrying before bottling. Available as Rare, Reserve and Jet, the latter two both 15-year-old de luxes.

King George IV • Blend formerly associated with now-defunct Glenury Royal distillery. The 'Royal' tag to the distillery was a matter of intrigue, whispers suggesting that the owner's putative partner, 'Mr Windsor', may even have been King George IV himself. Unlikely, since although foppish King 'Geordie' liked his dram of illegal Glenlivet (*qv*), he was dead before the distillery began production. The brand is popular in Denmark and a scattering of other long-held markets. Available as a standard.

Knockando • Highland (Speyside) single malt and distillery. Much of Knockando's production goes into the blending of J&B Rare but the self-whisky has acquired a following in its own right. The distillery was built in 1898 and, when it was bought by Gilbey's six years later, it was one of the first to be taken on by an English drinks firm.

Knockando is elegant, smooth, soft and aromatic. Releases are by vintage, which often jumps a year since the whisky can be 12 to 15 years old; maturation rates vary.

Knockdhu • Highland distillery which produces An Cnoc single malt. In 1894, during the distillery-building boom of the time, Knockdhu was located in a crofting community where there was pure water, fine peat, best-quality barley and available manpower. In the summer the crofters worked their smallholdings and over the winter (when the best spirit could be made) the distillery bought their surplus barley and employed them to make whisky. The whisky is soft, with fruit and spice tone and medium smokiness. Usually available at 12 years old.

Lagavulin • Single Islay malt and distillery. Lagavulin is one of the great malts in the classic style of Islay — big, powerful, pungent and smoky, but with a structure and elegance perhaps unsuspected in the shock of first encounter. Lagavulin is the sole survivor of a dozen or so illicit bothies which operated at this spot on the southern shore of Islay in the 1740s. The distillery was bought in 1867 by Peter Mackie, the creator of White Horse Scotch (*qv*), who used Lagavulin as the brand's core malt — just as it still is today. Mackie set up a second distillery within Lagavulin in 1908, called Malt Mill in which malt whisky was made using ultra-old-fashioned methods. The spirit it yielded was different to that of Lagavulin but production ended in 1960. Lagavulin is mouthfilling and splendid, redolent of the salty aromas of the seashore. Available as a 16-year-old.

Langs • Blend associated with Glengoyne distillery (*qv*). Lang Brothers have been blenders and merchants since 1850 and they bought Glengoyne in 1876 so they could have a core spirit for their products. It still is to this day. Langs' standard, Supreme, is a blend of around 25 different whiskies, none of which is less than five years old. Both it and the de luxe, Select, go back into oak after blending to marry for a further year. Langs hold the Royal Warrant to supply the Queen Mother. The company has excellent stocks and has begun issuing special editions. A Christmas Day distillation from 1967 and other interesting 'vintages' are among the recent releases. Available as standard (Supreme) and 12-year-old Select.

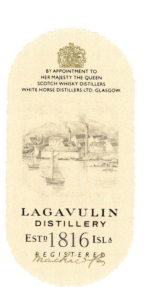

Laphroaig • Islay single malt and distillery. This is the epitome of Islay whisky — big, powerful, dramatic and glorious. It is the concentration of aroma and flavour in this style of malt that has made Islay a whisky category in its own right. The Kildalton shore in the south of the island became a real 'Distillers' Row' in the early 19th century, with five distilleries between Port Ellen and Ardbeg at one time. Laphroaig was a gaggle of white-washed cottages on a rocky inlet when the Johnson farming brothers began distilling in 1815.

The full-blooded nature of Laphroaig spirit made it greatly sought after as a core whisky when blends became important, and that circumstance continues today. Laphroaig still produces a percentage of its own malt with its floor maltings and drying kiln, the latter fuelled by local peat. Prince Charles, a great lover of Scotland, recently granted his Royal Warrant to Laphroaig's producers, who have also won the Queen's Award for Export Achievement. The whisky is smoky, salty and intensely peaty, but also silky and surprisingly approachable; it is aged exclusively in bourbon wood. Available at 10 and 15 years old.

Lawson's • Blend from company founded in 1849. Lawson's were blenders and merchants and, all told, never set the heather on fire in their business dealings. The company petered out and nothing of great import happened until 1972,

when their Belgian owners bought Macduff distillery (*qv*) on their behalf. Blenders with their own distillery are a much better commercial proposition and, in 1980, the General Beverage Corporation, holding company for Martini & Rossi, Benedictine and other international brands, bought Lawson's. The development money and large distribution now at Lawson's disposal is enabling the brand to grow as never before.

Available as standard and de luxe.

Ledaig • Highland (Island) single malt and distillery. Tobermory on the island of Mull, off the west coast of Scotland, began as a planned fisheries station in 1788. Two hundred years before that, a Spanish galleon sank in the bay and divers are still trying to find the treasure it was reported to have been carrying.

Ledaig operated successfully from 1798 until 1837 but during both last century and this, it has been closed for 40-year periods. Now owned by Burn Stewart (*qv*), who have been building its profile skillfully, the 'Ledaig' name is used for the (usually vintaged) single malt releases and 'Tobermory' for the vatted malts. Due to its recent intermittent silent periods, there are missing distillation years in the Ledaig inventory, but Burn Stewart's excellent mature stocks enable these gaps to be bridged so that the most may be made of the available Ledaig whiskies. Floral in scent, fruity, light and medium-peaty in flavour. Available as vatted Tobermory and 1974 'vintage' single malt Ledaig. Other vintages from the 1970s are expected to follow.

Littlemill • Lowland single malt and distillery, founded in 1772. Possibly the oldest distillery now in operation in Scotland, Littlemill is also one of the most interesting. It uses Highland peat and water, the latter piped in from the Old Kilpatrick Hills to the north. Jane McGregor, the licensee following the 1823 'new deal' for whisky, was one of the first female distillers in the industry, and Duncan Thomas, the American who bought it in 1931, was an inventor. He modified a Saladin Box malting system, lagged stills with aluminium and put rectifying

LAPHROAIG®
SINGLE ISLAY MALT
SCOTCH WHISKY
10
Years Old
The most richly flavoured of
all Scotch whiskies
ESTABLISHED
1815
DISTILLED AND BOTTLED IN SCOTLAND BY
D. JOHNSTON & CO. (LAPHROAIG), LAPHROAIG DISTILLERY, ISLE OF ISLAY

40% vol   70 cl

The rock-studded southeast coast of Islay is the home of four quite extraordinary peaty whiskies. Laphroaig is the best known of all.

columns on them instead of swan necks, to produce different styles of faster-maturing spirit. Littlemill was also triple-distilled until the 1930s. Today its whisky is the model of Lowland subtlety — gentle, sweet, a little herby, malty and rounded. Available at eight years.

*L*ong John • Blend historically linked to Ben Nevis distillery (*qv*). Long John McDonald was the founder of the distillery in 1825, the first in the area around the Ben, the highest mountain in Britain. He was a 'man o' many parts' — farmer, negotiator, improver, sportsman (he threw the wooden-shafted hammer in Highland games meetings) and distiller. His whisky was called Dew of Ben Nevis and, after Queen Victoria's visit to his distillery in 1847, demand became widespread and continuous. He died in 1856 and his grave, 'lost' for a long time, was recently relocated on a beautiful hillside spot overlooking a loch near Fort William.

Even without promotion, the brand has maintained sales of three-quarters of a million cases, but it was recently redesigned, relaunched and a 12-year-old de luxe version added. There are more than 30 malts in the make-up of Long John and its presentation is that of a quirky, unorthodox brand. Well, it was certainly a quirky thing for Long John's holding company to sell off Ben Nevis distillery to Japanese whisky-makers, Nikka, just before deciding to give the brand a new, higher profile. Available as standard and 12-year-old de luxe.

*L*ongrow • Campbeltown single malt produced at Springbank distillery (*qv*). Longrow is actually distilled in the same stills which yield Springbank spirit but, because its malt is entirely peat-smoke-dried, the resultant whisky is dramatically different. Longrow distillery (1824) pre-dated Springbank (1828) in licensing terms but both were involved in illicit distilling much earlier. It was run in conjunction with the Kintyre distillery nearby but closed in the 1890s. Longrow stood where Springbank's present car park is located. The whisky is rich, smoky, salty and medicinal — Islay-like, only more so. Available at 16 and 17 years.

*M*acallan • Highland (Speyside) single malt and distillery. Macallan is one of the great Highland malt whiskies, with great capacity for complexity, concentration and balance. When supplies of ex-sherry casks began to dwindle in the 1970s in Scotland, they were the first company to commission new oak barrels in Jerez and 'lend' them to sherry producers for fermenting and maturing their wines, often for four-year periods. Macallan wanted to work towards 100% sherrywood ageing for its malt whiskies and this (extremely expensive) system guaranteed it continuity of supply.

The distillery was built in 1824 and such was its reputation by 1892 that Roderick Kemp sold his share in Talisker (*qv*) on Skye to buy it. The present chairman, Allan Shiach, is directly descended from Kemp; as Allan Sharp he also writes Hollywood screenplays, among which were *Don't Look Now* starring Donald Sutherland and Julie Christie.

The sherrying masks the subtler facets of the malt, but not in order to conceal anything; with or without sherry, Macallan is a fine whisky. Instead Macallan has chosen a particular way to present its malt, substituting succulence and splendour for quieter attributes. Available at seven to 25 years.

Scotch

Left: Lowland spirit from Littlemill is pumped into casks to begin its three year journey into whisky. Below: Most casks maturing in Macallan's warehouses formerly held sherry. And it is from those that the distillery's single malts are chosen.

Macduff • Distillery where Glendeveron Highland single malt whisky is made. Macduff is a modern distillery, having been built in 1963, and its stills are lagged for heat-efficiency. The complex has its own cooperage. The whisky has fair body, spicy zest and some smoky/salty tone from the nearby Moray Firth. Clean and spot-on for drinking young, as in the five-year-old that goes to Italy. Usually available at 12 years old.

Mackinlay • Mainstream blended brand with high profile in Scotland, Europe and the Far East. It had its origins in Edinburgh in 1815, and 25 cases of the 10-year-old went to the South Pole with Ernest Shackleton in 1907. (He switched to Vat 69 for the 1914 and 1921 expeditions.)

Miltonduff • Highland (Speyside) single malt and distillery. The water source for Miltonduff was used by monks at Pluscarden Priory to make ale; since the settlement was founded in 1263, could they just possibly also have been making aqua vitae back in those days? Quirkily, the Catholic Church briefly part-owned Miltonduff in 1900 when it was bequeathed a share of the business. The malt is used in Ballantine's blends. The whisky is flower-fragrant and gently nutty in flavour. Available at 12 years old.

Oban • Highland single malt and distillery. Oban is one of United Distillers' Classic Malts range, a lilting, genteel malt from an isolated distillery that pre-dated the surrounding, now-thriving town. The Obanian culture in world archaeology is named for the 6,500-year-old human bones and artifacts exposed by blasting at the distillery when the yard was being extended. Gentle peat, smoothness and zesty fruit are its main features. Available at 14 years.

Old Elgin • Vatted malt from specialist merchants and bottlers Gordon & MacPhail. With its very large and mainly very old whisky stocks, the company can produce some extraordinary whiskies. This malt is mainly bottled at eight and 15 years, but there is a wide range of single-season versions that goes back to the 1940s and 1930s. Available as eight- and 15-year-old; also older 'vintages'.

Old Parr • Range of super de luxe blends. Thomas Parr was an old Shropshire man reputed to have lived to the age of 152, his lifetime spanning the 15th to the 17th century. He married at 80, was unfaithful at 100 and remarried when he was 122,

OLD PARR Æta. 152.
Sold by T. Jefferys in the Strand and W. Herbert on London Bridge.

harks back to the 'good old days' when smugglers' whisky was much better than the legally produced stuff. The bottle shape is based on the bell-shaped hand-lanterns used by shipboard smugglers at night to make contact with those waiting on shore. The Stodarts may have been the first to leave vattings to settle for a 'marrying' period in sherrywood barrels. Old Smuggler was latterly associated with Glenburgie distillery. Available as a standard quality.

*P*assport • Staple global blend which gets on quietly with being the 12th-top-selling Scotch in the world and selling almost 1.5 million cases a year in the process.

Owners Seagram introduced it in the late 1960s and spirit from the group's distilleries (which include The Glenlivet and Glen Grant [qqv]) is used in its making. Passport does well in the US, central and South America, southern Europe and some of the Far East countries. Available as a standard quality.

Left: Old Parr himself — if alive today would probably appreciate a well-aged blend.

and even credited with getting his wife pregnant. He was presented to King Charles I, was painted by Rubens and Van Dyck, and was buried among celebrities in Poets' Corner in Westminster Abbey.

Old Parr, the whisky, was marketed, mainly in Japan and the Far East duty free, featuring a very old blend. The brand is a top seller among de luxe whiskies around the world and the best seller in Japan where, a century ago, one of the country's government ministers is said to have introduced it when he brought a bottle home after a trip abroad.

The brand dates from the 1870s, and the blend of malt and grain whisky is one of the earliest on the market; its core malt is Cragganmore (*qv*). The bottle with the crackle finish is a reproduction of tavern bottles of Old Parr's era and the miniature portrait on the label is taken from the Rubens painting of him. Available as 12-year-old and other extensions.

*O*ld Smuggler • Value-for-money blend which is a great favourite in the USA and Germany. This brand name was introduced by the Stodart brothers in 1835, not long after commercial distilling was legalised, and

*P*ig's Nose • Blend which presents itself as the buffoon of whisky brands. It is the 'wot-a-laugh-eh?' kind of idea that aligns with radio-cum-toilet-roll-holders in bathrooms. It shows the product no respect, however — a shame, since the whisky is quite good. Begun in 1977 as a modest, own-brand bottling for a pub in the west country of England, the blend (and the companion malt, Sheep Dip [*qv*]), are now widely sold — and even exported.

Available as a standard swill.

*P*inch • Name in the USA for Dimple (*qv*), a de luxe blended whisky from Haig (*qv*).

*P*layer Special • Range of blends from small but vigorous independent blender. Under this licensing arrangement, Douglas Laing's of Glasgow offer a combination of above-average blends and packaging attractive enough to achieve consistent sales in its target duty-free and Asian Pacific markets. Available as standard and de luxe qualities.

100% SCOTCH WHISKIES
PASSPORT SCOTCH
IMPORTED SCOTCH WHISKY
WILLIAM LONGMORE & COMPANY
KEITH SCOTLAND
70cl e   40% vol

Poit Dubh • Vatted malt made in the 'old-fashioned way'. Praban na Linne on Skye blends whiskies in an authentic Highland style of the past so that they are not subjected to the final hi-tech rigours of modern chill-filtering. It means a mite more soupiness in the whisky from what are technically impurities, but it also brings extra flavour, aroma and texture.

The styles are very popular and sales increase by about 50% a year solely by word-of-mouth, (the company does not advertise). There is a brisk growth on the export side of the business, with regular shipments to France, Switzerland and Canada.

The company, founded in the 1970s, is owned by Sir Iain Noble, who also set up a business studies college nearby, where instruction is in Gaelic. All information on the bottle labels is in Gaelic. Poit Dubh means 'black pot' and refers to the sooty pots the old-time smugglers used all over Scotland to make their illicit spirit. Available at 12 and 21 years old.

Pride of Strathspey • Vatted malt, one of the 'Pride of' range from whisky specialists Gordon & MacPhail. Available as 12-year-old; some additional ages and 'vintages' go back to the 1930s.

Real Mackenzie • Subsidiary blend from Bell's (*qv*). The company originated in Edinburgh in the 1820s and bought Dufftown and Blair Athol (*qv*) distilleries during the whisky boom of the late 1890s. Bell's took over the company, complete with distilleries, in 1933. Available as standard.

Royal Citation • Super-premium blend from Chivas Brothers (*qv*). Five different types of oak are used in the maturation of this blend. Ex-sherry and ex-bourbon casks are conventional as ageing media; more unusual are remade bourbon and Scotch barrels, which combine seasoned and new wood to endow creamy oak tones and sweet complexity. Most unusual is new charred oak, which laces everything else with fresh, vivid vanilla fragrance. Lovely tone, multifaceted and mellow.

Royal Lochnagar • Highland single malt and distillery. The fortune of John Begg, distiller of the tiny village of Crathie in Aberdeenshire, was made the day new neighbours moved in next door. The Balmoral Castle estate adjacent to Begg's rented Lochnagar distillery site became Queen Victoria's summer residence. Begg had built his new distillery in 1845, and the Queen first arrived three years later. She visited 'the works' with Prince Albert and the children, soon granted Begg her Royal Warrant and the orders simply flowed in to what had become Royal Lochnagar.

In the late 1970s, the whisky was solely a worthy 12-year-old but a radically upgraded Selected Reserve was added for the international super de luxe market. It is a rare old malt from selected individual barrels and is correspondingly expensive. Selected Reserve is rich, generous and impeccably integrated. Wispy smoke and mellowed malt come seamlessly together.

Royal Salute • Super-premium blend from the producers of Chivas Regal (*qv*). The brand was created in 1953, to commemorate Queen Elizabeth II's coronation (a *cause célèbre* at the time was the fact she was Elizabeth I of Scotland). A military Royal Salute means firing 21 howitzers in tribute to special events and, accordingly, the brand is a 21-year-old. The Glenlivet, Strathisla, Glen Grant (*qqv*) and Longmorn are among the constituent malts and it is the best-selling super premium Scotch in the world.

Scapa • Highland (Island) single malt and distillery. Scapa stands above Scapa Flow, the great anchorage in Orkney under which still lie the hulks of the German war fleet from World War I. The captured fleet was scuttled in 1919 on the orders of the German admiral who lost patience with post-war negotiations. Scapa began distilling in 1885 and uses water which is naturally so peaty that the barley it brings in is left unpeated. A distinctive feature is the rare Lomond-type still used for the first distillation; it has a stubby top and yields heavier spirit. The bottled whisky is now more widely available than before, particularly in UK duty-free. It has the Island smokiness and saltiness but shows less peat. All maturation is in ex-bourbon casks. Available at eight years old.

Sheep Dip • Vatted malt from the producers of Pig's Nose blend (*qv*). The brand dates from 1974, when a Gloucestershire publican had special labels put on a worthwhile malt whisky which his customers insisted on ordering as, 'that there sheep dip'; now it is exported to more than half a dozen countries. Available as an eight-year-old dip.

Singleton • Term meaning a single malt and brand name associated with the Auchroisk distillery (*qv*).

Speyburn • Highland (Speyside) single malt and distillery. The little Highland town of Rothes had five distilleries by the end of the 19th century, and in 1897 Speyburn, the fourth of these, was wedged into a picturesque, sloping site on the floor of the glen. Due to the lack of elbow room the distillery comprises two- and three-storey buildings, most unusual in Scotland, where ground-level construction round a central

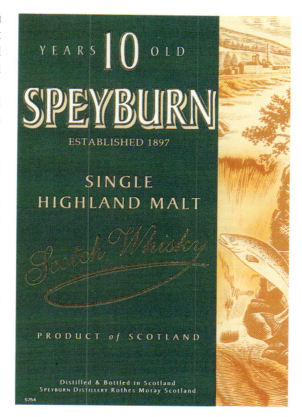

courtyard is almost universal. The first distillation took place at the very end of 1897, before doors and windows were in place, because some spirit of that year was wanted to commemorate Queen Victoria's Diamond Jubilee. The men worked in overcoats and mufflers in a snowstorm and managed a single barrel. It was not until 1950 that a tractor finally displaced the horse-and-cart cask-transport system between the station and the distillery. The whisky is malty-sweetish in aroma and shows dry, spiced fruit in flavour; silky texture too. Available at 10 years old.

Speyside • Upmarket blends from independent firm which has recently completed building its own distillery. The Speyside Distillery Co. Ltd (distillery in the Highlands and office in Glasgow) has taken just under 40 years to reach the point of beginning to produce its own whisky, but it has been creating fine blends in the interim. Under its Speyside label it has a wider-than-usual range and Glentromie vatted malt (*qv*) has recently been building up its profile. Available as standard and eight- to 21-year-old de luxes.

Above right: Scottish tranquillity around Skipness chapel, with the granite island of Arran and the Kintyre peninsula in the distance.

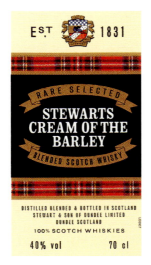

Springbank • Campbeltown single malt and distillery. Springbank, at the tip of the Mull of Kintyre in southwest Scotland, is notable for being able to carry out the entire whisky-making process *in situ* — from malting the barley and cutting local peat, right through to bottling the whisky. The three stills are used in complicated sequence to distil the final spirit but it is not triple distilled. A naked flame used to heat the wash-still creates a toasted quality which comes through the distillation and enhances the end spirit. The distillery is still owned by the descendants of the smugglers, who first produced illicit whisky on the site in the early 1800s; it was 1828, or even as late as 1837, before Archibald Mitchell bothered to get a licence for the business. Springbank was, until recently, the top-selling Scotch malt in Japan.

The whisky is full flavoured (chill filtering is avoided) but not heavy, and there is a salt-and-pepper, zesty, silky elegance to it. It is a medium-peated whisky but the distillery also produces a heavier malt called Longrow (*qv*). Springbank malts are always well aged, the main range covering 15- to 30-year-old bottlings.

S.S. Politician • Super de luxe blend which contains whisky from the real *Whisky Galore* ship. In 1941, the *SS Politician* foundered on the rocks of Eriskay island to the north west of Scotland, where Bonnie Prince Charlie had skulked after the Battle of Culloden. The ship had been bound for the USA with (among other luxury goods) a cargo of whisky, and having rescued the crew from the stricken vessel, the islanders began to plan the rescue of at least some of the Scotch. They were even able to discuss the details among themselves in Gaelic in the hotel bar beside crew members waiting on the island for a ship to pick them up. The book, by Sir Compton Mackenzie, and the movie tell the full story of the 'salvage' operation, but not all of the whisky was taken at the time. More inaccessible bottles lay deep in the wreck and, in 1990, a number of these were retrieved by Glasgow blenders Laing (*qv*). They incorporated a small amount of the *SS Politician* whisky in a special blend made from stocks of the time and made a limited-edition bottling in a fine decanter called S.S. Politician.

Stewart's Cream of the Barley • Mid-price blend with loyal and substantial following in its native Scotland. Stewart's were blenders established in a Dundee tavern in the 1830s, and their whisky gained a following which has never really fallen away, despite the advent of the international standard brands like Bell's and Grouse. Available as a standard.

Strathisla • Highland (Speyside) single malt and distillery. This, the oldest distillery in continuous operation in Scotland, is also one of the most picturesque, with its unusual twin pagoda chimneys and waterwheel. It was established in 1786, and has had many owners. The original proprietor made illicit whisky in addition to his licensed production from a second, hidden still; another, in the late 1940s, was imprisoned for tax evasion. Both were fined swingeing amounts. The present owners are Seagram and Strathisla goes into their Chivas Regal, Royal Salute and 100 Pipers blends (*qqv*). The whisky is fruity, sweet and herby, with some peat intensity and mouth-filling texture. Usually 12 to 21 years old with some high strength and old vintage alternatives.

Talisker • Highland (Island) single malt and distillery, the only one on the Isle of Skye. It was built at Carbost on Loch Harport in 1831, by two brothers who lived over the hill in splendid

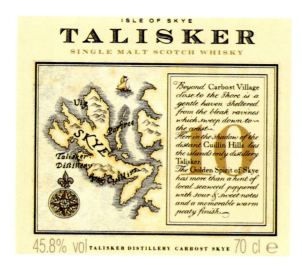

Talisker House. Sir Walter Scott, Boswell and Johnson were among the celebrities who had visited when it was the home of the son of the Clan Macleod chief. Part of the rent used to be paid in whisky to the chief at Dunvegan Castle. In 1892, one of the partners, Roderick Kemp, sold his share and went to Speyside where he established Macallan distillery (*qv*). The Talisker community has long been Gaelic speaking and the only English spoken there in recent times was to accommodate a former distillery manager who was… an Englishman! Robert Louis Stevenson liked his Talisker, describing it in an 1880 poem as 'king o' drinks'. The whisky is peaty, full-bodied and smoky, broadly in the way of Islay, but with its own particularity. A highly spiced, medicinal but silken malt. Available at 10 years old.

Tamdhu • Highland (Speyside) single malt and distillery which is possibly the last authentically local whisky. Tamdhu is made from local barley, produces all its own malt and dries it in its own kiln from local peat. For the malting, it uses a now very rare Saladin Box system, a development of the traditional floor maltings, in which the germinating barley lies in troughs and is turned by mechanical 'stirrers', which travel up and down the troughs. The distillery dates from the surge of construction that took place in the Highlands in 1897 and is built round its own spring. Tamdhu is an important constituent in Famous Grouse blend (*qv*). The whisky is light, quite sweet and faintly smoky. Usually 10 years old and available intermittently at other ages.

Teacher's • Blend closely associated with Glendronach distillery (*qv*). After branching out from the licensed grocer business in Glasgow, William Teacher became famous for his 'dram shops', simple, clean pubs where men could drink (although smoking was forbidden). The success of the idea made him the largest licence holder in the city, with 18 outlets. Teacher's sons began blending for their own shops but soon demand from other businesses led to them supplying blends to the industry. The

next step was the creation of a brand for general sale and, in 1884 Teacher's Highland Cream was launched. It became a bestseller and today is the number three brand in the UK. Teacher's has always had a high malt content, with 45% declared as minimum; indeed, for a period in the overstocked 1970s, it had a blend which boasted 60% malt content.

Ardmore distillery was built by the company in 1897 to guarantee the supply of malt spirit at a time when there was frenzied interest in whisky. Glendronach, whose whisky had also long been used in the blend, was bought much later in 1960. Just before World War I, William Bergius invented the wooden-topped cork now widely used in the industry. During Prohibition, Teacher's was exported to Canada, whence it was smuggled into the USA. As a result, Teacher's was well known there when Prohibition was repealed and continued to grow. The brand sells around two million cases a year, most of it within the European Community. Available as standard Highland Cream and 12-year-old de luxe.

Andrew Usher — the pioneer of blended Scotch whisky.

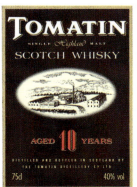

***T**e Bheag* • Blend produced to 'old-style' character without chill filtration. Te Bheag is the blended partner to Poit Dubh (*qv*) vatted malt from the small Skye company Praban na Linne.

The brand was created in 1976 to supply old-fashioned 'whisky fit for Highlanders' and to give a boost to the island's economy. The focusing upon, and use of, the Gaelic language was also deliberate. The brand continues to grow both locally and in export markets; it goes to a number of British embassies, including those in Washington and Paris. Goods going into Canada are required by law to carry bilingual labelling, normally in the country's own official languages, French and English. When Te Bheag began to be exported there, the Canadian Liquor Commission accepted French and Gaelic as appropriate to the product. Available as a standard quality.

***T**omatin* • Highland single malt and distillery. Tomatin was built in 1897, just as the whisky boom was about to collapse, and the company went into liquidation before the decade was up. New own-

ers took it through to the 1980s, when a Japanese partnership bought it. With a view to establishing high-volume production, the still capacity had been doubled from 11 to 23 units in 1974 by adding a second large stillhouse.

The malt is elegant and understated, with sweet, floral aromas and taste. It is used in the firm's Big T blends. Available at 10 years.

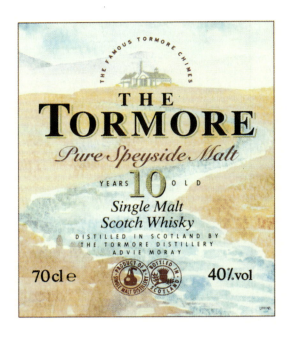

***T**ormore* • Highland (Speyside) single malt and distillery. Tormore is an unexpected architectural feature of the road that runs with the Spey at Advie — a cross between an art gallery and a concert hall, designed by a past president of the Royal Academy and built in 1960. The great chimney was originally to have been fashioned as a giant whisky bottle but (perhaps just as well) the idea fell through. Tormore has its own cooperage and is energy efficient by using bulk woodchips from the local forestry industry for fuel.

Tormore has a short track record but its whisky has already shown itself to be fine, with a light and velvety texture and a malty, nutty aroma and taste. Tormore is used in the Long John blend and is available at 10 years old.

Usher's Green Stripe • Blend from the company that invented modern blended Scotch whisky. Andrew Usher established a wine and spirit business in Edinburgh in the early years of the 19th century, a time when whisky was drunk water white and unaged, just like young grappa in Italy today. Usher knew of the improvement that took place when spirits were matured in casks and he began to consider the possibilities of blending together complementary types of whisky in the way brandies were combined in cognac. He methodically blended — vatted — a number of malts around George Smith's Glenlivet, to which he had the agency, and did well with it.

The continuous still had been invented in 1827; it produced lighter grain whisky faster and more cheaply than malt whisky and it was Usher's son, also Andrew, who began to tinker with blending both types of spirit. The motive was partly to save money in whisky production, since the London government was again raising duty rates for Scotch, but there was also interest in creating lighter whiskies which were more consistent from batch to batch. Usher's new-style blend was created in 1853 and found a wide and enthusiastic clientele, particularly abroad. Exports began to grow and by the turn of the century Usher's was a very big brand. Today it is one of the stable of brands belonging to United Distillers and goes to a number of developing Scotch markets. It is a firm favourite in Venezuela, where it is brand leader. Available as a standard.

Usquaebach • Successful US-based brand specialising in premium blends for duty-free markets. The brand name is based on a spelling mistake in a 1768 London auctioneer's list, a near-enough-for-jazz rendering of usquebaugh, which had been in use since Elizabethan times to indicate whisky (in Gaelic, *uisge beatha*, 'water of life'). It is doubtful that Usquaebach functioned as a brand back in the 18th century, but it has achieved a high profile since 1969, when Scotch collector and hobbyist Stan Stankiwicz set up the Twelve Stone Flagons company in Pittsburgh to market fine blends in prestige packaging. Usquaebach was served, alongside Bunnahabhain (*qv*), at the US Presidential Inauguration Luncheon in 1989, and for

President Clinton's toast to John Major when the British Prime Minister visited Pittsburgh in 1994. The firm has no distillery, but a Glasgow office sources mature whiskies and arranges the vatting of the core blends, which have 85% malt content, are 18 to 27 years old and are finished for a minimum of 18 months in sherrywood. Available in a wide range of bottles, hand-blown decanters and flagons.

VAT 69 • Blend from United Distillers. William Sanderson, a young and energetic wine and spirit merchant in Leith, near Edinburgh, was an early believer in the merits of blending malt and grain whiskies. Just 10 years after Usher's (*qv*) groundbreaking ideas, Sanderson was an accomplished blender. He had his own branded whiskies by 1870 and, in 1882 he carried out some early consumer research to enable him to launch a new brand. He commissioned 100 different blends from experienced blenders and these were tasted by Sanderson and a group of friends who finally chose the blend in the number 69 vat. Vat 69 was retained, launched in a new-style bottle like those in which port was sold (the Sandersons had close connections with the port trade), and the brand proceeded to become very successful. It continues to sell consistently in markets around the world. Available as a standard.

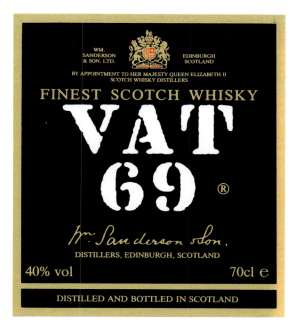

Born 1820
—Still going strong.

JOHNNIE WALKER : "Well, how are you?"
MR. TOMMY ATKINS : "Like yourself, Sir—Fit to go anywhere."

JOHN WALKER & SONS, LTD. SCOTCH WHISKY DISTILLERS, KILMARNOCK.

'Like yourself, Sir — fit to go anywhere' comes the reply to the 'striding dandy' Johnnie Walker, acknowledging its massive export success.

Tom Browne. The slanting label and the square bottle completed a very strong identity for the new, lighter blends which the company were launching. They had signal success: today one bottle in five of all Scotch whisky exported has a Johnnie Walker label on it.

The individual brand variations have their own stories, too, among them Blue Label, which has some 60-year-old whisky in its blend, and a bottle that is a recast of the original Johnnie Walker bottle. The Swing bottle was designed in 1920, specifically for the luxury transatlantic liners of the time. Its curved base enabled it to 'swing' with a ship's movement and avoid toppling. Over 2,500 bottles of whisky were consumed on every crossing. Available as standard, 12-year-old, Blue Label, Swing and other restricted-distribution de luxe qualities.

Walker • Blend that is the world's best-selling Scotch. Johnnie Walker Red Label, that is. For good measure, Johnnie Walker Black Label is the world's seventh-best-selling Scotch and combined sales of both amount to well over 10 million cases a year. Black Label used to be the de luxe version but so many super de luxes have been added at the expensive end in the past few years that it is now merely 'Extra Special'.

John Walker was a grocer in Kilmarnock in south-west Scotland who dabbled in whisky retailing through his shop. It was his son who saw the unlimited potential of good blends and, within six years of his joining the business in 1856, almost half-a-million litres a year were being sold. Walker's bought Cardhu distillery (*qv*) on Speyside in 1893 to ensure continuity of supply, and its malt whisky is still the heart of the Walker blends. The Red and Black Labels were created in 1908, together with the Johnnie Walker 'striding dandy' logo, painted by commercial artist

White Horse • Blend that is a top-seller in a number of world markets. The White Horse Inn in the Canongate in Edinburgh was the terminus of the twice-weekly stagecoach service from London that was established in 1742. It had belonged since the early 1600s to the Mackie family, who became distillers and, when they decided to create a new branded whisky blend, it was named after the tavern. The Mackies already produced blends but only in bulk for the brewing and retail trades. The idea of a Mackie proprietary brand had been kicked around since 1883 but was not implemented until 1891, when Peter Mackie, a particularly dynamic young man, registered the brand name. He had studied whisky-making at Lagavulin distillery (*qv*), which the family owned, and the plan was to make a blend from Islay malt (from their own Lagavulin), Highland malt (from Craigellachie, which Mackie was also helping to build) and patent still grain spirit. The blend is much more complex these days but Lagavulin is still the core malt to White Horse.

The brand was immediately successful and sold almost 30,000 cases in the first year, all of these as exports. Mackie later established one of the first scientific laboratories in the whisky business at Hazelburn distillery in Campbeltown in 1920. A visiting Japanese student there was Masataka Taketsuru, who then returned home, not only with the knowledge that would help him establish both the Suntory and Nikka whisky firms (*qqv*) in Japan, but with a pretty Scottish bride, doctor's daughter Jessie Cowan, from near Glasgow.

After abdicating as King Edward VIII of Britain, the Duke of Windsor used to telegraph his orders for supplies of White Horse from wherever his European base happened to be. Word got into the Austrian papers once when someone caught a glimpse of a telegram and reported he had sent to London for the splendid white horse he used to ride when he was king. In 1926 the company became the first to use the screw cap closure bottles.

White Horse is one of the world's top ten whiskies in terms of volume — around two million cases a year — and is the standard brand leader in Japan. Available as a standard quality.

Whyte & Mackay • Blend associated with Dalmore and Fettercairn distilleries (*qqv*). The brand had its origins in an unlikely sounding partnership between a chemical engineer and a ham-curer, John Poynter and William Allan, who warehoused food-stuffs and, latterly, whisky in the mid-19th century. James Whyte and Charles Mackay began as employees in 1875, but were able to buy the business in 1881, when a subsequent owner died. Whyte and Mackay concentrated on whisky and had just set up an ambitious blending operation for export markets when the Whisky Crash took place and all but scuppered them. They, and their newish brand, survived and indeed the business managed to build sales throughout the opening years of the new century. Export markets like the USA, Australia and New Zealand waxed and waned, with war and rationing playing their part, but sales began to build on the home market and in the 1960s the brand made inroads into the dominant Bell's and other brands.

Whyte & Mackay marry their malts and grains separately before blending, as well as resting the blend after it has been made, practices which create a lissom gentleness to the finish of the whisky. The company pioneered the large 40-ounce bottles (equivalent to 1.5 normal bottles) which were mounted upside down on bar gantries. The brand sells over a million cases a year. Available as standard; and 12- and 21-year-old de luxe qualities.

Ye Monks • Blend introduced in 1898 by the Donald Fisher firm in Edinburgh. Fisher was ahead of his time in his readiness to use older, mellower whiskies in his blends, and his preference for ex-sherrywood casks. The sweet richness they endowed gave him his house style. Brand leader in Paraguay. Available as a standard blend.

With the loading and unloading of fine malt whisky, even in the early days of motorised vehicles, it was the big brand name which gained the publicity. In this case, White Horse.

Ireland

in more than a dozen distilleries all over Ireland. In recent years there has been a third, Cooley's near Dundalk, where a combined pot and continuous still distillery began production in 1989 with a business development grant. After the mandatory initial minimum three-year ageing phase, its brands are now starting to appear in the marketplace.

A century ago, Irish, not Scotch, was the whiskey that was exported round the globe. The Portuguese used it to fortify their port and there were said to be 400 brands of Irish on sale in the USA at the peak of its popularity. During World War I, so concerned was the Irish government about drunkenness that it was made illegal to stand a round of drinks in a pub. Other wartime restrictions, Prohibition and lack of foresight in building up stocks to service demand after Prohibition's repeal finally put an end to its dominance. Irish distillers had also been reluctant to accept non-pot-still spirit as genuine whiskey (as the Scots had done) and Dubliner Aeneas Coffey, who approached many Irish distillers with his version of the continuous still, could get no backers and had to go to Scotland. By the time Irish distillers relented, Scotch had grabbed the market.

Above and below: The Irish pub comes in all shapes and sizes and it is seen as more than just somewhere to have a drink. More often than not it is the very social centre of the community.

Right: Rural Donegal — long recognised as the home to many a skilled poteen maker.

IRISH WHISKEY'S ORIGINS CAN BE TRACED BACK TO THE SIXTH CENTURY AD, when it was introduced by missionary monks, probably from the Middle East. Peter the Great of Russia and Queen Elizabeth I of England liked it and Sir Walter Raleigh stopped off in Cork to pick up a cask of it on his way to Guyana in 1595. Irish whiskey is produced from one end of the Emerald Isle to the other but, unfortunately, these days there is very little that gets made in between. Whereas once Ireland had more than 2,000 distilleries, there are now only three, although technology has enabled the survival of a score or more different brands.

The Irish whiskey industry in recent years has been based on a single traditional distillery in Northern Ireland (Bushmills, whose heritage goes back to 1608 and beyond) and a space-age complex near Cork in the south of the Republic (Midleton, built in the 1970s) which is clever enough to re-create exactly, in its 140 different fraction receivers, distinct whiskeys which evolved over the past century

CLASSIC SPIRITS OF THE WORLD

seeing but not worth going to see. The water of St Columb's Rill rises in peat and runs through that same basaltic rock on its way to the distillery. Although there has been a licence to distil in the Bushmills area since 1608, the present operation began in 1784 and, despite production having always been of traditional pot-still malt whiskey, bottled Bushmills Single Malt dates only from 1985. About 20 per cent of the distillery's casks at present are sherrywood. New spirit goes into sherry-, new bourbon-, first-, second- and third-fill casks for its entire maturation and these are then combined to produce the Bushmills malt house style.

The visitors' centre is festooned with relics and utensils from the old days at Bushmills. A still from the old Coleraine distillery up the road looks like a space machine from a Jules Verne novel and there is a letter from George Bush paying tribute to the, 'magical elixir Black Bush'. US presidents are to Northern Ireland as British royals are to Hanover; the ancestral homes of 11 of them are located hereabouts.

Six whiskeys are conjured from the 10 stills — four blends (Original Bushmills, Black Bush [*qqv*], 1608, and Coleraine) and the two malts. Bushmills single malt is aged almost exclusively in bourbon oak so you get straight to the malty core of the flavour with minimum sherry overlay. Vanilla fragrance is tempered by combining new and old oak, with even third-fill casks playing their part. It is graceful, sweet, oaky and malty. Available at five and 10 years old. Bushmills 1608 is an elegant, well-flavoured 12-year-old premium blend, aged in a very high proportion of sherrywood, presently exclusive to duty free.

By 1966, there were only five distilleries left. Four of them — Jameson, Power, Midleton and Tullamore — drew together to form Irish Distillers in a desperate effort to save themselves and the 18 brands they produced from extinction. Six years later, the fifth, Bushmills, joined the rest. That meant that the entire generic production of Irish whiskey belonged to a single company but that circumstance has now begun to change, albeit to a modest extent, with the advent of the Cooley operation.

Irish whiskey is made from both malted and unmalted barley as well as grains but, with the exception of Cooley, the malts are not peated. The spirit is made in both pot and continuous stills but the former types are, at Bushmills and Midleton, triple distilled, not double distilled as in Scotland. Minimum maturation is three years by law but in practice some premium whiskeys are at least 12 years old.

Black Bush • Blend from the Bushmills distillery. Like Original Bushmills (*qv*), Black Bush is also a blend but the malt content is higher (80% of total) and aged for longer (up to nine years), predominantly in oloroso wood. Rich malt and sherry nose with zesty, malty, gently oaky taste.

Bushmills • Brand name, single malt and distillery in Antrim, Northern Ireland. The distillery is close to the Giant's Causeway, the famous basalt rock formations grouchy Dr Johnson described as worth

Cooley Distillery • Independent distillery set up in 1987 in Dundalk under the Irish Republic's Business Expansion Scheme. John Teeling spent £4 million on buying plant, warehouses and brand names of famous but defunct distilleries with a view to building up a 'second force' in distilling outside the Irish Distillers group. He began distilling at Cooley in 1989 and the first whiskey, the Tyrconnel malt (*qv*), went on sale in 1992. Two blended whiskeys, Kilbeggan and Locke (*qv*) have now been added to the range. Cooley also imports a Scotch called Glen Millar.

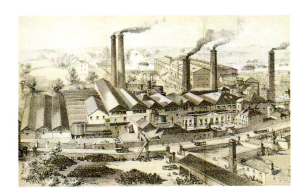

Irish Distillers • Company, part of the Pernod Ricard group, which owns the main brands of Irish whiskey, namely Jameson, Bushmills, Paddy, Power and Midleton (*qqv*). It recently sold the Tullamore Dew brand (*qv*) to Allied Distillers in the United Kingdom, for whom it still produces the whiskey. The five brands were the last remaining distilleries in the country in 1966 and they joined forces as Irish Distillers to relaunch Irish whiskey. They held a complete generic monopoly until 1989 when Cooley distillery (*qv*) began distilling in Dundalk.

Jameson • Blend and the world's biggest-selling Irish whiskey. Scot John Jameson established his distillery in Bow Street, Dublin, in 1780, just 200 metres from St Michan's church, where Handel used to play the organ. His wife was one of the distilling Haigs of Edinburgh and a grandson was Guglielmo Marconi, who invented wireless telegraphy. Jameson liked body and flavour in his whiskeys so he made a point of acquiring great numbers of ex-sherry casks in which to mature them. With expansion impossible at its city-centre site, production at

Bow Street was transferred to the Power distillery (*qv*) in 1971 and, eventually, to Midleton (*qv*). Round and well flavoured, graceful. Available as standard and 12-year-old de luxe '1780'.

Kilbeggan • Standard blend from the Cooley firm (*qv*). Kilbeggan distillery, in the County Westmeath village of the same name, was originally known as the Brusna distillery and became Locke's (*qv*) from the 1840s. The whiskey is one of two blends in the Cooley range at present and has 30% malt content. Both its pot- and continuous-still whiskeys are distilled at Cooley.

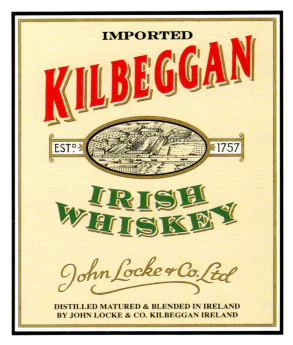

Locke's Distillery • Premium blend and former distillery at Kilbeggan, now used to warehouse the maturing spirit distilled at Cooley (*qv*). Locke's was called Kilbeggan, prior to John Locke taking over the business in the 1840s, before that it was named Brusna and the site has had a licence since 1757. The Locke family never quite shook themselves free of the problems brought about by Prohibition and the Depression. The opera singer Count John McCormack was linked to the family through marriage just before their era drew to a close.

Top: A Victorian line drawing of William Jameson's distillery in Marrowbone Lane. William set up business in opposition to his brother John.

Bottom: In the 1920s, John Jameson whiskey was sold by the cask rather than the bottle.

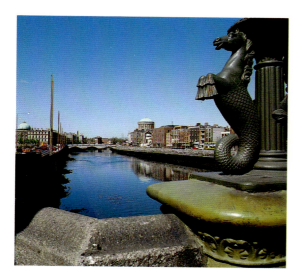

The distillery was never modernised during the 20th century so the plant and machinery on view to visitors all dates from the period 1870-1900. It was powered by water wheel, with a steam-engine for use only in the summer when water was low. The mash tuns (1892) are in good condition and millstones and pumps date from the 1870s. Locke's last distilled in 1953, but there are plans to produce eventually a traditional heavy Irish malt in a 'boutique' operation, to which end the distillery now contains the three pot stills formerly used to distil Tullamore Dew. There is a cooperage at Kilbeggan where Scottish coopers prepare oak casks imported from the USA for filling.

*M*idleton • Brand name and distillery near Cork. New Midleton was built in 1975, using the latest technology to produce under the one roof the different brands belonging to four of the five distilleries that had merged to become Irish Distillers. The four pot stills and seven different-sized continuous stills are all interlinkable to produce the spirit mix required. With 140 spirit receivers of varying sizes and different malted/unmalted barley/grain options available, over 1,000 spirit combinations are possible; most brand styles are going to lie within these boundaries, as indeed do the Irish big five. The distillery's production rate is so great that the maximum grain-storage period is six hours. Lorries arrive every 15 minutes to discharge full loads into the grain hoppers, with massive penalties incurred if a maltster's lorry is even minutes late.

Old Midleton was designed as a woollen mill in 1796 and, after serving as a military barracks during the Napoleonic wars, was converted into a distillery in 1823 by the Murphy brothers. It was displaced by the new distillery immediately adjacent in 1975. Old Midleton had the world's largest pot still — nearly 32,000 gallons (150,000 litres) capacity with its upper skin supported by struts attached to the ceiling — which remained in use until 1975 and is still on display *in situ*. It had a bell which was rung when all hands were needed to rake out fires from underneath during boiling. Everyone would drop what they were doing and come running; you don't hang about if there is a risk that the biggest still in the world might overheat. On one occasion a still exploded when someone was passing through the still-room. He was stunned but otherwise unhurt — and left wearing only his shoes, socks and necktie. Old Midleton is now the Jameson Heritage Centre, a museum devoted to Irish whiskey.

Midleton Very Rare is Ireland's most expensive whiskey, vintage-bottled in limited batches. It is well merged and silken in texture, with toasted, intense malt and oak flavours. Available as a super premium.

*O*riginal Bushmills • Blend of grain and six-year-old malt whiskey, aged principally in ex-bourbon casks. With its delicate, sweet-edged cereal notes, the whiskey succeeds in being distinctive of its sources because, unlike most whiskey blends which may have 40 or more constituent distillates, Bushmills has only two: its own single malt and single grain from Midleton (*qv*), in the Republic. Wine-like, sweet nose and malted, slightly toffeed flavours.

*P*addy • Brand from the Cork Distilleries Company formed in 1867 at Midleton (*qv*). In the 1920s, sales rep. Paddy O'Flaherty was apparently so enthusiastic in his description of the company's whiskey that repeat orders came to be made for 'Paddy Flaherty's whiskey' and it was not long before the name made it on to the label. Paddy's role within the company's range is to attract attention as an approachable whiskey, a recruitment brand, and indeed it is light, slightly spirity and gently malty. Available as a standard.

Top left: The River Liffey, bisecting Dublin and the old Power and John Jameson distilleries.

Power • Branded blend that is the biggest-selling whiskey in Ireland. The distillery was founded in 1791, at the western gate of Dublin City. It incorporated an inn from which the mail coaches left for north and west Ireland. Power pioneered the miniature bottle ('Baby Power') which needed special legislation. He was also the first in Ireland to sell whiskey in bottle instead of cask. John's Lane distillery was dismantled in 1976, prior to moving to the open fields of Midleton (*qv*), County Cork. Rounded, with good, prominent flavour. Available as a standard.

Tullamore Dew • Blend founded in 1829 in County Offaly. Word-play seems especially associated with the brand. 'Give every man his Dew' was a pleasing joke, particularly since it also fitted neatly with D. E. Williams, who subsequently came to own the company; throughout Europe, where the brand is very successful, '*Tout l'amour*' seemed to indicate thoughts that lay in other directions.

Daniel Williams spent 60 years at the distillery from the age of 15 and did much to build its success throughout the 19th century. His family became major shareholders and also went on to create Ireland's first liqueur, Irish Mist, in the late 1940s. Irish Distillers sold the whiskey brand to UK firm Allied Distillers in 1993 but will continue to produce the spirit for the new owners. Tullamore Dew has high malt content and a flavour that is very delicate, smooth, nutty and quite urbane.

Tyrconnell • A celebrated brand name from the defunct Watt's distillery in Derry, revived in 1992 as a single pot-still malt from the Cooley Distillery (*qv*) in County Louth. It is the first new independently produced Irish whiskey this century and is particularly aimed at the UK, US, European and Far Eastern export markets.

The Andrew Watt distillery, which originally owned the Tyrconnell brand, is thought to have begun trading in 1762, but not much more is known until the 1830s, when it was also a wine and spirit merchant. Tyrconnell is double distilled, in contrast to its triple-distilled Northern Ireland counterpart at Bushmills, and is five to six years old until Cooley's old whiskey stocks mature a little more to give greater options. The original Tyrconnell was exported to the USA, where early films of baseball games at the Yankee Stadium show it ringed with Old Tyrconnell hoardings. Such was the dependence on the US market that Prohibition caused the company to collapse, and the Watt distillery closed in 1925. The new-generation whiskey has a fresh, malty nose and delicate, dry flavour with a sweet edge.

United States

THE EARLIEST AMERICAN WHISKEYS WERE MADE IN PENNSYLVANIA, MARYLAND AND VIRGINIA by the Scots and Irish who brought distilling with them from the old countries. In the early days, whiskey was money, medicine and means of celebration. Two casks slung across a horse's back and taken out to be sold made six times more money than two sacks of grain. Within the family, as one historian put it, the newly born got weak toddy, the mother got it stronger, the father straight and the old and cold bathed their limbs in it.

It was government moves to tax spirits in 1791 that brought on a three-year Whiskey Rebellion; tax officers were tarred and feathered and people rioted. George Washington had to muster more soldiers to put down the rebellion than he had needed to send the British packing. Back in the Scottish Highlands, similar dramas were unfolding at the same time, only the rebellion there was quieter and lasted 120 years! The taxation caused many of the American distiller families to move on to Kentucky, with its *vegas* (large open expanses) of native Indian corn, where they formed the basis of what became the bourbon industry.

The Rev Elijah Craig, a Baptist minister in Bourbon County, was said to have already originated the whiskey style in 1789; it is largely a convention, however, and there is no real evidence for it. The county was given its name in tribute to the French for assistance given in the Revolutionary War against the British. It was 1840 before the whiskey became known officially as bourbon, 1870 before trade 'in bottle' as opposed to 'in cask' began, and 1964

The open plains of the United States became a perfect home for the making of whiskey, especially when settlers began growing rye, wheat and corn.

before the US government laid down regulations to define production of the whiskey. At one time there were 2,000 distilleries producing bourbon; now there are no more than a dozen in Kentucky, where 95% of it is made. Since many of the distilleries are in 'dry' counties, visitors are not guaranteed a taste of the whiskey they see produced or even the opportunity to buy any. Often you may buy whiskey from a shop but not in a restaurant, and it is illegal to drink from your hotel minibar during the night.

Straight whiskey is made from at least 51% corn (in the case of bourbon), with subsidiary grains, and has not been stretched by mixing with neutral spirit. If the corn content is over 80% it becomes corn whiskey and not bourbon. (Straight rye whiskey is similarly made from 51% rye and subsidiary grains.)

Blended whiskey need only contain 20% straight whiskey, the rest being silent spirit and/or other whiskeys. If it contains a minimum 51% straight whiskey it may be called blended bourbon, blended rye *etc*. There might be 70 different whiskeys in a blend and they are often bland and similar in character from one brand to another. Blended whiskey, however, is highly popular in the USA.

Light whiskey is distilled at a minimum 80% vol and stored in used barrels. Flavours are faint and the category is unexciting. Sour mash is a production method in which some yeast residues of a previous distillation are carried over to the next to achieve consistency of flavour and style. A completely new, fresh yeasting is called sweet mash.

Bourbon and Tennessee together comprise the dominant whiskey style in the USA; they are similar, but not identical, in production.

Bourbon

Bourbon is minimum 40% vol (80° proof) whiskey made mainly in Kentucky, principally from corn, and aged for at least two years in new charred-oak barrels. The remaining content may be a mix of rye (which gives a bitterish taste), barley malt and sometimes wheat. Better quality bourbons have about 70% corn, but good flavour is tied up with the grain mix rather than with just corn content; 90% corn whiskey, for example, is one-dimensional, dull — and cheap. Although most bourbon is made in Kentucky, it need not be bottled in the USA and much is exported in bulk for bottling abroad.

The grains are ground and mixed into a mash with hot water and yeast, the latter being each distillery's 'secret recipe', since it influences the detailed flavour of the final spirit. Most are made by the sour mash method. Kentucky sits atop a great limestone shelf so the water quality is excellent.

The mash ferments, a type of beer results and this is distilled, first in a continuous 'beer' still, then in a 'doubler' still, into bourbon spirit. In the past, bourbon was not a highly regarded spirit like Scotch or cognac because there was no law against it being sold as soon as it was cool from distillation. After Prohibition was repealed in 1933, whiskey was frequently made and sold on the same day. Eventually, when it came to legislation, two years' ageing was seen as ample minimum delay before allowing consumption to go ahead. Now, however, with the whiskey's potential for fine development more widely recognised, maturation periods of up to a dozen years are being implemented. Barrels for ageing bourbon may only be used once — not a quality requirement,

Top right: Bourbon Street in the famous French quarter of New Orleans.

Right: Bourbon barrels maturing. Old men and rocking chairs pop up only when the PR department is around.

nor even a protectionist stance over full employment for coopers, but a tax ploy by the authorities — 'X barrels out the door, so X dollars in duty, please.'

One of the reasons bourbon is not aged for very long is that new oak can make the whiskey over-woody. New wood gives the whiskey pronounced oak (vanilla ice cream) aroma and flavour, and the char endows a toasted, caramel-like characteristic. These are signature features of bourbon whiskey. High strength is an indicator of quality in bourbon and US Proof is twice the alcoholic strength by volume. Unlike Scotch, which loses strength during maturation in damp warehouses, bourbon gains strength in the hothouse phases of its maturation in Kentucky.

Quaintly, Bourbon County in Kentucky is a dry area with no distilleries; its connection with the whiskey was as a shipping-out point in the early days. Christian County, next door to Bourbon County, on the other hand, is wet. During Prohibition (1920-33), demand for medicinal alcohol resulted in more than 10 million prescriptions making a million gallons of alcohol available to 'patients' every year.

Ancient Age • Brand from the Leestown company. The town was founded as a pioneer settlement in 1773, but distilling did not begin until 1869. Young Albert Blanton joined the already thriving company in 1897 and, under his stewardship, over the following 55 years the distillery became one of the most notable in America. Leestown was the first company to issue a single-barrel bourbon named, appropriately, after Blanton.

Within the distillery lies the smallest bonded whiskey warehouse in the world. When it was built in 1953, it received a single barrel, the two-millionth produced by the company since the repeal of Prohibition in 1933. As each landmark total is reached, a new barrel displaces the previous, the current occupant being the five-millionth. The main bottling hall handles 10,000 bottles an hour but elsewhere in the grounds there is a smaller bottling house where Leestown's celebrated single-barrel bourbons are hand-bottled. Blanton's was the first, but Rock Hill Farms, Hancock's Reserve, Benchmark and Elmer T Lee (named after Leestown's master distiller) follow on. Leestown also makes two 10-year-olds of different strengths and a blended whiskey.

Jim Beam • The world's best-selling bourbon. In the 1780s, Jacob Beam and his family farmed the bluegrass hills of what was later to become Kentucky, raising corn, fruit and hogs. Beam ran a grain mill, grinding grist for himself and neighbours and he was usually given a portion of the weight in payment. He used it to make whiskey for the family's own use but, in 1795, Beam began distilling on a commercial basis. The Jim Beam brand name was not used, however, until much later.

Successive batches of Beam whiskey are made with fresh cultures of a yeast that has been kept alive for over 60 years to endow consistency. It is said to have been first developed by Jim Beam himself on the back porch of his Nelson County home. 'It makes a better bourbon,' says Booker Noe, master distiller and grandson of Jim Beam. The fermented mash is distilled in a column still, then put through a doubler still. Jim Beam is aged for four years before reducing to 80 US proof (40% vol) and bottling. Production is such that 600 new barrels (17,000 cases) of whiskey are stored and 600 barrels come out of the maturation warehouses for blending and bottling every day.

Early Times • Brand name and distillery. Early Times was established in 1860 and became the biggest-selling bourbon in the USA in the 1950s. It continues to do well as a popular-price brand and the company was the first to promote bourbon's mixability; the brand is closely associated with the popular Pussycat and Tomcat drinks. In the 1970s, the whiskey was reduced in strength from 43% to 40% vol in response to the growing interest in lighter spirit drinks.

Early Times uses a type of 'accelerated maturation' process based on the whiskey expanding and contracting into and out of the 'red layer' behind the char in the cask. This occurs with temperature change during the year and a normal cycle is twice every 12 months. By controlling temperature and humidity in their brick warehouses, the company creates its own weather and can insert up to five cycles a year to bring the maturation on faster. The whiskey is aged for a minimum of three years in this way. In 1987, a 'vatting' of bourbon and spirit aged in second-fill wood was introduced to give a smoother, lighter style; it must be termed Kentucky whiskey, not bourbon, due to the unconventional casks.

Elijah Craig • Brand from the Heaven Hill company (*qv*) which commemorates the distiller credited with creating the generic bourbon style. Craig was a preacher distiller in Bourbon County who, the story goes, used an over-charred barrel in 1789 to store some new spirit, perhaps an old fish barrel which needed extra burning to remove persistent smells. Bourbon took up to two months to deliver to more distant customers and a third of the colour and flavour transfer in the spirit occurs in the first three months. Since the whiskey would slosh about inside the barrel on its journey by flat wagon, it is perhaps not surprising that 'that' Bourbon whiskey tasted different and probably better than the others. Heaven Hill's Elijah Craig is a richly flavoured, aromatic 12-year-old super premium (94° proof).

Bottom right: The Kentucky homeland headquarters of the tastefully labelled Four Roses bourbon at Laurenceburg.

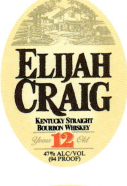

Four Roses • Brand and distillery established in 1888 at Laurenceburg, Kentucky. Four Roses is the third-largest export bourbon, third-largest in Japan and brand leader in Europe. The main brand is the Yellow Label, aged for five years and showing rich, nutty flavour with fruit edge; Black Label has its own yeast-strain, is aged six years and has a distinctive spicy-apple character; and the Single Barrel Reserve, which has more corn in the mash, is aged eight years and shows the spice and flowers that tends to emerge in older Four Roses bottlings. Rich and settled, too.

I.W. Harper • Brand created in 1872 by Isaac and Bernard Bernheim. The brothers had great entrepreneurial spirit and set themselves up as whiskey traders in Paducah, Kentucky, with a single barrel of bourbon and their combined life savings of $1,200. From the outset, Isaac wanted to remove bourbon's stone-jar image, writing in 1875, 'Clear glass gives whiskey a shine never seen before.' I.W.Harper went into glass bottles not long after. The sound as well as the sight of the brand was important to Isaac, and the 'Harper' name was grafted on to his own initials simply because it was 'euphonious'.

The business moved to Louisville in 1888, where the brothers bought their own distillery two years later. Harper's was well regarded and won several gold medals at turn-of-the-century international competitions. It was a medicinal bourbon during Prohibition and grew dramatically as a brand after repeal. Largely an export brand today, it is the best-selling bourbon in Japan. The millionth barrel was distilled in 1962. Late in life, Isaac Bernheim funded a number of public facilities for Louisville, including the 14,000-acre Bernheim Forest nature reserve.

Heaven Hill • Brand and distillery. The company is of comparatively recent foundation, having been set up in 1935 by the Shapira family and named after William Heavenhill, a former owner of the distillery site. The Shapiras distrust technical innovation as far as bourbon production is concerned, double distilling in traditional copper stills and using no temperature or humidity control in their open-rick

maturation warehouses. The closest they get to a high-tech operation is to open and close the windows at different times throughout the seasons to let the weather get at the casks. Most age for six to eight years and about 13% of the bourbon market's future supplies currently rest under Heaven Hill's roofs. Heaven Hill is bottled at a range of strengths and ages, the six-year-old 80° proof the most popular.

Kentucky Tavern • Brand established in 1903 by James Thompson as his premium bourbon alongside Old Thompson, a blended bourbon. Thompson arrived in Kentucky from Ireland in 1871 and formed a company with his cousin, George Brown, which subsequently became Brown-Forman. In 1916, during World War I, all production of Kentucky Tavern was stopped at the Glenmore distillery to put resources into supplying the French military with alcohol for the manufacture of gunpowder. Production was resumed in 1917 and maintained throughout Prohibition due to Glenmore's Federal permit to make medicinal bourbon. Kentucky Tavern was the brand chosen for use in the Federal Government's ex-service hospital and homes. When

Bottom left: A taste of Heaven Hill — from one of the last nine distilleries in Kentucky, and one of the most fiercely independent.

1933 came round, the distillery had 31,000 barrels of mature stocks which enabled it to market the brand immediately, and by the end of World War II Kentucky Tavern was one of the top sellers in the USA. Today it is in the top dozen domestic brands.

Maker's Mark• Celebrated small-batch brand and distillery near Loretto, Kentucky. Bill Samuels' life was transformed on the day in 1980 when *The Wall Street Journal* ran a front-page story on his family's distillery and everyone wanted to try it. Maker's Mark was producing 38 barrels a day in an industry where the big boys made 1,300, but that was the point. The theory had belonged to Samuels' father back in 1953: what if they made a little at a time, slowly, with wheat instead of rye in the subsidiary grains? And Samuels Snr was right — you did get a better bourbon. The Samuels' ancestors are like a roll call from American history, including Frank and Jesse James, the outlaws, and Daniel Boone, the frontiersman. The family has Frank James's gun in its collection but just a couple of years ago the gun Bob Ford used to kill Jesse surfaced in Sussex, in England, making £105,000 at auction. The Boones had a distillery whose stillman, Tom Lincoln, father of Abraham, had a reputation for drinking his wages away.

Maker's Mark scores for its smoothness, body and intensity of aromas and flavour, a combination which stems from the lower proof at which it is distilled (more congenerics) and the use of wheat instead of

Top right: Maker's Mark distillery, compact with its black and red livery, is unquestionably Kentucky's most attractive distillery. Below: To add to the whiskey's distinction, and aid against tampering, each bottle is hand sealed in plastic-wax.

rye in the subsidiary grains (more flavour and aldehyde-free). The bottling age is based on seven years, although about five per cent of the whiskey is deliberately over aged to put a little bite into the flavour. The wax seal was to emphasise the traditional feel (a bonus was its being tamper-proof) and the bottle shape did not fit in the wells out of sight behind American bars, so it had to be displayed on the shelves.

The brand tends to figure in White House banquets and it turned up at the recent Japanese court dinner held for the heads of state at a summit meeting in Japan. Today, Maker's Mark distillery, dating originally from 1889, is a National Historic Landmark. Available as Red Cap, the universal style at 45% vol, and Gold Cap at 50.5% vol in duty-free outlets. A Black Cap so-called special blend for Japan with a more robust flavour has 47% vol. A rich, rounded, tasty whisky (their spelling) with vaulting oak-spice fragrance and velvet finish.

Old Charter • Companion brand to I.W. Harper. The Chapeze brothers began distilling their whiskey on the farm at Long Lick Creek, Kentucky, in 1867 and Old Charter was a sizeable brand by the turn of the century. How extraordinary it must have been during Prohibition for doctors to be writing prescriptions for 12-year-old bourbon as medicine. It was obviously a valuable marketing exercise for the company, since the 12-year-old was first introduced during Prohibition and remains part of the range today. The brand is known for the longer ageing all of its bourbons undergo, resulting in rich, full-bodied whiskeys. Eight-, 10- and 12-year-old are currently available.

Bourbon

64

Old Crow • Brand and distillery which claims to have invented the sour-mash production technique prevalent in Kentucky and Tennessee whiskey production. Old Crow was James Crow, a Scottish doctor who established the distillery in 1835. His scientific abilities and insights, including the invention of a saccharometer, enabled him to make a number of improvements in production methods, which he is credited with passing on to the industry. There is no actual evidence that he was the first to use sour mash in production, although the claim is openly made on the label and several competitor distillers do acknowledge it. Other distilleries have made similar claims, also apparently unsubstantiated. The Old Crow house style is exuberant and well flavoured.

Old Fitzgerald • Brand founded in 1870, specifically for the American steamboat and railroad dining-car industry. It did well enough by the turn of the century to be exported to European capital cities and up to World War I was still being mashed in single-barrel batches and distilled in small copper pot stills heated by a naked flame. The distillery at Frankfort closed for good with Prohibition, but the brand name was bought by the maker of Old Weller (*qv*) and became one of the era's medicinal bourbons. Old Fitzgerald, now distilled at Louisville, is one of the frontline bourbons and has been marketed as 'The most expensive bourbon made in Kentucky.'

Old Forester • Brand that was the first bourbon to go on sale in bottles around 1872. William Brown was a scout with frontiersman Daniel Boone and settled in Kentucky when bourbon distilling was starting to be noticed. His grandson, George Brown, began producing Old Forester near Louisville in 1870, a time when whiskey was transported in cask with an empty bottle, stamped with the distiller's name, which the retailer filled with whiskey and displayed in his window. Brown took that idea a stage further by filling and sealing bottles at the distillery for delivery to retailers. The business eventually developed into the Brown-Forman drinks giant of today. During Prohibition, Brown-Forman was able to sell its whiskey for medicinal purposes, one of only 10 distillers licensed to do so. While many distilleries were closed, never to reopen, Old Forester's Treasury Permit helped Brown-Forman get through the difficult Prohibition years. Old Forester is aged for four years. Its corn content is around 72%, with 18% rye and 10% malt. Available at 86 and 100 Proof (43 and 50% vol).

James E. Pepper • Brand recently relaunched for the export market by the makers of I.W. Harper (*qv*). The Pepper dynasty possibly goes right back to the birth of the industry, when Elijah Pepper is thought to have been the first distiller in Kentucky, round about 1780. Grandson Oscar later had a distillery at Versailles, Kentucky, and was responsible for bringing Dr James Crow into the industry. Crow was Oscar Pepper's distiller and he created the Old Crow brand (*qv*) in recognition of the good doctor's achievements.

James E. Pepper enters the frame with successive operations on a site at Lexington, Kentucky, in 1858 and 1879. He kicked against the cask-sale dominance of wholesalers who blended different whiskeys before selling on and, in 1890, Pepper, who wanted

The Old Forester water tower, a long-time landmark of Louisville.

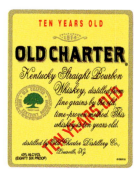

A shot of whiskey — this old photo of a Wyoming bartender gives some idea how a barrel on the bar kept troublesome frontier drinkers under control.

Yell has a higher wheat content, is distilled to a lower strength and is matured to a lower strength than most bourbons, so endowing greater richness to the final flavours, according to the distillers. The company also prefers its traditional 'open-rick' maturation warehouses to the modern temperature-controlled kind.

Southern Comfort • It may be the grand old drink of the South, but it ain't a bourbon, nor even a whiskey. See under Liqueurs.

Weller • Brand and distillery originally located in Louisville, Kentucky. Daniel Weller arrived in Kentucky by flatboat from Maryland in 1794, and was possibly one of the Whiskey Rebellion refugees. The family's living was distilling but it was not until 1849 that William L Weller began actively marketing their own product. It went into bottle after a while and by the 1880s they had customers across the USA.

The Wellers invented the standard 'open rick' warehousing universally used by the bourbon industry until recent hi-tech developments in climatically controlled environments.

The Weller house style uses wheat instead of rye in its grain mix, giving softer whiskey without the characteristic rye bitterness. The company's 'whisper of wheat' slogan is used for all Weller brands, including Rebel Yell (qv). The brand can claim to have been continuously marketed since 1849. W.L.Weller is 43% vol and Old Weller is 53.5% vol; both are aged for seven years.

to sell his product unblended, obtained a licence to bottle his own whiskey. He was thus, together with George Dickel (qv) in Tennessee, one of the first distillers in the country to produce his own brand. He mashed his grains a bushel at a time in small tubs and double distilled his spirit over an open fire.

The brand was well established by the turn of the century and boxer Jack Johnston celebrated his world-championship victory over Jim Jeffries in 1910 with Pepper bourbon. The owners shipped 30,000 cases and 4,000 barrels of Pepper to Germany in 1919 to escape confiscation when Prohibition was introduced, but the company succumbed like so many others.

Rebel Yell • Brand and distillery in Louisville. During the American Civil War, the 'rebel yell' of attacking Confederate troops — only authentic on an empty stomach — used to chill the blood of the waiting Union soldiers. William Weller began making bourbon in 1849 and, as late as 1984, the whiskey remained a local brand, not even sold north of the Mason-Dixon Line (the old frontier between the free and the slave states). The Rebel Yell distillery was one of 10 licensed to continue medicinal-purposes production during Prohibition in the 1920s. Rebel

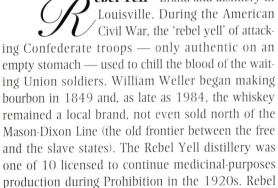

Wild Turkey • The USA's best-selling premium bourbon from Boulevard distillery, Laurenceburg. The Ripy family established their distillery in 1855, coincidentally the same year that Austin Nichols, later to own the business, began trading as a wholesale grocer. The Ripy house style was better than most and their whiskey was chosen out of 400 to represent Kentucky at the World Fair in 1893. The distillery was modernised in 1933 before re-opening after Prohibition, but it was not until 1940 that the brand name came about. Some 101° proof bourbon supplied for a businessmen's wild-turkey shoot in North Carolina went down so well that the idea of marketing it as Wild Turkey took shape.

In addition to local corn and water, the company brings in barley from Montana, rye from Dakota and oak from the Ozarks for the barrels. The spirit is made in a continuous still 40 feet-high and a second doubler still before distilled water is added to the spirit and it goes into new thick char casks. During maturation, casks are rotated between the hot upper storeys of the warehouses and the cool lower storeys.

Master distiller Jimmy Russell, 'born within sniffin' distance' of the distillery, has worked there for over 40 years. The whiskey is tasted annually by his teams from the end of the second year, to monitor continuing correct development. Eight-year-old 101° proof (50.5% vol) Wild Turkey is the original bourbon style produced by the Ripy brothers in 1893, and by their successors in 1933 with the repeal of Prohibition. The 80° proof, introduced in 1974 for those who did not like high-proof bourbon, is aged for at least four years. Latest in the range are a 12-year-old and limited-release Rare Breed, a blend of six-, eight- and 12-year-old stocks. Wild Turkey delivers generous flavours of vanilla, caramel and woody sweetness.

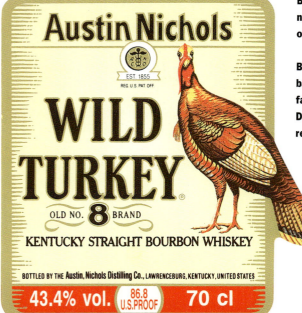

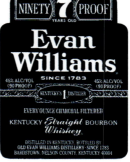

Bottom left: Wild Turkey — named in commemoration of a turkey shoot.

Bottom right: Yet another barrel of Tennessee's most famous export, Jack Daniel's, is found a quiet resting place.

Evan Williams • Flagship brand of the Heaven Hill firm (qv) and named for Kentucky's first distiller who was an immigrant from Wales, where his family were distillers. Williams opened for business in Nelson County in 1783 and the brand is the second-top-selling bourbon in the USA. It is matured for seven to eight years and bottled at 90° proof.

Tennessee Whiskey

Tennessee whiskey is made in a similar manner to bourbon but a special filter process with charcoal and woollen blankets, introduced in the early 1800s and carried out before the spirit is matured, gives it a lighter, smoother texture and a touch more smokiness in the flavour. Sugar maple slats are stacked in the open air and burned and hosed down with water to create charcoal, which is stacked in vats 10 feet-high and the distillate passed through it. Tennessee whiskies are now aged at least four years by law. There are only two Tennessee whiskey distilleries although there are a number of brands with a range of styles.

Tennessee's undulating country is criss-crossed with small roads, once the highways of bootleggers. Now, occasionally, you might find trucks carrying a more legal cargo.

Jack Daniel's • Brand and distillery in Lynchburg. Jack Daniel the man was born in 1846, bought his own still when he was 13 years old and registered his own distillery in 1866, when he was just 20. At just 5 feet 2 inches in height, he cut a dash by dressing in a knee-length frock coat, bow tie and wide-brimmed hat every time he stepped out of doors. He had a natural flamboyance and would have approved of the statue to him that stands in the distillery grounds beside the cave spring he found and around which he built the distillery.

When hometown bands were in vogue, he bought an entire set of musical instruments on Lynchburg's behalf and then set about finding musicians to play them. In 1904, he entered his whiskey in a tasting competition of world whiskies at the World Fair in St Louis and came away with the top award. He never had children and the distillery passed to his nephew, Lem Motlow, when he died —

the result, incidentally, of gangrene in his foot, caused by kicking a safe he was unable to open. During Prohibition, Motlow turned to mule auctioneering and made Lynchburg an important trading centre. After World War II distillers were only allowed to use inferior grains so Motlow held off reopening until the restriction was lifted in 1947.

The 'beer' stills are 100 feet high and produce spirit of 70% vol strength which then goes into the charcoal-mellowing vats (10 feet high). The spirit that emerges is systematically tasted and the charcoal replaced when necessary. The distillate goes into barrels at 55% vol and ages for four to six years. The No. 7 black label at 45% vol is the 'standard' Daniel, which is the top-selling premium spirit in the USA. There is a green label, also No. 7, which is 43% vol.

George Dickel • Brand and distillery. George Dickel was an immigrant from Germany who became a Nashville whiskey merchant in the 1860s during the Civil War. His whiskey sold well and in 1870 he became a licensed wholesaler; he built his distillery at Cascade Hollow, a backwood site near Tullahoma, in 1879. At the time proprietors branded their whiskeys with their own name but Dickel wanted to draw attention to the location and its fine water, so his product became Cascade Whisky (no 'e'), one of the earliest brand names in the industry. The name and the label were trademarked in 1895.

His distillery was closed during Prohibition but his whiskey was passed as suitable to be sold for medicinal purposes. Tennessee remained 'dry' until 1958, when a master distiller called Ralph Dupps, who had been impressed by the whiskey as a young man, built a new distillery near Dickel's original.

Dickel noticed that he made his best whiskey in winter so he latterly only distilled in the winter months; today, Dickel spirit is chilled before it passes through the charcoal. Both Tennessee distilleries use 'charcoal-mellowing' but a Dickel refinement is to place virgin wool blankets at top and bottom of the charcoal vats. Normally, runnels of whiskey use the same descent paths and the charcoal is unevenly used but Dickel found that the blankets diffused the permeation of the water uniformly through the charcoal. It takes 10 days for the spirit to pass down through the 10-foot vat. The whiskey is smooth, rich and dryish, with oak, smoke and spice flashes all through. Available as No. 12 (45% vol) and No. 8 (43.4 vol).

Gentleman Jack • Brand from the Jack Daniel distillery at Lynchburg. Introduced in 1988, it was the first new whiskey from the Daniel distillery in over a century and the formula is based on early work carried out by Daniel himself. The whiskey is charcoal mellowed twice, once before and once after the maturation period, and it is in limited production with hand-finishing. The bottle is based on the decanter designed by Daniel to celebrate his whiskey winning the gold medal at the St Louis World Fair tasting. The extra process gives smoother texture over an already rich flavour in comparison with mainline Jack Daniel and, in quality terms, the brand is being aligned with cognacs and malt whiskies. 40% vol.

Far left: The old world Dickel General Store doubles up as the distillery's shop and Dickel Station post office.

Left: A typically glorious sunset brings another distilling day in sleepy Tennessee to a close.

Canada

Above: Canada — a vast country, sparsely populated but with all the natural elements to make whisky. Below: The whisky may be different, but the spirit safe remains the same.

IN THE 17TH AND 18TH CENTURIES GIN AND RUM WERE THE SETTLERS' SPIRIT DRINKS, the one arriving as ballast in lumber ships from Europe, the other brought in from the Caribbean. The first home-made spirits were largely fruit brandies and at the tail end of the 18th century, whisky production began at Kingston, on Lake Ontario. As cereal farming developed along the St Lawrence and Lakes area, so did distilling in parallel. In 1875, government regulation specified exclusive use of cereal grains as raw materials, continuous still distillation and three years' minimum ageing in oak — at the time the strictest spirit legislation in the world.

Early adoption of sales in sealed bottles built confidence in the Canadian product and Americans' access to it during both their Civil War and Prohibition saw them develop a liking for it. Throughout Canada's Prohibition period, even high-class hotels served whisky in silver teapots and water in matching cream jugs; while visiting during this period Winston Churchill insisted upon — and was given — similar service. Today, Canadian whiskies are a succession of spirituous mosaics, each brand painstakingly put together to great effect in the way of an artist starting with a mound of stone chips in the corner of his studio. While most whiskey cultures acknowledge an important role for blending, Canadian whisky is wholly based upon it to the extent that the constituent spirits in the blends are never marketed as self-whiskies. The generic style is light, smooth, soft and sweetish, with a counter-balancing rye zest.

Canadian whisky is made from a wide range of grains — rye, barley, wheat and, of course, corn. The mix for each brand decides the flavour profile and is a proprietary secret, as are details of the yeasts used. Dominant wheat endows sweetness while rye brings a bitter, spicy tang that is attractive as long as it is kept under control. Continuous stills are used but variation in product occurs with different lengths of column, the use in some cases of doubler stills as in the USA, and Coffey stills.

Three years in oak is still the minimum ageing period, although most spirits mature for much longer. Each constituent whisky in a blend has its particular optimum maturation age, from three years for a light grain to six, 12 or even more years for a more complex rye spirit. Ex-brandy, -bourbon, -sherry, new and charred casks are used, adding to the list of variables which go into building a house style. The blender assembles typically about 20 whiskies in the proportions he needs to make up his recipe. Canadian styles evolved out of a desire to combine good flavour with softer spirit impact.

'Whisky' without an 'e' is the normal spelling for the Canadian spirit.

Black Velvet • International brand with sales of 2.5 million cases a year. In the 1950s, the master distiller at Gilbey Canada first produced a soft, silky whisky that was easy to name Black Velvet. Rye spirit is aged for two years in oak and then blended with another whisky base before going on to age for a further four years. This blending procedure, carried out before, rather than after, the main maturation period, as widely done elsewhere, is thought to be the secret behind the smoothness and generous flavour of this and other Canadian whiskies. Black Velvet (40% vol) is now in the top-35 segment of best-selling spirits in the world.

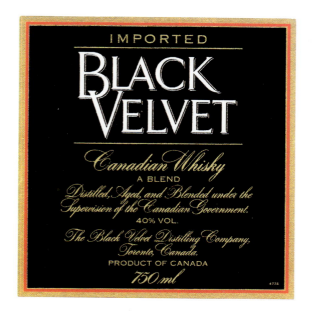

Canadian Club • Leading international brand. The brand was introduced in 1858 by Hiram Walker, a grain merchant turned distiller, and by using a very slow distillation technique he produced a clean, tasty and soft 'master whisky' which he then blended with silent spirits. The blend is based on triple-distilled silent spirit and two flavouring spirits, one of them double distilled, the other distilled once. Most Canadians are blended after maturation, but Canadian Club blends are assembled beforehand and go on to six years' ageing. There is also a 12-year-old Classic. Not too full bodied but well mellowed, lightly smoky and clean.

Women's chores — bottling at Seagram, as with most other Canadian distilleries, remained very much a female occupation until the advent of full mechanisation.

Canadian Mist • World's biggest-selling Canadian whisky. Brown-Forman obtained the brand in 1971 and sales increased from 850,000 cases a year to almost 3.5 million by the mid-1990s. A popular-price brand, Canadian Mist is made from corn and barley malt and distilled at Collingwood, Ontario. Light and smooth in style.

Bottom right: A simple message in 1914 to encourage emigration from Britain to Canada.

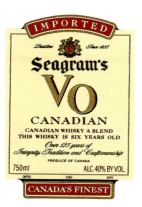

Crown Royal • De luxe brand from Seagram. In 1939, King George VI and his Queen travelled across Canada during their state visit in a special Canadian-Pacific train. They enjoyed the best of the country's fare — antelope steaks, lake trout, river salmon and a specially blended de luxe whisky created by Seagram to celebrate the tour. Crown Royal, with its crown-shaped bottle, is based on that special whisky. A specific corn-dominant grain-mash and yeast ferments out and the beer goes through a continuous still before filling into new and seasoned (used) white oak barrels. Little colour is taken from the wood by the end of the 10-year maturation period and rye whisky is added to darken the colour and fill out the flavour. Smooth, full bodied and mellow, with settled wood aromas. 80° proof.

Seagram's V.O. • In 1904, a batch of 40 casks of Seagram whisky was set aside for longer-than-usual ageing. In 1909, Joseph Seagram tasted the casks and instructed that they be left for a further three years. When the batch was finally bottled in 1912, the whisky was marketed as V.O., which is understood to mean 'very own', although some think it is short for 'very old'; either way, no-one is really sure. Corn, rye and malted barley play important roles. Once the mash is ready for fermentation, it then travels through a mile and a half of cooling coils on its way to the great fermentation tanks. Cultured yeasts are used. V.O. is made by continuous distillation and the still's columns rise to the height of a five-storey building.

The blend is marketed at six years old now but the type of ageing is important and takes place in small oak barrels. The blenders choose the constituent whiskies with an eye to producing a light, delicately fragrant final blend which can still offer richness of flavour. V.O. has good texture and soft flavour and finish; 40% vol.

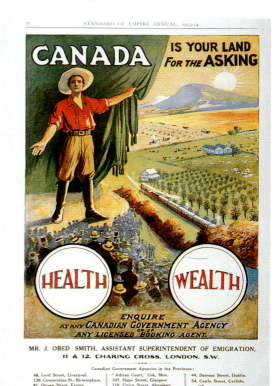

Japan

WHISKY PRODUCTION IN JAPAN GREW OUT OF TWO TURN-OF-THE-CENTURY CIRCUMSTANCES: the almost religious reverence of the Japanese for the real substance historically conjured out of sooty black pots in distant, misty Scotland, and the local Japanese 'pretend' whisky made from coloured-up neutral alcohol. When young Masataka Taketsuru went to Scotland in 1918 and was let in on the inner secrets of making 'real' whisky his feat was regarded with awe and reverence, as if the meaning of life itself had been revealed to him.

Two men are regarded as the 'fathers of Japanese whisky' — Taketsuru, ultimately founder of Nikka, and Shinjiro Torii, founder of Suntory, who gave him the opportunity to make prototype spirit when he returned to Japan. Taketsuru was the heir to a sake brewery but he was more interested in whisky. He studied applied chemistry at Glasgow University, then worked in a distillery at Rothes. No-one knows which one, because Taketsuru documented it only as 'Glenlivet' and three of Rothes's five distilleries (Glen Grant, Glenrothes and Speyburn) hyphenated their names with the word 'Glenlivet'. He also worked in Campbeltown before returning (with a Scottish bride, Rita) to Japan in 1920.

Kihei Abe, president of the Settsu brewery who had financed Taketsuru's distilling studies abroad, was unable to continue with the whisky project due to recession. Shinjiro Torii, at that time a successful wine producer, contacted Taketsuru and appointed him to set up whisky production at what became the Suntory company, in exchange for a 10-year contract. Production began at the new Yamazaki distillery in 1924 and whisky first went on sale in 1929.

Suntory was largely responsible for creating the whisky-drinking culture in Japan, displacing at least part of the traditional shochu (schnapps-type spirit,

see Fact File) industry. After World War II, Japanese youngsters aspired to the American lifestyle of baseball, sloppy joe sweaters, chewing gum — and whisky. The Japanese could not afford the Scotch the Americans drank, so Suntory established the Tory whisky bars nationwide, with a facsimile American ambience and their own tariff-free local whiskies behind the counter. They became very successful.

A feature of today's bars is the 'owner's bottle' — a customer's personal pouring bottle kept for him or her, ticketed on a shelf like left luggage and untouched until the next visit.

The spelling used in Japan is that of 'whisky' without the 'e'.

Mount Fujiyama overlooks the Kirin-Seagram whisky distillery. Japan imports vast quantities of Scotch to blend with its native grain spirit, but cannot produce its own distinctive malt whisky.

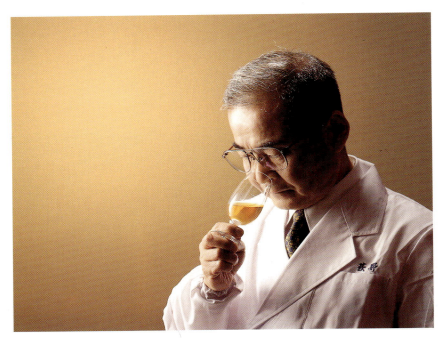

Hi • Soft-textured blend from Nikka (*qv*), which is aimed at younger consumers.

Hibiki • Premium blend from Suntory (*qv*). Hibiki contains about 30 different malts from the Yamazaki distillery (*qv*) with an average age of 20 years, and grain whiskies. This is one of the company's top five prestige brands and priced accordingly. 'Hibiki' means 'harmony'; the whisky has fair body, vivid rich fruit-and-smoke nose; gently woody but more bite than expected.

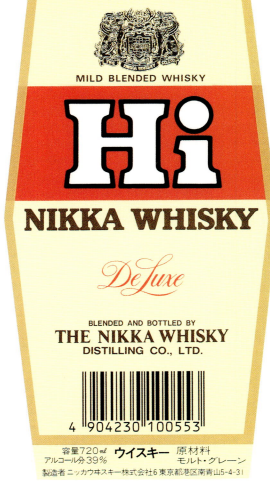

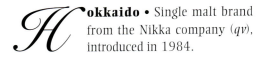

The art of blending malt whiskies is not restricted to the Scots, as this blender at Kirin-Seagram demonstrates.

All Malt • Vatted malt from Nikka (*qv*). Introduced in 1990, this is a combination of two malts, one produced in a pot still, the other in a Coffey continuous still. It makes for soft, easy-to-drink whisky, at once rich in malty flavour and delicate in texture.

Corn Base • Bourbon-style whisky from Nikka (*qv*). It is made from American-corn spirit, aged in charred new oak and blended with other whiskies specially produced by the company. All the constituent distillates are aged for a minimum of eight years. Extrovert and big in flavour but well enough mellowed.

From the Barrel • High-strength blend from Nikka (*qv*), introduced in 1985. It is bottled from the barrels to which the blend is returned to 'marry' after being assembled. Aromatic and 51.4% vol.

Gold & Gold • Blend of pot- and Coffey-still whiskies from the Nikka company (*qv*).

Grand Age • Super-premium blend brand from the Nikka company (*qv*), introduced in 1989.

Hokkaido • Single malt brand from the Nikka company (*qv*), introduced in 1984.

Kakubin • Standard blend from Suntory (*qv*). Kakubin is a pre-war brand, its introduction in 1937 representing an acceptable attainment level in the company's early efforts to produce a worthwhile blended whisky. The industry in Japan had only got under way in 1923 when construction of the first distillery began, and first sales were as late as 1929. Today, Kakubin (meaning 'square bottle') is the company's top-selling whisky (3.5 million cases a year), partly as a result of being upgraded in 1989 with additional malt content and higher average ages of the whiskies in the blend.

Nikka • Brand and company founded by one of Japan's 'fathers of whisky', Masataka Taketsuru. After studying distilling in Scotland (see introduction above), Taketsuru set up whisky production at Suntory (*qv*) before establishing his own company in 1934. He was 40 years old when he left Suntory and set up a fruit-juice company, Dai Nippon Kaju, to support him and his family as well as finance his continuing project to make whisky. The factory

was located at Yoichi, on the northern island of Hokkaido, where he had wanted to build the Suntory distillery 10 years earlier. Yoichi was a herring fishing and orchards locality with the humidity, cool climate, peat and good water Taketsuru felt were

Left: Scottish roots — Mr and Mrs Taketsuru, the founders of Nikka's malt distillery.
Below: The Suntory distillery towers at Hakushu combine the chimney design of Speyside drying kilns with elegant Japanese style.

right for making and maturing whisky. The local apple trees provided fruit for the juice production although the brand was not a big seller.

In 1935, Taketsuru had a pot still installed at Yoichi. Normally these are set up in pairs, one for each stage of the double-distillation process, but Taketsuru could only afford the one. It meant more work, but a bonus was the greater artisanal authenticity going right back to the original single-still part-time whisky production of Scottish Highland farms. His first whisky went on sale in October 1940, exactly 20 years after he and his Scots bride, Rita, arrived in Japan together, and just 14 months before Pearl Harbour and the concomitant economic disruption of the ensuing war. Taketsuru survived into the post-war whisky boom in Japan and went on to develop a range of different brands.

In 1952, he renamed the company, taking the initial syllables from NIppon and KAju to form Nikka. Rita died in 1961. In 1962, he bought his first Coffey still from Scotland to produce softer but not totally neutral spirits for blending, thus creating the broad company house style. Nikka, as quality-orientated as any company, makes what it calls 'hybrids' from products it imports, *ie* no local Japanese spirit is added but the final products are fashioned for the marketplace in Japan by blending

The pagodas of Nikka's Yoichi Hokkaido distillery reflecting the founder's deep love of Scottish whisky tradition.

according to Nikka's own specific techniques. This policy is in contrast to other Japanese whiskies, which blend local Japanese and imported spirits.

In addition to Yoichi on Hokkaido, where pot still 'Highland' malt is produced, and Sendai in Miyagikyo (built 1969), which yields pot still 'Lowland' malt (all of the stills coal-fired), Nikka has its Coffey still grain distillery at Nishinomiya, Hyogo, and its blending and ageing plant at Tochigi. Taketsuru died in 1979, at the age of 85, and his adopted son, Takeshi, succeeded him as president of the company. Nikka has just under 20% of the Japanese market.

*O*ld • Popular-price blend from Suntory (*qv*). Introduced in 1950, Suntory Old was, for long, the company's key brand, selling four million cases a year. Recession and up-grading of other Suntory brands, Reserve and Kakubin (*qqv*), have cut that by half but it is still the company's third top-seller. Old was the brand which established the widespread *mizu-wari* drinking style of one part whisky/three parts water and is nicknamed *tanuki* (the badger) or *daruma* (the doll) because of its distinctive, dumpy bottle. Malts and grains drawn from all three Suntory distilleries are used in the blend, which has good body and a fruity texture.

*P*ure Malt Black • All-malt Nikka (*qv*) whisky. Japan's first 100% pure malt whisky, it was intro-

duced in 1984 in tandem with Pure Malt Red (*qv*). Black comprises malt spirit, most of which is distilled at Nikka's Yoichi distillery on the northern island of Hokkaido, regarded as producer of the company's robust 'Highland'-style malt. Described as 'manly and strong' by an enthusiastic Japanese publicist who perhaps misses the point, it is certainly rich in aroma, with malty intensity of flavour.

Pure Malt Red • All-malt Nikka (*qv*) whisky, partner brand of Pure Malt Black (*qv*). In contrast to it, Red is a gentle, understated whisky from Miyagikyo in Sendai, seen as Nikka's 'Lowland' type malt distillery. The company encourages consumers who buy both Red and Black to carry out their own blending experiments with them to make their own personal whiskies. Red is soft, subtle and well textured.

Pure Malt White • Islay-style all-malt whisky from Nikka (*qv*). White is made from 100% imported Scotch malts, principally from Islay, and is vatted by Nikka's own blenders. Smoky, peaty and resonant in aroma and flavour.

Reserve • High malt-content standard blend from Suntory (*qv*). Reserve was introduced in 1969 to commemorate the company's 70th anniversary, and is its second-best-selling whisky, with sales of 2.5 million cases a year. Good rich flavour, touch of sherry and fruit, clean malty finish.

Royal • Premium blend at a standard price from Suntory (*qv*), created by Shinjiro Torii, founder of the company. Introduced in the 1960s, Royal has become popular as a 'customer's bottle', the practice in Japanese bars of holding over personal bottles for customers pending their next visit. Royal contains over 20 malts, the core spirits being 10-, 12- and 15-year-olds, and the average age 12 years. Good wood fragrance from American white oak casks, soft vanilla and malt on flavour.

Bottom: The grace of Nikka's second distillery, at Sendai.

R ye Base • Canadian-style blend from Nikka (*qv*). A core rye whisky blended with support whiskies, all produced and aged for six years at Nikka. Soft and smooth, with authentic tart fruit rye edge.

S untory • Brand and company with almost 70% of the Japanese market. Shinjiro Torii produced a port-style sweet wine called Akadama in the early years of the century. He felt he could establish a whisky market in Japan and, in 1921, employed a young chemist, newly returned from studies in Scotland, to set up a distillation project (see Nikka and introduction above).

Torii sought sites for a distillery throughout Japan, trying to find an environment that was as 'Scottish' as possible and collecting water samples for analysis and comparison with distilling waters in pure water and its formative influences on the Japanese tea ceremony. Three rivers converge at Yamazaki and their differing temperatures create a misty atmosphere conducive to maturing whisky. The distillery was built and the whisky marketed in 1929, although it was not until 1937, with the launch of the Kakubin brand (*qv*), that there was satisfaction with product

quality. In the post-war years Torii built whisky awareness among the shochu-drinking Japanese with his Tory whisky pubs and today the company markets more than 20 different whiskies.

Suntory's Hakushu plant, built in 1973, became the biggest malt distillery in the world, with 55 million litres of cask-strength spirit production a year; a third distillery, also at Hakushu, was built in 1981.

S untory White • Blend that was the very first modern Japanese whisky. Introduced in 1929 as Shirofuda, it quickly became known as White Label and the name stuck. Still available as one of the staple range.

Super Nikka • Blend from Nikka (*qv*), and the company's best-known product. It was introduced by the founder of Nikka in memory of his wife Rita, whom he met and married when a student in Scotland, after her death in 1961.

Super Session • Take-home blend from Nikka (*qv*), which was introduced in 1989.

The Blend • Blend from Nikka (*qv*). The brand was introduced in 1986, putting the emphasis on more vivid-tasting malt content in a blended whisky instead of grain. The Blend has majority malt content and The Blend Selection, introduced in 1989, is a de luxe version in decanter packaging. Fine intense flavours and silky texture.

Tsuru • Super-premium blend. This is the Nikka (*qv*) company's flagship whisky, the name deriving from the name of the founder of the company, Masataki Taketsuru. Tsuru means 'crane' in Japanese, hence the crane bird motifs on the packaging. It normally sells in a porcelain decanter but goes into a slim glass decanter for duty free, where display space is at a premium. Elegant, mellow finish.

Yamazaki • Suntory single malt and distillery. Yamazaki, built in 1923 by Shinjiro Torii, founder of Suntory (*qv*), beside Tennozan mountain, Kyoto, was Japan's first malt distillery. Its founding also marked the birth of the Japanese whisky industry with Torii's expansion beyond the wines in which he had previously specialised. Malting was initially done at the distillery but, as in Scotland, malt is now brought in. Suntory barley malt is imported and ranges from light to heavy peating to serve a wide scatter of blending and vatting functions. Different yeasts, wood and steel fermentation vats and a bewildering array of still shapes are used to create a wide range of malt spirit-types, all from the same distillery.

The distillation is all two stage, in copper pot stills and there are two distillation lines, each using a different yeast and having three versions of both the wash and the spirit stills, the swan necks having differing contours. Each kettle produces a unique distillate. Both naked flame and steam heating methods are used. The diversity of spirit types from a single source is akin to that of Midleton in Ireland (*qv*) but at Yamazaki, every one is a malt. Hence, the 'single malt' from Suntory is but one of many which could be offered. The rest are used as building bricks to form other final whiskies.

The variation continues with the choice of wood, both in terms of size and type; ex-sherry, bourbon and charred new oak barrels are used. All this diversity of production means that Suntory has 1.6 million casks of 100 different varieties of malt whisky maturing in four different locations at any given time. Suntory has two other malt distilleries, both of them at Hakushu, a hilly forest area west of Mount Fuji.

Yamazaki bottled single malt matures in seasoned white oak but has also used ex-sherry casks. Elegant, medium concentration, whiffs of peat, smoke and spice. Available as a 12-year-old.

Bottom: Yamazaki, like other Japanese distilleries, enjoys wild forested locations. Doubtless the builders regarded this as being as close to Scotland as they could find.

Whiskey from Other Countries

The Canterbury Plains of New Zealand's South Island. Many Scots settled this part of the world, but it was further south at Dunedin that organised, legal distilling was to begin.

WHISKY, WHISKEY, CHWISGI, VISKI — it is produced all over the world in so many different ways from combinations of bulk imports, local spirits and neutral alcohols. What distinguishes even modest-quality whiskey from vodka, schnapps, arrack and so on is that it is self-contained: it carries, or should carry, its own aromas, flavours, balance and resonances, rather than rely on mixers to add excitement. In short, it has a character to discover and, hopefully, savour. If you produce a whiskey you are aspiring to a certain excellence, whether it be through the individuality of your own local raw materials or the facsimile you can assemble from international brokers' lists.

The following gives an idea of the difference in approach of some of the world's other whiskey makers — from a large group like UB Spirits in India, producing 14 million cases a year, to a small, island distillery off the English coast, making 'white' whiskey.

Brazil

Natu Nobilis • Brazilian blend from international giant Seagram. Its Scottish style derives from malts from the company's own Highland distilleries imported and blended with local Brazilian grain spirits.

Czech Republic

King Barley • Single malt. The Tesetice distillery in Moravia has been making whiskies for 20 years now, King Barley deriving from different malts smoked over imported Scottish peat. It is the only Czech whisky produced by double distillation in pot stills and maturation is in oak casks for a minimum of six years (43% vol). Smoke on nose, sweet edge and full flavour.

India

Bagpiper • Bestseller in the Indian standard whisky category. The brand sells more than three million cases a year, mainly in its own domestic market. Bagpiper promotes by maintaining close links with the Indian film industry, and male film stars such as Ashok Kumar, Pran, Jackie Shroff and others, who are associated with the brand, attract a lot of attention to the whisky. Bagpiper runs national talent contests with screen tests as prizes and has a weekly 'Bagpiper Show' on satellite television about the life stories of the male Indian film stars; 42.8% vol.

Maqintosh • Blend from Amrut Distilleries in Bangalore. The actual blend is made up of Indian malt, five-year-old Scotch (presumably malt and grain already blended) and Indian neutral spirit.

McDowell's • Range of whiskies amounting to annual sales of several million cases on the domestic market. Their No.1 brand, a mainline quality, sells nearly 1.7 million cases each year while Diplomat, a popular-price brand, reaches 1.4 million cases. The McDowell range also includes India's 'first and only authentic' single malt produced in pot stills and aged in charred ex-bourbon oak casks. Robust aromas and rich texture. There are also two premiums.

Men's Club • Blended whisky introduced to the domestic market in 1974. A popular-price brand, it sells well in southern and western India to the extent of around 250,000 cases a year.

White House • Introduced in 1983 as a popular-price brand, a blend of Indian malt and imported (already blended) Scotch. In addition to domestic sales, it achieves a number of export markets, particularly in eastern Europe where it crops up in Latvia and Russia.

The best of both worlds — Indian tradition and western culture meet head on as Bagpiper whisky is given the glamour treatment by advertisers.

The delightful Isle of Man, home to The Gregneish Village Museum and a very popular whiskey.

New Zealand

Lammerlaw • New Zealand Single malt from Wilson Distillers (*qv*) in Dunedin, South Island. Lammerlaw was introduced in 1984 and achieves distribution throughout the Pacific basin and to the UK through the network of its owners, Seagram. The water used in production runs off the Lammerlaw Ranges through peat and moss bogs forming Deep Creek, the distillery stream, and Southland barley is grown in fertile alluvial soil. A pleasing artisanal element is the single pot still used for both stages of the double distillation. The spirit matures for a minimum of 10 years in American oak casks in warehouses on the Taieri Plains, outside Dunedin. Good peaty, oaky nose; full, sweet-edge flavour and fine length. Available at 10 years and 43% vol.

Wilson's • Blend and distillery in Dunedin, South Island. Dunedin (Gaelic for Edinburgh) was the landing point of the first Scottish settlers in New Zealand in 1848 and, of course, they brought distilling skills with them. Two men, Howden and

Isle of Man

Glen Kella • White whiskey from Isle of Man, a tiny dependency of the British Crown in the Irish Sea with its own parliament and currency. Glen Kella take Speyside malt and grain whisky which are already aged and redistil them on the island to create what is effectively a triple-distilled colourless whiskey with full nose and taste characteristics. Experiments had taken place with Canadian whisky but it tended to 'disappear' after the redistillation.

The first commercial distillation was in 1980, first sales were released in 1984 and the first malt was introduced in 1990. The spirit is reduced to 40% vol bottling strength with local Manx water. There are three- and five-year-old blends (with 40% malt content), and both eight- and 12-year-old vatted malts.

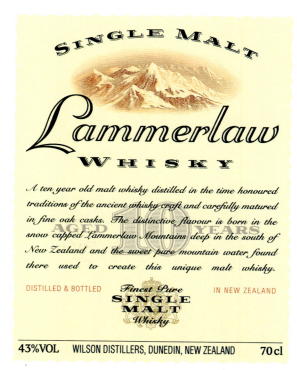

SINGLE MALT

Lammerlaw WHISKY

A ten year old malt whisky distilled in the time honoured traditions of the ancient whisky craft and carefully matured in fine oak casks. The distinctive flavour is born in the snow capped Lammerlaw Mountains deep in the south of New Zealand and the sweet pure mountain water found there used to create this unique malt whisky.

AGED 10 YEARS

DISTILLED & BOTTLED   Finest Pure SINGLE MALT Whisky   IN NEW ZEALAND

43% VOL   WILSON DISTILLERS, DUNEDIN, NEW ZEALAND   70 cl

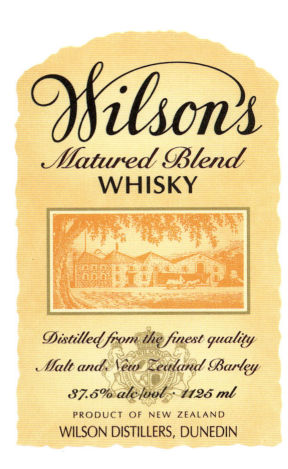

Robertson, went into partnership and built their Cumberland Street distillery to make Highland-style malts. In 1875, the government effectively closed what had developed into a thriving business by imposing excessive rates of duty. New Zealanders had to get by on illicit whiskey (including the famous Hokonui made in the wild and beautiful Southland) and imports for almost a century until 1968, when Wilson, an existing malt-extract production company, opened a distillery in Dunedin's old Willowbank brewery. The first matured whisky finally went on sale in 1974, this time in a fully fledged New Zealand style based on the distillery's own locale. Wilson's blended is now the top-selling brand in New Zealand.

Wilson's blend has a high malt content which is a combination of light and medium peatings. The minimum age of the malt spirits is six years; that of the grain is three years. Clean malty fragrance and warming flavour, with some alcoholic snap.

Slovenia

Jack & Jill • Blend from the Dana company in Mirna. Dana grew from a small specialist brandy distillery set in the Dolenjska vineyards and now produces a wide range of local and international spirit styles. Jack & Jill is a blend of imported 'Skotch' malts and local grain distillates. Fullish bodied and medium intensity of flavour.

South Africa

Teal's • South African standard blend. Teal's was introduced in 1990, and is a blend of Scotch malt and South African grain whiskies. It is three years old.

Three Ships • South African standard blend. Three Ships was launched in 1977 as a value-for-money three-year-old, a blend of imported Scotch malt and local whiskies. It has become one of the country's best-selling whiskies. In 1992, a five-year-old was introduced, the only one of its kind in South Africa. The malt content is high and the brand has won a number of international competition medals .

Whisky

DESTILERIAS

DYC

WHISKY

FINO BLENDED

Destilado, envejecido y embotellado por

DESTILERIAS Y CRIANZA DEL WHISKY, S.A.

PALAZUELOS DE ERESMA - SEGOVIA - ESPAÑA

D&C

REGISTRO EMBOTELLADOR
Nº 1-SG.1

70 cl.   - ELABORADO EN ESPAÑA -   *40% vol.*

Right: Experiments for Turkish whisky production involved the University Agricultural faculty at Ankara.

Spain

DYC • Best-selling Spanish blend produced in Segovia. The DYC stands for Destilerías y Crianzas (del Whisky SA), the brand-owning company which also owns the Lochside distillery in Scotland.

DYC

WHISKY

FINO BLENDED

8
AÑOS

70 cl.   *40% vol.*

DESTILERIAS Y CRIANZA DEL WHISKY, S.A.

Palazuelos de Eresma ~ Segovia.

ELABORADO EN ESPAÑA

Distilling began at Palazuelos de Eresma in Segovia in 1959, and the brand was launched in Spain in 1963 to general consumer approval.

Peat-dried malted barley and pot stills are used in an artisanal process based on Scottish production and ageing takes place in American oak in brick-built earth-floored warehouses. 40% vol.

Turkey

Ankara • Turkish whisky (or Turk Viskisi as the label says) from the country's state enterprise directorate, Tekel. The Faculty of Agriculture at Ankara University began experimenting in whisky production at the Ankara Brewery in 1956. By 1961, the whisky produced was ready for assessment and foreign experts, invited by Tekel to sample it, pronounced it 'better quality than many foreign whiskies'.

Wales, renowned for its rugged natural beauty may soon once again boast its own indigenous whisky.

Wales

Prince of Wales • Malt whisky bottled in Wales. The Welsh Whisky Company has actually never yet dealt in Welsh whisky — or 'chymreig chwisgi' as they say locally. To date, the product has been cask-strength Scotch tankered into Brecon, filtered through local herbs and reduced to bottling strength with fine Brecon water. However, the energy and enterprise have been entirely home produced by ex-Lufthansa pilot Dafydd Gittins and his wife, Gillian, who began blending whisky in 1974 in a small cellar and finally began distilling their own in 1994. Maturation requirements mean that the first home-produced spirit will not be marketed until 1997 or 1998 at the earliest.

Whisky making in Wales can be traced back to the fourth century, when a form of it was made by monks on Bardsey Island, off the Lleyn Peninsula. The first commercial distillery in Wales was founded in the early 18th century, by the family of one Evan Williams from Pembrokeshire, and a little later the kin of a Jack Daniel from Cardigan began a similar venture. We know these names now as the very people (*qqv*) who went on to emigrate and establish two of the greatest brands in American whiskey production. In fact, Williams was also the first commercial distiller in Kentucky when he set up his still there. After the Williamses and Daniels, a small Welsh whisky industry existed until the temperance movement snuffed it out in 1906. Swn y Mor, a three-year-old blend, is the best seller, with Prince of Wales Special Reserve, a four-year-old malt, said to be catching up fast. Prince of Wales 10-year-old is confusingly labelled a 'single vatted' malt, by which is meant a malt from an individual Scottish distillery (although they do not say which) that has been vatted with herbs before bottling. Exports now reach several countries in Europe and the Far East.

Brandy

BRANDY IS SPIRIT DISTILLED FROM FRUIT. JUICE, PULP AND SKIN from any kind of fruit that will ferment may be used in different ways to produce brandy. The name comes from the Dutch word *brandewijn*, meaning 'burnt wine' from 'burning' or boiling wine to distil it. The most familiar type of brandy comes from wine made from grapes. Wine brandy is distilled and usually aged in oak barrels, a process which mellows the spirit and adds colour, aroma and flavour to it. Provided the spirit itself is good, the longer a brandy remains in wood, the better and finer it is likely to become. However, after about 60 years even the best get too woody and are transferred to large glass jars.

An age statement on a bottle gives an idea as to the quality — two years old is very young, 10 to 12 years should mean good brandy anywhere — but some countries favour a coded system like the Three-Star, VSOP *etc* ratings used in France. Such quality-indicators, however, must be subject to some kind of legal control, otherwise they are open to abuse. Ages must refer only to time spent in wood since spirits, unlike many wines, do not improve in bottle. Brandies are made in every wine- and fruit-producing country and usually there is some kind of regulatory structure to define styles, production, and so on.

In France, the word *fine* on a label indicates a brandy from a less well-known region which is still subject to regulation. A *fine* can also be used to indicate any good quality brandy in a bar or restaurant.

A type of brandy is also made from the mass of grape skins and stalks left behind after grapes have been pressed, and/or juice has fermented, to make wine. This is called pomace brandy and, although often an acquired taste, it is widely popular. It has the merit of carrying the fresh aromas particular to the grapes from which it has been distilled, and is thus often drunk very young, *eg* at six months, with no wood ageing. Italian grappa and French marc are the best-known examples of pomace brandy. On French labels, the word marc is usually followed by the vineyard region where the grapes used in its making were grown. Marc, however, is of local importance only.

Brandy made from fruits other than grapes is called, predictably, fruit brandy. Mirabelle, quetsch and slivovic are all plum brandies, poire William is made from pears, apple (or cider) brandy from apples and so on. Some fruit brandy styles are hidden behind other names, like applejack in Canada and the USA, and calvados in France, both of which are apple brandies.

It is worth remembering that natural fruit distillates are essentially dry in style, so liqueurs and cordials with names like apricot brandy and cherry brandy are misleading; these are not brandies but sweetened fruit essences mixed with silent spirit. Kirsch, on the other hand, is a true cherry brandy distilled from fermented cherries.

Opposite page: The Ugni Blanc grape (St Emilion) gives good yields with low alcohol, copes well with frost, and has high acidity. It is one of the three authorised varieties that can make a wine base for cognac.

Left: The tranquillity of barrel ageing is no distraction for the vigilant record keeper.

France

Cognac

COGNAC HAS COME TO DOMINATE THE CON-
CEPT OF BRANDY to such an extent that
the word is widely used in other countries as a synonym — *coñac* in Spain, *conhac* in
Portugal, *konyak* in central Europe and so on. In the
16th century, the Dutch traded in salt and wine along
the west coast of France, La Rochelle being one of
their stops. They distilled the wine back in the
Netherlands but eventually designed a still so that the
French could distil it for them and save storage space
on board their ships. Distillation began in the area

around 1530, and the still became the traditional
pot charentais in use to this day.

Cognac, like the great wines of France, has its
own *appellation contrôlée*, which states that brandy of
that name must come from six designated vineyard
areas (Grande Champagne, Petite Champagne,
Borderies, Fins Bois, Bons Bois, Bois Ordinaires)
around the town of Cognac in the Charente region of
western France. It also specifies the grapes to be used
(mostly Ugni Blanc, some Folle Blanche and Colombard)
and that the brandy be distilled twice in a traditional
pot still, the idea behind all this being that the broad

characteristics of cognac brandy will always be identifiably similar no matter who makes it. *Appellation contrôlée*, however, has nothing to do with prescribing or indicating excellence; that is left to the individual producer, and it has to be said that there are many extremely modest cognacs on the market.

Cognac is normally blended for it to be at its best; even a single-vineyard bottling will be an amalgam of several casks. Age statements are not used for cognac and quality indicators like VSOP, XO *etc* are inexact; they correspond only very broadly when comparing different brands. The youngest spirit in a Three-Star cognac might be a raw three years or a mellow five years old; in a VSOP it could be five or 15 years old, and so on. Ageing is always in oak, usually from the Limousin and/or Tronçais forests, and both new and old wood are used.

Bisquit • Alexandre Bisquit was just 20 years old when, in 1819, he set up his cognac firm in Jarnac. He hailed from Limoges, and knew well the special properties of the local Limousin oak for ageing brandy, so he brought in quantities of it to build his maturation vats. Soon all his competitors were using the same wood, and today Limousin oak casks are in demand worldwide for ageing wines and spirits. Bisquit has vineyards and distils its own cognac in a large, modern still house at the Château de Lignières, north of the town of Cognac. The casks of spirit used to age on the banks of the Charente river in Cognac but now do so at Lignières, where the storage *chais* (ground-floor cellars) are temperature- and humidity-controlled to simulate riverside conditions. Bisquit spirit runs off the still at a lower strength than most others, giving it a fuller, grapier flavour. Normal range of qualities available, plus occasional 50- and 100-year-old bottlings and single-vineyard Château de Lignières.

Bouju • Fiercely traditional artisanal producer who uses only his own Grande Champagne grapes (the vintage is hand-picked) and makes small batches in a tiny still. It is only the third still the little family business has had since it began making cognac in 1805, a fine example of 'If it ain't broke, don't fix it'. Small stills mean more emptying and refilling but allow

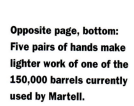

more control over the final product, which is what M. Bouju likes. The still is wood fired and during the winter distillation runs someone has to sleep in the still room to keep an eye on things. Blending decisions are easy for M. Bouju since his stocks amount to 17 times his annual sales rate.

No caramel or sugar is added and the cognac has the mouth-filling style of armagnac — 'virile, rustic and substantial', as M. Bouju himself puts it. Long, patrician and dry finish. There is a Four-Star quality (following an old tradition whereby each star indicates a year's ageing), many different average ages and a spread of cask strengths.

Camus • The company specialises in top-end cognac, much produced in its own distilleries. Sixty per cent of Camus' turnover is in Napoléon-quality and a fifth of all Napoléon sold has the Camus name on it.

The firm began in 1863, as a small consortium

Opposite page, bottom: **Five pairs of hands make lighter work of one of the 150,000 barrels currently used by Martell.**

Below left: **The tranquil Château du Plessis in the Borderies is the home of the Camus family with their award-winning cognacs.**

he sailed into exile and the company was later also purveyor to the court of Napoléon III.

In the course of the 20th century, Courvoisier was owned by an English family, confiscated by the Germans during World War II and projected to best-selling status in France in the postwar years by the Braastads, a dynamic Norwegian family. Today, Ivar Braastad works with the brand and Alain Braastad is chairman of Delamain (*qv*). Courvoisier takes grapes from the four best growing zones, and the combination of these yield full-bodied, well-flavoured cognac.

formed by a grower to compete with the large buyers. Jean-Baptiste Camus wanted to retain full control of the final cognac and from the outset sold on quality. To this end, the trademark, La Grande Marque, was created and export markets were cultivated; today, more than 85% of Camus' sales are outside France. The company has four large vineyards, each with a château and its own distillery, but mature brandy at least 20 years old is also bought in. The opulent and elegant Camus house style is created by combining distillates principally from Grande Champagne and the Borderies vineyard zones; the latter's brandies tend to be big and fuller flavoured. The company has done well in recent years in the International Wine & Spirit Competition in London: three entries, three gold medals awarded, these being for Vieille Réserve, Extra and XO, the latter two packed in decanters.

Château-Paulet • Established in 1848, the business is still family-run and in the hands of the grandsons of the founder. Château-Paulet's XO won the trophy for 'Best Cognac' twice in three years in London's International Wine & Spirit Competition in the early 1990s. The XO is an elegant Fine Champagne but the company also concentrates to some degree on blending well-flavoured brandies from the Borderies vineyards with old cognac from its stocks (part of which are over a century in age).

Courvoisier • Brand which is closely associated with Napoléon during his latter, imperial days. Emmanuel Courvoisier had a wine and spirit business in Paris in the late 18th century, and he became supplier to Emperor Napoléon's court. Napoléon is said to have taken a supply of Courvoisier cognac with him when

The firm has two distilleries of its own and commissions 400 independent distillers to make spirit to its specifications. Since wood is so important, Courvoisier even chooses the trees for its casks and the staves are seasoned in the open air for three years before being made up into barrels.

At the top end of the range are the decanters designed by Russian art deco artist Erté (*aka* Roman de Tirtoff). The cognac museum in the Courvoisier château on the river bank in Cognac is excellent.

Top left: Subtle nuances detected by the nose confirm the success of the blending to an experienced taster.

Bottom right: Courvoisier's elegant head office in Jarnac, on the bank of the river Charente, upstream from Cognac.

Davidoff • High-quality blend developed to complement fine Havana cigars. For the past 30 years, Zino Davidoff's cigar shop in Geneva has been a place of pilgrimage for Havana smokers the world over. In that time, he has formed strong opinions as to the best style of cognac to accompany the best cigars and this blend embodies his preferences. His 'Sélection' goes against the grain of current and recent trends towards lighter and subtler cognacs; his is rich, intense of aroma and oaky. Taste is big, mouth-filling and a little pungent, with good length.

Delamain • Delamain specialises in old cognac exclusively from the top delimited production zone, Grande Champagne. It has no vineyards but buys brandies with a minimum age of 15 years and ages them gently in old wood for a further 10 to 40 years before careful and gradual blending. The Delamains have long been travellers in search of their fortune; a member of the family was part of the court of Charles I of England in the 17th century, another established a porcelain factory in Ireland, and in more recent times Delamains have distinguished themselves in the modern arts and sciences. There is a family connection with Courvoisier (*qv*).

The Delamain house style is light and elegant, as befits Grande Champagne distillates. Three noses are involved in approving blends and there must be unanimity regarding approval of quality; a two-to-one majority is never accepted. Grande Champagne cognac can take 60 years to mature fully. Many of the brandies in the Delamain cellars are so old that they are removed from wood and stored in glass demijohns.

Flavour and balance at Delamain are close to perfect. The 'youngest' version, Pale and Dry, is minimum 25 years old, light and mellow in flavour and fine in texture. Top of the range of four is from a single cask so perfectly balanced it remains unblended.

Delon • Luxury brand using the fame of, and actively promoted by, French film star Alain Delon. It is an XO Réserve Spéciale from Grande Champagne, Petite Champagne and Fins Bois, with an average age of 30 years, and aimed at prestige outlets, particularly duty free. Delon made a personal appearance at a big tax-free industry exhibition in Cannes recently to boost his cognac as well as a new women's perfume and a cigarette brand, all of which bear his name.

Dor • Remarkable small company which, in addition to a fine current range, has cognacs going back to the year of Napoleon's victory over the Russians and Austrians at Austerlitz. There are several pre-phylloxera cognacs which have dropped naturally in strength to between 31% and 37% vol and which, due to the special circumstances, are allowed to be sold with a year of vintage indicated.

Frapin • Prestigious brand that distils its own Grande Champagne wines. François Rabelais was a member of the Frapin family, and Pierre Frapin was apothecary to Louis XIV. The coat of arms the king granted him appears on the labels of

Top: Contrasting different samples can be enjoyably hard work.

Bottom left: The art is to select, balance, and finally assemble the house style.

Frapin cognac today. The family has lived in the Charente since 1210 and today own the largest vineyard in the Grande Champagne. There was a link through marriage with Rémy Martin (*qv*), to whom they used to sell cognac, but following an inter-family feud in the 1970s, that arrangement came to an end. Frapin now has its own distinguished niche in the top-end cognac market, all of its qualities (bar the Three-Star) comprising 100% Grande Champagne eaux de vie. When well developed, the style is soft, slightly oaky and earthy with a mellow fruit *rancio* and succulent finish.

Godet • A family firm still run by the Godets, who descend from the Dutch who settled around 1600 in the La Rochelle area to show the local growers how to distil 'burnt wine' — brandy — for export north to the Netherlands. Not only did King Henri IV buy the Godet's cognac, he granted them the right to carry swords, a considerable honour in those days. For a small firm, Godet has a high profile in the USA and international duty-free outlets. The range includes an innovative bottle design which is square in cross section but uniquely long and slim, in order to fit snugly into a standard businessman's briefcase.

Bottom: Nosing a cognac in a typically suitable tulip-shaped glass.

Hardy • The Hardy brand became the third-top-selling cognac in France in the 1950s, within only six years of appearing in bottles for the first time; previously, it had been sold only in bulk. Anthony Hardy was a London wine merchant who moved to Cognac in 1863. He closed his office in London when sales dropped off due to a rise in UK duty and concentrated instead on selling in bulk to eastern Europe. Today, the brand's main markets are the USA and the Far East, and fifth-generation sisters Bénédicte and Sophie Hardy have taken over much of the marketing. There is a family link with the Hardys who own the famous wine (and brandy) company (*qv*) in Australia. Both the top-end cognacs and the decanter designs from Hardy are very fine, and there is also a small range of Pineau des Charentes. El Sublimado is Hardy's own brand of hand-made, cognac-impregnated corona cigars from the Cibao valley in the Dominican Republic.

Hennessy • Mexican *bandido* Pancho Villa used to say that 'Hennessy' was the only gringo word he liked. Today, this is the best-selling cognac brand in the world, with sales now approaching three million cases a year.

The company has 2,600 growers under contract to produce grapes and 27 distilleries producing spirit for it exclusively. At any given time, there are more than a quarter of a million casks of distillate maturing in Hennessy warehouses, yet for a while they had to suspend supply of certain categories of cognac to the duty free market due to stocks running dangerously low. The company even owns a forest in the Limousin, to ensure resources for oak casks.

Captain Richard Hennessy, an Irish nobleman from Cork, had served in the French army and, having liked his surroundings when he was stationed near Cognac, subsequently settled there. In 1765, he began shipping cognac to British and Irish aristocrats and did very well out of it. The brand has never been embraced by the French and 98% of production is still exported. Talleyrand and Alexandre Dumas, however, are two Frenchmen known to have regularly drunk Hennessy cognac.

Hennessy had much to do with the origination of the descriptive codes that are used on cognac bottles today. In 1817, the British Prince Regent began ordering 'very superior old pale' cognac from Hennessy and, latterly, this was shortened to VSOP in orders and to describe shipments of this type bound for Britain. A little later, Hennessy was also the first to use stars and the term XO on bottle labels to indicate specific qualities of cognac. All of these terms are recognised in French law today.

The Hennessy house style is opulent and well flavoured, for which a high percentage of Borderies is added to the Champagnes and Fins Bois in the blending. More than 100 different brandies go into the blending of Hennessy's XO, the oldest of which is almost 100 years old.

*H*ine • High-quality cognac from a company also associated with 'early-landed late-bottled' vintage cognac. Thomas Hine went to France from Dorset in the late 18th century and was stranded there, at least to begin with, by the effects of the French Revolution. He joined the cognac firm of Ranson & Delamain (*qv*), married the boss's daughter and eventually became its proprietor. The firm's name was changed to Hine in 1817, and a logo of a hind, punning his surname, was introduced. This was later changed to the splendid stag emblem which now adorns Hine cognac labels.

Today, cousins Jacques and Bernard Hine buy in both young and mature brandies for blending and ageing in small casks. The first eight months are spent in new wood, followed by long-term maturation in used casks seasoned with cognac. The Hine style is light, elegant and silky, from Champagnes and Fins Bois origins. The starter quality, Signature, is not designated Three-Star because it is at least as good as other firms' VSOPs. The middle range is Fine Champagne and the top-end qualities are exclusively Grande Champagne. Napoléon Old Réserve was recently relaunched.

*L*andy • Brand with spun-glass sculptures set within glass-globe decanters. There are two series of 12 sculptures — famous ships and the animals from the Chinese zodiac — and they are seen as 'collectables'. Prices of up to US$480 do not seem to dent their popularity, particularly in duty-free outlets.

*M*artell • With sales of two million cases a year, the world's second-largest cognac brand after Hennessy (*qv*) but, unlike the latter, it has a high profile in France, where it is the top seller. It was the cognac served after the signing of the World War I armistice in 1918. The company owns vineyards in the Champagnes, the Borderies and the Fins Bois, but

their contribution to Martell's production volume is nominal. Even an army of almost 2,500 growers providing wines for distillation (some of them for the past two centuries) furnishes only half of the annual requirements; the other half is bought in, in the form of young spirit. This all comes from the top four vineyard zones, but Martell's distinctively full and nutty core flavour comes from an emphasis on Borderies spirit; in fact, 60% of the entire Borderies production is taken up by Martell. For maturation, Martell prefers Tronçais oak, which has a very tight grain and imparts less tannin to the spirit. The evaporation known as 'the angels' share', which empties about 3% of the volume from Cognac's casks every year, costs Martell alone 2.5 million bottles each season.

'La Coquille', the modest building where Jean Martell set up in business on his arrival from Jersey in 1715, is now surrounded by the company complex in the centre of Cognac.

The company dates from 1715, when Jean Martell went from his native Jersey to Cognac; within five years, he was exporting 40,000 barrels a year to Hamburg, Liverpool and London. The first use of the term 'Extra' to indicate better quality was used for an order being sent to London. Towards the end of the century Martell began using a starring system to further indicate quality ranking.

Today, the brand is sold wherever cognac is drunk but Martell continues to seek out new markets. It is creating super-premium editions for the Far East and duty free (including the recent Classique in a Baccarat crystal decanter) and working, like many of the large drinks companies, to develop the enormous untapped potential of mainland China, where cognac has great prestige. New distilleries are also being built to produce non-cognac brandy outside France in countries like South Africa and Mexico.

Meukow • The founder of the company was originally the Russian tsar's wine buyer, who went to Cognac each year to buy distilling wine to be shipped to Russia. Eventually he was based there permanently and, in 1862, set up his own company. The brand became well known in the Far East, still the company's core market, where the bottle with the great cat motif on the glass echoes Jin Bao, the 'golden leopard' which symbolises success to the Chinese. During the German occupation of World War II, the Commandant in Cognac was a member of the family who had sold Meukow to the Shepherd family just 20 years before. He kept the Germans off the townspeople's backs by having them supply 'brandy' — made not from grapes, but from vegetables.

Otard • The smallest of the big brands, or biggest of the small brands, as the company itself puts it. The Otard lineage is stiff with history, family ancestors including a Viking noble and a Norman soldier in William the Conqueror's 1066 invasion of England. The Otards were latterly Scottish Jacobites, who fled to France when the Stuart Rebellions failed.

Jean Otard was sentenced to death in the French Revolution but he escaped and, in 1799, set up in partnership with a local grower in Cognac where he had land. The company has no vineyards or distillery, but buys in young brandies for ageing and blending. The historic Château de Cognac in the town is the company HQ and what is now the town hall used to be the Otard family home. The distinctive Otard bottle was inspired by the 'teardrop' shape of the brandy that runs down the inside of a glass after being swirled.

The VSOP is a Fine Champagne of up to eight years of age and the higher qualities bring in cognacs from other zones to round out flavour and aroma. The Napoléon is up to 15 years old and the top quality, Extra, has some 50-year-old brandy in it.

Polignac • High-profile brand of the largest cooperative in Cognac. The growers' membership is around 3,600, most of it in the Fins Bois and Bons Bois vineyards, so the house style is quite light and soft. The spirit is made in more than 100 stills in nearly 30 distilleries. The de Polignacs are one of France's

LA VOUTE-POLIGNAC

oldest and most distinguished families and they gave permission for their name and escutcheon to be used for the brand. It has been very successful since its introduction in the late 1950s, business in the USA doing particularly well. Japan, the UK and duty free are also important markets, which have given the company opportunities to introduce presentation packs and de luxe editions.

Rémy Martin • Founded in 1724, the Rémy Martin house specialises in blends exclusively from the two top-ranked vineyard zones of Cognac — Grande Champagne and Petite Champagne. When a blend contains at least 50% of the former, it is called 'Fine Champagne', and this description is to be found on almost all Rémy Martin labels. The specialisation began in the 1920s with access that the owner, André Renaud, had through marriage to the Frapin (*qv*) vineyards in, and mature cognac stocks from, the two Champagnes. By emphasising the lightness and elegance of Fine Champagne, Rémy Martin acquired a reputation for 'specialness'. After the last war, emphasis was extended to the VSOP to encourage consumers to trade up from Three-Star, and this has been very successful. It is the top-selling VSOP in the world and one in every three bottles of VSOP or higher quality is Rémy Martin. The wine is distilled on its lees in small stills to give better aroma and fruit presence. Ageing is in small Limousin oak casks made by Rémy's own coopers in the traditional way.

Normal range available, plus some special editions and decanters. Louis XIII has an average age of 50 years, meaning two generations of cellar masters have been involved in tending the brandies that go into it. The decanter is a replica of a flask found on the site of the Battle of Jarnac in 1569.

The family name of de Polignac has given a stylish lift to a classic brand.

Renault • Important brand in Scandinavian and duty-free markets. Jean Renault founded his company in 1835, and he was one of the first to export cognac in bottle. In the 1970s, the company used the Castillon brand name for an expansion programme in some export markets but the Renault branding is now firmly established. By concentrating on a single high quality — Carte Noire Extra has an average age of 20 years — the brand is well understood and appreciated. It is round, soft and has a pleasant wood fragrance throughout.

Robin • The first cognac company to sell in bottle and the first to register a bottle label. Customers were slow to convince on the merits of bottles and to begin with Robin had to insist on them buying six cases of bottled cognac for every cask they bought. The label was to protect against counterfeiting once the idea caught on in the trade. Hubert Germain-Robin, who produces small-batch brandy in the USA (*qv*), is a member of the family. The company is now part of Martell, and specialises in top-end editions such as their soft and gracious Extra.

Armagnac

ARMAGNAC, THE 'BRANDY OF D'ARTAGNAN' MADE IN THE SOUTH-WEST OF FRANCE in the Gers (Old Gascony) actually predates cognac. Distilling skills fostered by the Arabs in what is now Spain had crossed the Pyrenees by the 12th century and there is documented reference to distillation in the region in 1411. Armagnac has its own official appellation and there are three delimited vineyard zones — Bas Armagnac, Ténarèze and Haut Armagnac, in order of importance.

There are similarities with cognac, such as the main grapes used, although the Folle Blanche has a local name, the Piquepoul, and the Baco is also highly successful. However, the latter grape happens to be a hybrid, something disliked by Brussels, so no matter how much the growers like it, up it will have to come eventually. Also, the traditional armagnac still is different. It is a form of continuous still, which distils to much lower strength (55-60% vol, compared to 70% vol for cognac) and produces a more rounded, flavourful spirit. Cognac stills, too, are now permitted in Armagnac to give wider blending options but the best armagnac is made with a traditional still.

Top: Gabarret is the first town you meet travelling south-west into Bas Armagnac, the zone with the best production of the three delimited areas.

Right: This traditional Armagnac still, at Distillerie Lafontan, near Eauze, is different from those in Cognac in both shape and output.

Like cognac, most armagnac is blended, but single vintages — some going back to the 19th century — and single vineyards can be found. Quality indicators (VS, VSOP *etc*) are also used and correspond roughly to those used for cognac, although often with armagnac the blends are a little older, mellower and better value for money. Oak ageing as in Cognac but since the native 'black' oak of Monlezun is now scarce, Limousin and Tronçais casks are taking over. There is a tendency for those who do not know any better to dismiss armagnac as a cheap substitute for cognac. There is also a tendency for those who know what they are talking about to prefer it to cognac.

mouth-filling brandy. Joseph Vaghi, an Italian, bought the Château de Lamothe in Gascony in 1924 and his son Bruno established the vineyards there.

Baron de Sigognac • Very traditional distillers with extraordinary old armagnac stocks, including every vintage from 1984 back to 1920 (£192 per bottle) and another 10 vintages going back to 1866 (£652 per bottle), the year in which the Treaty of Prague ended the Austro-Prussian War. Vaghi 1975, a single vintage from the Bas Armagnac, was distilled at the ancient norm of 55% vol (*cf* cognac at 70%-plus vol) and has been aged in local 'black' Monlezun oak. It is bottled at its natural strength (49% vol) and colour. With the low distillation strength, it is overbrimming with tangy, rooty, fruity, toasted complexity — a wonderful,

Chabot • Large brand with high profile in duty-free shops and specialist in top-end qualities. It is a sister brand to Marquis de Puységur (*qv*) under the Camus cognac umbrella (*qv*) and they both use brandies from the company's vineyards in Bas Armagnac, the best growing zone. They are produced in traditional stills. The range offers nothing below Napoléon quality.

Château Garreau • Family-run estate distillery that produces prize winning armagnacs by a secret blending process. This is a very traditional operation with M. Garreau growing his own vines and distilling in three ancient classic local stills (although his son has invented a new electrically heated still with the help of a state research grant). The casks in which the brandy ages are from trees on his own estate. The range states ages from five- to 20-year-olds, apart from the Three-Star.

Château de Laubade • Single estate and old-vintage specialist. The Lesgourgues family have Folle Blanche grapes in their Bas Armagnac vineyards, and the different grape types are distilled separately on the lees in a traditional armagnac still to enhance flavours.

Festival time in Gascony, where stilt walking is a traditional way of celebrating another year free of the old scourge of flooding.

Château du Tariquet • Elegant, classic armagnac from a small-batch production specialist who exports widely. Yves Grassa produces from the 'grape to the bottle' on his vineyard in Bas Armagnac. The produce of his traditional wood-fired still includes a sumptuous, fragrant Folle Blanche at 45% vol.

Clés des Ducs • An early brand on the export markets, it made its name when armagnac was first launched as a cheap alternative to cognac. A bestseller in France and in duty-free outlets but owners, Rémy Cointreau, are trying to reposition it higher up the quality scale. Most of its distillation wines are from the top two production zones but the still spirit (mainly cognac) is blended young for the volume market.

Château de Laubade uses Folle Blanche vines for their estate-bottled production.

The brandies spend three years in new oak, then go into local 'black' oak from Monlezun. The Lesgourgues range starts with VSOP because they do not deal in young armagnac. Château de Laubade is a single-property, estate-bottled brandy and vintages go back to 1886. There is also a clear, unaged Folle Blanche eau de vie with fine authentic grape aroma which may not be called armagnac since it lacks oak ageing.

Château de Malliac • The Bertholon family has distinct ideas on the making of armagnac and commission a distiller to make its distillates to precise instructions. These distillates spend up to a year in new oak and then go into gentle old casks. The final stages of maturation take place in the cellars of the splendid château, built in the 12th century by Jehan de Malliac, a crusader knight. The de Malliac house style is fragrant and zesty but very fine. The Bertholons also manage to produce some brandy from Folle Blanche, the now-rare original armagnac grape which has become particularly susceptible to disease in recent decades. The company has an extraordinary range of vintage armagnacs and its Ultimate bottling is a blend of the best years of the century. Château de Malliac has been served on Concorde and at the Elysée Palace in Paris.

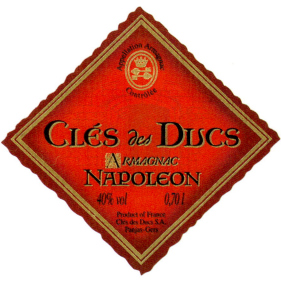

Dupeyron • Vintages specialist and populariser who will blend to order and personalise bottles. The jazzier side of Dupeyron's business belies a serious approach to buying Folle Blanche wines from the best two growing zones and commissioning a distiller to make the brandies. These are aged in local Monlezun oak. He also buys old armagnacs for further ageing, blending and bottling. Dupeyron's bottles travel far, thanks to his vintage club, Armagnac du Collectionneur, mail-order office, an armagnac boutique in Paris and duty free presence. Vintages go back to 1850 but those bottled separately date from 'only' 1904.

CHATEAU de LAUBADE
J.J. Lesgourgues Propriétaire en Bas-Armagnac

Janneau • Pre-eminent brand and family who have done much to proselytise for armagnac as a quality brandy in its own right. The company dates from 1851, and the present stocks have been built up over the five generations of the family distilling since then. Topping up of casks depleted by evaporation — 'the angels' share' — is done by brandy from the same vintage. Today, Janneau is the best-known name in armagnac and the brand the biggest selling. Both traditional and *cognaçais* stills are used, the latter for younger spirit that makes up most of the large-volume Three-Star. Above VSOP, all the brandy is from traditional stills and the higher qualities make up over 60% of the company's sales. Domaine de Mouchac is a vintaged single-estate armagnac from the family's own vineyards. Some other vintages and special gift presentations in porcelain and decanter supplement the conventional range to XO and Extra.

Larressingle • Family firm established in 1837, and the first to sell armagnac in bottle. The Papelorey family buys in eaux-de-vie under 20 years old from both classic and cognac-type stills, and ages them in cellars which were once part of a convent in the town of Condom. These are finally blended with older stocks held at the Château de Larressingle. This is a beautiful *bastide*, a type of fortified hamlet to be found all over Old Gascony. Larressingle was built by the Bishops of Condom and finished in 1250; the Papeloreys bought it in 1896 and are thus able to say, perhaps tongue in cheek, that their house was established in the 13th century. Small but distinguished range including the Comte de Laffite XO, available in duty free and Japan.

Marquis de Caussade • The first bottle of armagnac to enter the USA bore this name and it was taken there by the then-marquis himself. He took it with him on the maiden voyage of the *Normandie* liner in 1934 to introduce the 'brandy of D'Artagnan' to the Americans. He was an appropriate courier, since many of his ancestors served as musketeers to the French kings. The brand is now the fifth biggest on the market and high profile in many export markets. The mature stocks are among the largest in the industry and give great scope for old ages and vintages. Conventional range plus vintages, and several stated-age bottlings, including 21- and 30-year-old.

Marquis de Montesquiou • Brand and company founded by a descendant of the original D'Artagnan. Pierre, Marquis de Montesquiou, set up the company in 1936, to market armagnac distilled on his estate. Among his ancestors is Charles de Batz Castelmore, who was a captain of the 18th century French Compagnie des Mousquetaires and the original on whom Alexandre Dumas based D'Artagnan, the hero of his novel. The brand is now one of the top half-dozen in the world and widely exported. It is the top seller in Japan. The company has vineyards in Bas Armagnac (which include Folle Blanche grapes) but also buys in wines from the top two zones. The traditional stills produce real, old-fashioned armagnac spirit with a distillation strength of just 55% vol, which ultimately mellows into rich, aromatic brandy. The spirit is stepped through different woods, from a few months in new oak to a long final lie in benign old casks. Normal range and some vintages going back to the 1930s.

Château de Larressingle, spiritual home of the Papelorey family brand, is an Old Gascony bastide dating back to the 13th century.

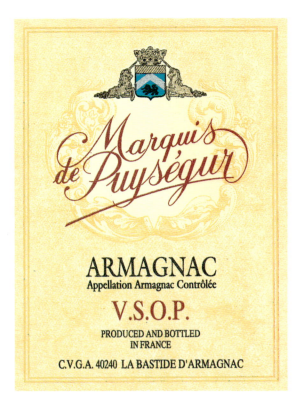

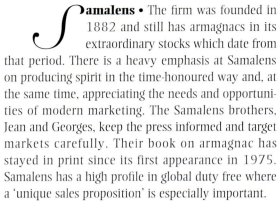

Samalens • The firm was founded in 1882 and still has armagnacs in its extraordinary stocks which date from that period. There is a heavy emphasis at Samalens on producing spirit in the time-honoured way and, at the same time, appreciating the needs and opportunities of modern marketing. The Samalens brothers, Jean and Georges, keep the press informed and target markets carefully. Their book on armagnac has stayed in print since its first appearance in 1975. Samalens has a high profile in global duty free where a 'unique sales proposition' is especially important.

Each of the four traditional armagnac stills is over 100 years old but the company also makes lighter spirit from cognac stills, only for use in the VSOP where it makes up 30% of the blend. The brothers still use local black oak from Monlezun in the cellars.

There is a large range from the tasty VSOP, through a noble 15-year-old, to a centenarian which has spent 70 years in oak. There is also a good choice of vintages going back to last century.

Marquis de Puységur • Companion brand to Chabot (*qv*), armagnac brand leader in global duty free. They may well have been making armagnac at the Château de Puységur in the 1500s, and an ancestor of the family is claimed to have introduced Louis XIII to armagnac brandy. Five of the Puységurs have been Knights of Malta. The group owns vineyards in the Bas Armagnac and distils in traditional apparatus.

Vieille Plus is 20 years old minimum age and richly fragrant, and there is a range of single vintages.

de Montal • Small firm with short track record but already a fine pedigree in offering good armagnac. The de Montal cousins buy brandies from the local cooperative and age them at their Château de Rieutort in Eauze. The blends are well put together and widely exported. They have older average ages than most, such as their VSOP, which is eight to nine years old. The cousins also offer vintage armagnacs from a wide scatter of properties throughout the three growing zones.

Sempé • Henri-Abel Sempé was a French war hero decorated by the British government for his underground exploits in the last war. His armagnac has been decorated too, the 1965 vintage receiving the Grand Prix du Président de la République. The Sempé family have vines (in the Ténarèze) and a pair of small stills, but most of their wines are bought in and distilled by a retained specialist in a traditional still. Ageing is in local Monlezun oak casks. Normal range, as well as some gift presentations and a number of vintages.

Calvados

CALVADOS IS APPLE (OR CIDER) BRANDY and takes its name from the orchard-dotted *département* in Normandy where it is made. Calvados has its own *appellation contrôlée* which requires the best style (from the Pays d'Auge) to be double-distilled in Charentais (cognac) stills, while lesser calvados, which is smooth but light, may be produced in continuous stills. Maturation is in oak barrels and ages on labels are permitted. 'Produit Fermier' or 'Production Fermière' on the bottle indicates the equivalent of single-property calvados. Three-Star is about two years old, VSOP about four years old and higher qualities from six years up.

Over 48 different types of apple are used to make calvados and they are graded from sweet to tart. The small, nuggety pears grown in Normandy may also be used for distillation. *Le trou normand* in a Norman meal is a short drink of calvados after each course to cleanse the palate and help anticipate the next dish.

Boulard • Brand of Pays d'Auge calvados, double-distilled in pot stills and aged in seasoned oak casks. Pierre Boulard established his company in 1825 and his brand has gone on to become one of the top brands, both in France and abroad. Exports have been going out from the distillery at Coquanvilliers for the past 40 years and now constitute almost half of the firm's business. Boulard also produces continuous still spirit (from an armagnac still) for a subsidiary brand, Dumanoir. It also uses up to 10% of pears in the fruit mix to help boost acidity. The company recently formed links with Martini and Rossi greatly enhancing distribution potential, but the family still retains control of the business. Small range, from Three-Star to XO.

Busnel • The world's best-selling calvados brand, with very large blending stocks of old brandy. Busnel was founded in 1820 and is one of a number of Norman country distilleries 'with ancestral know-how' bought in recent years by the Pernod Ricard group, to produce sufficient volume of calvados to make international branding feasible. The Busnel name is used on the labels and all of the spirit is pot-still produced in the top *appellation* zone, Pays d'Auge.

The damp Normandy climate produces over 48 different types of apple suitable for a classic brandy.

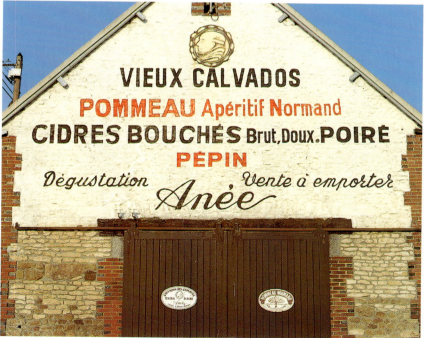

The Vieille Réserve is a warming five-year-old VSOP with good, musky bouquet and full, slightly spirity flavour; the Hors d'Age is minimum six years old, with up to 20-year-old brandy in it, and is more mellow, with finesse and medium body.

Château du Breuil, magnificently secluded among clusters of trees and apple orchards for over four centuries.

Château du Breuil • Small brand of carefully made Pays d'Auge calvados, recently sold by the Bizouard family to a Swiss family of distillers, the Affentrangers. The château is a delightful 16th-century Norman manor house. Only local apples are used (no pears) and these are hand-picked.

Very slow distillation teases out great finesse and subtlety in the spirit. The Hors d'Age is 14 to18 years old, gently flavoured (and great with chocolate!); Réserve des Seigneurs is 16 to 22 years old, muskier and richer; Royal is a special old single-cask calvados. There is also a fine old brandy in a hand-blown bottle which features a spun-glass apple sculpture inside.

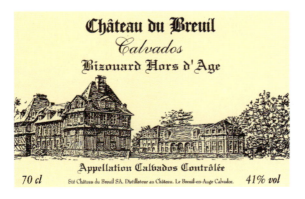

Château du Breuil
Calvados
Bizouard Hors d'Age

Appellation Calvados Contrôlée

70 cl   Sté Château du Breuil SA. Distillateur au Château. Le Breuil-en-Auge Calvados.   41% vol

Cœur de Lion • High-quality hand-made calvados from a little artisanal distillery in the hills near Honfleur. Christian Drouin (*père*) distilled and aged his spirit for 20 years before deciding, in 1979, that his stocks were sufficient to set up in business. Christian (*fils*), took over things as the business began to develop. Double-distillation in a wood-burning pot still is followed up by ageing in small ex-sherry and -port casks. The 50-year-old apparatus was once a travelling still but now sits with its wheels on blocks in the front yard. The Drouins' vintage calvados — currently 1968 and 1969 — are distilled in a given year from matured cider produced in the preceding two seasons. Typically, these remain in the wood for about 18 years. There is also a VSOP, which is a blend of six- to 14-year-old spirits.

Père François • Growing brand, now part of the Berger group. The original Père François was an itinerant distiller in Normandy, having used his wife's dowry to buy his first still. Range comprises three qualities: VS, VSOP and Hors d'Age, which won a silver award in the 1993 International Wine & Spirit Competition in London.

Père Magloire • A well known calvados, both in France and abroad, with exports going to more than 65 countries. The firm was founded in 1821 and was essentially a local product until the early years of this century. Both the cider-making plant and the distillery are at Sainte Foy de Montgoméry. The spirit then goes to the Pont-l'Evêque cellars, where it is put into Limousin oak barrels for ageing. New spirit in new barrels means that every year a tenth of the barrels that contain the total maturing stocks are replaced. There are the equivalent of 15 million bottles in the cellars, contained in 2,300 barrels and casks, enabling the cellar master to blend for consistency from year to year. During the last war, the Russian-French fighter squadron made up of Yakovlev Yak-9s was nicknamed the Pères Magloires. There is a small museum at the distillery.

Range runs from Three-Star to XO and 20 years old.

French Brandy

FRENCH BRANDY IS A BLEND OF HIGHLY RECTIFIED GRAPE-SPIRITS from non *appellation contrôlée* vineyards. These are bought from the French alcohol monopoly and aged

in oak for different lengths of time, picking up flavour and aroma as any spirit will do. They can be blended with cognac, other brandies, wine, grape juice, *boisé* (an oak essence) and suchlike to create a smooth, soft spirit drink which is quite acceptable but short on character.

There are no production regulations specific to French brandy and each manufacturer has his own recipe. These brandies are essentially export products and as such are not drunk in France. On average they cost about half what is normally asked for a VSOP cognac.

All of the large cognac houses and many of the small ones have French brandies. The following are some of the more widely distributed brands; unfortunately, there is little to say about them since they are basically industrial products and all produced in similar manner.

Bardinet • A leading brand in the French Brandy category and one which focuses on the higher-priced end of the market, with XO and Napoléon editions. Bardinet vies with Raynal/Three Barrels (*qv*) for the position of brand leader and is widely distributed in duty-free outlets worldwide. The Bordeaux-based firm of Bardinet is also a well-known producer of rum and liqueurs.

Beehive • Brand from the Adet Seward wine and spirits group in Bordeaux. Beehive does well in a number of export markets as well as in duty free. The range is from Three-Star to Extra, which is very soft and light.

Cortel • One of a number of non-*appellation* French grape-spirit brandies which are gaining a higher profile in international markets, particularly in duty free. Cortel is well presented but its 'Napoléon/VSOP'

Top left: French brandy is aged in various oaks for different lengths of time.

description on the label is meaningless; brandies for which these terms are controlled must use one quality indicator or the other. The company says the 'Napoléon' reference is to emphasise the Frenchness of the product.

Cortel is smooth and light in both weight and flavour and consistent in style. There is an XO quality in a decanter which is probably aged longer.

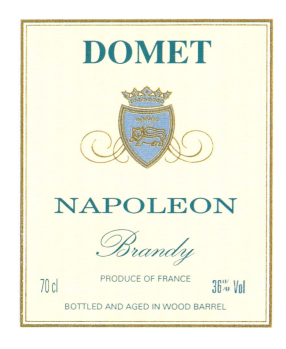

Domet • Brand from the Godet cognac house (*qv*), a family firm with a long history of distillation.

Dorville • Brand which specialises in porcelain and decanter editions for gift presentations.

Grand Empereur • One of a number of French Brandies from the Rémy Cointreau group which owns Rémy Martin cognac. This brand enjoys a high profile in duty free outlets.

Kleber • High-profile brand in eastern Europe, duty free and military markets.

Raynal/Three Barrels • The market leader in non-*appellation* grape-spirit brandy from France. The company was set up in 1974 and is owned by the Moët-Hennessy group, whose distribution range and expertise it enjoys. It is growing in popularity in duty free outlets, the USA, the Far East and the UK, where the Three Barrels name is used. The brand has done much of the work in pioneering the French brandy market, indicating the potential for well-packaged, inexpensive-but-still-French alternatives to cognac and armagnac.

Ronsard • Brand attaining a growing profile in export and duty free markets. There is a five-year-old as well as two Napoléon editions.

Ruche • Brand aged to minimum five years and indicated thus on the label. This is an above-average age in the French brandy sector, where spirits attain smoothness through high-strength rectification rather than through maturation in cask. One of the reasons cognacs do not display ages is because the *average* age of brandies in a blend is what is important regarding balance. La Ruche means 'beehive', which links it to the main brandy brand of the Adet Seward house in Bordeaux.

de **V**alcourt • Brand from the Seagram company which owns the Martell cognac house.

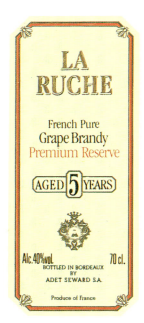

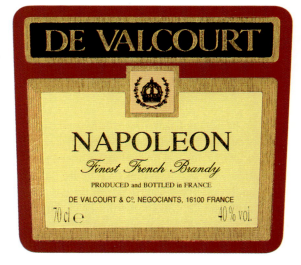

Germany

DISTILLING IN GERMANY HAS A LONG PEDI-GREE. Medieval monks and surgeon-barbers distilled herbal potions and the German Wine Distillers Federation was formed in 1588. However, traditionally all of Germany's grape production went into making wine, so brandy distillers began importing wines. Today, *vins vinés* (semi-fortified wines) are brought in from France and Italy for distillation. Brandy made in Germany is called *weinbrand* (see Asbach) and must be aged for at least six months in oak; *uralt* or *alter* means brandy that has been aged for at least a year in oak. All batches of distillate are numbered and samples stored for examination in case of later complaint.

Conventionally, there are German and French styles produced. German types are quite full-bodied and sweet to varying degrees; French styles are made after the manner of cognac in pot stills, and often from Ugni Blanc wines sent from the Charente.

Burg Stahleck, one of the many castles overlooking the Rhine vineyards. German brandy, however, has a tradition of being made from imported wine.

Chantré • Top-selling brandy in Germany, with mild and smooth house style. It is in the same style league as sister brand Mariacron (*qv*) but lighter and less expensive. It was introduced in 1953, when Ludwig Eckes saw the potential for a smooth brandy at a reasonable price, and it sold well from the outset. It now sells nearly 22 million cases a year. Chantré was Eckes' wife's maiden name.

Dujardin Fine • French-style brand made from wines produced in the Fins Bois vineyards of Cognac. It is double-distilled in Germany, in Charentais pot stills, and aged for eight years — longer than Three-Star and even a few VSOP cognacs — in small Limousin oak casks. The heritage is there in the Racke company, which owns the brand; its founders were French immigrants called Raquet, who began trading in wines in the Rheingau in the 1600s. The Dujardin family in Cognac were suppliers of distilling wine to the company. Dujardin Imperial is aged for a minimum of one year in oak.

Eckes Privat • One of the few German brandies produced from local wines. It is an *alter* spirit (aged for at least a year in oak) and, since it is supplied exclusively to the catering trade, is normally obtainable only in restaurants and bars (*qv* Mariacron).

Asbach Uralt • Premium brand from the firm that invented the modern German word for 'brandy'. In 1907, Hugo Asbach coined the term *weinbrand*, meaning 'wine brandy', to describe his own product. However, in 1971 the word was officially adopted to signify wine or grape brandy made in Germany. *Vins vinés* arrive at Rüdesheim by train from Armagnac, Cognac and Italy and are piped under the road from the station to the distillery. Hugo Asbach built his distillery in 1892, and blended his brandy to appeal to Anglo-Saxon palates. It is a combination of pot- and continuous-still spirit, which picks up oak fragrance from two years in small new casks and finishing in larger, gentler oakwood. Prune juice and other enhancers are added for flavour.

Asbach is Germany's highest-profile brandy and has a reputation to protect. During the last war, when harsh counterfeit 'brandy' in Asbach bottles was being sold on the black market, Asbach advertised regularly in newspapers, requesting people not to buy it since the genuine product was unavailable.

Asbach Uralt is a 'home' brandy, rich and round with good zest and oaky fringes. It is 38% vol and around seven years old.

Below: Peter Eckes started what is now Germany's largest brandy firm, as a small family business at Nieder-Olm in 1857.

Jacobi 1880 • Successful commercial brand distilled from imported Charente and Armagnac wines. The brandy is double-distilled and aged in small Limousin oak barrels. The VSOP is aged for at least two years and is smooth and grapey. The 1972 Selection is aged for 20 years and is mellow and settled. The 1880 refers to the year that Jacob Jacobi of Weinstadt ('Wine Town') in Swabia announced to the Royal Court in Stuttgart that he was in the business of brandy production.

Eckes is Germany's largest spirits producer and a specialist in brandy production. One out of every two bottles of brandy sold in German food stores and supermarkets is an Eckes product. All Eckes' brandies are 36% vol in strength. The company was founded in the 1850s, and also makes a range of health drinks. Mariacron Premium is an *alter weinbrand* and aged longer; Attaché is also an Eckes brandy.

Melcher's Rat • Mild, soft brandy from the Racke company. Henricus Melcher began distilling in 1743 in Urdingen and was supplied with distilling wine from Cognac by the Dujardin family (*qv*). The latter name is used by Racke for its main brandy brand.

Mariacron • Germany's number two top-selling brandy, produced in the distillery of an old Cistercian monastery. The brand's selling point is its smoothness and accessibility, due to high-strength distillation and low bottling strength. It undergoes nominal ageing (less than a year) and was the German bestseller until ousted by stablemate Chantré (*qv*), which is milder and has a little less body. The brand sells nearly two million cases a year.

The distillery at the Mariacron monastery at Oppenheim on the Rhine had produced brandy since 1894 and the Eckes company bought it in 1962.

Zinn 40 • Water-white wine schnapps from Eckes (*qv*) with faint aroma and taste from high-strength distillation. Bottled at 40% vol strength.

Italy

The Camel distillery in Udine, sandwiched between the Gulf of Venice and the Alps, was founded in 1951 by master distiller Giuseppe Tosolini.

THE ITALIANS THINK THEY MAY HAVE INVENTED THE WORD 'BRANDY', pointing to *branda* in old Piedmontese, the translation for aqua vitae. The Dukes of Savoy had distilleries on their estates by the 1500s, and the local Jesuits, who dispensed brandy to the poor as medicine, became known as the 'Brandy Fathers'. Many of today's main distilling firms in Italy were established during the 19th century when brandy became very popular; the composer Paganini liked it so much that he made plans to have his own distillery built on his estate at Gaione.

Italian brandy is well made and can be both interesting and of very high quality. The regulations governing its production are demanding and there is the Italian Brandy Institute to oversee the maintenance of high standards. The trouble is, there is no geographical identity to the brandy, no production heartland or vineyard delimitation areas, as there are with cognac, to lend cachet or focus. That said, there are a number of brands in export markets whose merit and elegance are increasingly attracting the attention of serious consumers.

With light and approachable styles to the fore, most of the distillation is by continuous apparatus, although there are a number of small artisanal producers now making pot-still brandies. Maturation in oak is one or two years' legal minimum, depending on how the final brandy is to be used. However, there are tax benefits which encourage firms to age their spirits for longer. Given the lightness of the prevailing style, extended ageing confers no special benefits and six or seven years is usually regarded as ample. Greater ageing usually indicates a difference in the production, perhaps pot-still spirit or a blend of two types. Label terms like *vecchio* (old) and *stravecchio* (very old) are cosmetic. Oak infusions may be used to enhance aroma.

Branca • Brand from the producers of the famous Fernet bitters (*qv*). The noble Branca di Romanico family established a distillery in 1845 in Milan and soon did well with their bitters product. In 1892, 'Vieux Cognac Croix Rouge', with its overtones of medicinal respectability, was successfully introduced. Branca Stravecchio is the mainstay product, for which a (secret) flavouring technique is used. The spirit is aged for four years in oak and emerges with a quite round bouquet and a soft, smooth texture.

Carpenè Malvolti • Small range from a respected sparkling wine producer. Antonio Carpenè founded the company in 1868 and Angelo Malvolti subsequently joined him as partner. Carpenè was Italy's answer to Dom Perignon, his original researches into sparkling wine and oenology in general leading him to correspond with Pasteur and Koch. Although brandy was being produced by the partners right from the outset, the wine has tended to attract the greater attention at home and abroad. The brandies are understated, fine and harmonious.

Fogolâr • Traditional north-east Italian brand from the Camel firm (see Vite d'Oro, Grappa). There is a six- and a 12-year-old, the latter nicely woody and mellow, with succulent flavour and draw. The Vecchio 800 is top of the range, one version being high strength.

Inga XO • Vintaged 12-year-old brand, aged in Piedmont in very small casks from Slavonian oak. Soft, warming and mellow in character.

Oro Pilla • Highly visible range of brandies from Bologna firm first established in Veneto in 1919. Scudo Bianco is a young *normale*; Scudo Nero is six years old; Scudo Oro is a minimum of eight years (and has spicy appeal); and the Speciale Selezione is a 20-year-old with a gentle and quite full flavour.

Stock • One of Italy's top-selling brands, increasingly well known in export markets. Stock carries a small range of attractive, amenable brandies, which is occasionally tweaked to keep up with consumer tastes. Some of the brandy in more distant markets is locally produced to their specification, as in Australia, where Penfold's distil for the company from local grapes. This is the modern equivalent of Stock's historical policy of building factories in its export markets.

Lionello Stock established the company in 1884 in Trieste when it was still part of the Austro-Hungarian Empire. When he realised local wines were being shipped to Cognac for making eau de vie in the wake of the destruction of the Charentes vineyards by phylloxera, he exclaimed, 'So we, too, here in Trieste, can make cognac!' The company has always been energetic and innovative, taking maximum advantage of opportunities to promote and publicise. They were among the first to advertise on radio and television.

VSOP 1984 is three years old, Gran Riserva six years old and the XO has the best part of nine years' ageing in large vats. Stock's 'brandy cathedral' at Portogruaro has rows of vast double-decker vats containing spirit up to 20 years old.

Never publicity shy, the distinctive Stock barrels are left to mature in one of their ageing cellars.

*V*ecchia Romagna • Prestigious range with high profile in international markets. The company was founded in Bologna in 1820 by Frenchman Jean Bouton who came from the Charente and went into business with a local man, italianising his name in the process to Giovanni Buton. The company uses both continuous and double-distillation and has some beautiful old swan-neck pot stills in its distillery. Trebbiano (Ugni Blanc) grapes are used and maturation is in small oak casks.

In the 1950s, Buton began building brandy reserves which in the intervening 40 years have become an enviable, mature inventory. They are the basis of the exceptional old brandies now marketed by the company. The pot still qualities are classy and fine, with pleasing, complex aromas and finishes. Visitors can browse in the company's City of Brandy.

Etichetta Nera (Black Label) is pot and continuous still spirit, three to five years old; all the better qualities are from the pot stills — Oro (Gold Label) seven years old and Riserva Rara, minimum 15 years old. There are some very old 25- and 35-year-olds which sell in prestigious outlets.

*V*illa Zarri • Small-batch vintaged brandy in the cognac style. The *acquavite di vino*, as it is called, was the hand-made premium in the portfolio of the late Leonida Zarri's high-volume Oro Pilla brandy brand before the latter was sold.

Wine from Ugni Blanc grapes grown in the hills near Chianti are double-distilled in pot stills and aged in both new and old French oak for up to three years. During that time, it is gradually reduced from 70% vol to its bottling strength of 43% vol. The brandy has only been produced since 1986, however it has attracted considerable attention. The-mustard-and cream coloured villa is 16th-century with its own little chapel and park, and sits amid the industrial spread of the Oro Pilla maturation warehouses at Castelmaggiore.

The brandy style is firm, a bit austere, but with good aroma and a certain dry fruit succulence.

Top right: Autumnal terraced vineyards in the Friuli hills where artisanal grappa is produced by anyone with a still.

Grappa

*G*RAPPA WAS ORIGINALLY THE POOR MAN'S BRANDY, made from the skins, stalks and pips left over after grapes were pressed and/or wine was made. Last century in northern Italy, portable stills travelled from village to village after the grape vintage, distilling the growers' pomace. The distiller received as payment his *mondure*, a proportion of the spirit produced, which he would sell on. Historically, grappa was rough, fiery and clutched you by the throat, but it also warmed you throughout the merciless Alpine winters. Nowadays, there are also very fine, elegant grappas, many of them sold at high prices in hand-blown bottles and flasks; both styles are valid.

Grappa is made by adding a little water to the mass — the pomace, *vinaccia* (*vinacce*, plural) in Italian — fermenting it and distilling it. It can be a large-scale operation or a small-batch obsession, particularly when one bears in mind that it takes 12 kilos of *vinaccia* to make a litre of *grappa*. Some small distillers in Italy use a local type of steam-heated *bain-marie* still with double walls, which requires two distillations just like the Charentais pot still.

Grappa may be aged in oak or bottled young and zesty, the latter water-white style carrying more vivid aromas of the grape. Large brands, like Stock's Julia, sell by their brand name; artisanal and smaller-batch grappas will indicate the single grape type (*monovitigno*) from which they are made — Grappa di Moscato, di Chardonnay and so on. *Acquavite di vinaccia* is an alternative name for grappa; *invecchiata* means aged.

Grappa production is mainly small scale and

artisanal. Very few grappas have brand status and even fewer enjoy other than local distribution, so availability depends where you are when you are buying. The following listings indicate the national brands and some examples of good smaller operations.

Lic. U.T.I.F. N. 690/TO – gradi 45-Anidri cc. 315 – cl. 70e

Ceretto • Small range of single-vineyard varietal grappas from distinguished producer of Barolo and Barbaresco wines. Bruno Ceretto is a single-vineyard specialist and his grappas derive from three of these.

Ceretto was the first in the Langhe area to offer varietal grappa back in 1974. Brunate and Zonchera are the best-known vineyards and the grappas are from Nebbiolo grapes and carry a year of distillation on the labels. Rossana vineyard's vines are Dolcetto. The double-distillation takes two hours each run.

Con Senso • Brand name of the Bonollo distillery in Formigine. This unaged grappa from Chianti grapes is light and zingy with a spicy nose. Among the company's brandies is a toffee-nosed, sharp-textured 20-year-old. Bonollo also runs a grappa information centre.

Gratacul • Hand-made grappa from dog roses that grow at 1,600 metres above sea level in the Sestriere Alps. The delightful name means 'bum-scratcher', no doubt referring to the contacts made with the roses as you walk among them. The Chaberton distillery in the Susa Valley collects fruits, roots, berries and plants, both wild and cultivated, from the Alpine slopes and meadows that go right up to the glaciers. A wide range of grappas, distillates and bitters are produced, and the owners have an ancient collection of 15,000 formulae for drinks and potions, many of which would be illegal if they were to be made up today. Gratacul has a delicate but long fragrance and pleasing flavour that balances acidity and sweetness.

Inga • Range of fine, *monovitigno* (varietal) grappas. The majority of the pomace comes from Piedmont, where the distillery is located, and the Oltrepò Pavese, in Lombardy. Hence the range features grappas produced in small, steam-heated pot stills from grape types used in the making of Barolo, Gavi, Asti spumante and other distinguished Piedmont wines. Top of the range are Brachetto and Nebbiolo, in Murano glass hand-blown bottles. These are all unmixed, single-vine grappas.

Glistening steel and copper at the immaculate Ceretto distillery, a distinguished producer of grappa.

The company dates from 1832 under its old name, Gambarotta, but the present title was introduced in 1938. Inga launched the award-winning Libarna grappa brand (*qv*) in 1966, but it passed to Giovanni Buton in 1982.

Julia • Brand leader from the Stock company. Grappa does not easily lend itself to large-scale production, since pomace is best distilled fresh, *ie* on the spot. Stock gets round this by commissioning lots of small distillers during vintage time and buying the spirit in for bottling and/or ageing. Julia is aged for two years but Stock has young grappas with fresh, clean scent and zesty fruit pungency.

Romano Levi • One of the original grappa gurus, who emerged in the initial boom of the 1970s. Romano Levi is an artist in distillation; he produces grappa as an artefact. Amid a confusion of books, bottles and cats, he distils, bottles and handwrites individual labels deep in the Piedmont countryside. The labels are charming and look like a page from a child's story-book. For his 'Grappa della Donna Selvatica che Salta le Montagne' he draws stick figures in colour of the countrywoman — la Donna — crossing the mountains. His eaux de vie vary from one distillation to the next, depending on the *vinaccia* he is using, but they are all superb, graceful and polished examples of slow, patient production.

Libarna • Two complementary, continuously distilled styles from the proprietors of Vecchia Romagna brandy. Libarna Cristallo is young and unaged from Barbera, Dolcetto and Cortese grapes, probably grown in Piedmont. Smooth, strong and clean in taste. Libarna Invecchiata is made from selected but unspecified pomace, although it must include Moscato, the Asti spumante grape, going by the ripe, muscatty nose. Clean, softish and smooth in its finish.

Lungarotti • Small, fine range from one of Italy's best wine makers. Giorgio Lungarotti has been something of a tail wagging a dog. The non-*appellation* red Rubesco and white Torre di Giano wines he produced near Perugia were so good that the authorities were eventually obliged to create a delimited zone around him and base it on his methods. The Rubesco Riserva is now one of the country's very best red wines. His grappas are from Sangiovese, Canaiolo and Chardonnay grape pomace, collected from individual vineyards close to the distillery — important for freshness — and distillation is all done in pot stills.

The Grappa di Chardonnay uses pomace from the single-vineyard Vigna I Palazzi wine; it is unaged and has a rich, floral, fruit fragrance and full, clean taste. Grappa di Rubesco, also unaged, is from Sangiovese and Canaiolo pomace with fresh grape aromas and soft, round flavour. Grappa Riserva 'L' is made in very small quantities from similar pomace from the single Monticchio vineyard that yields Lungarotti's élite Rubesco Riserva wine. It is briefly aged in old oak and comes in a hand-blown glass ampoule. Smooth, elegant and lengthy.

Marolo • Artisanal production from pomace yielded by a number of famous vineyards, among them Gavi La Scolca, Brunello Lisini and Barolo Montez-emolo. The Marolo brothers make over a score of grappas, including a rare Arneis, at their little Santa Teresa distillery in a *bain-marie* type of still traditional in Piedmont, where they are located. Their bottles (31,000 a year) are in great demand and a

10th-anniversary Barolo grappa produced in 1987 fetched £1,200! The grappas all show intensity of aroma, particularly the Moscato and the Barolo, although the latter is a bit austere. Acacia, as well as oak, is used in ageing.

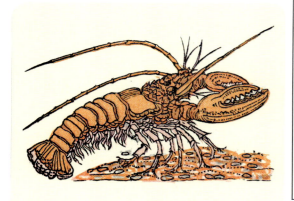

GRAPPA di VERMENTINO

Nardini • Respected and long-established brand in the Veneto. With a pedigree going back more than 200 years, Nardini tended to stand out in a marketplace filled with rustic and unambitious products. It is now surrounded by up-market achiever brands but still holds its own — just. Both the unaged and the aged (three years in gentle oak) sell widely.

Nonino • Prestige range of distinguished grappas from family firm. Back in the 1880s, Grandpa Nonino was an itinerant distiller in Friuli, and the present generation began distilling in 1973. Nonino introduced the new idea of distilling whole grapes (the spirit is called 'ue) and, to encourage growers to plant near-extinct local vines, it instituted an annual award. The battery of small pot stills has overflowed from the old forge where Benito Nonino's father-in-law used to make ploughs. Vuisinar is perhaps the most widely available type but the Picolit, from a local vine rare through floral abortion, is the most famous. The specialities are very expensive, the beautiful bottles hand-blown in Murano glass.

Vite d'Oro • Wide and interesting range of commercial grappas from the Camel firm in Udine, northeast Italy. The brand comes in *classico* style (waterwhite and unaged) and *stravecchio, ie* aged for three years in casks made of ash — a light wood which removes the fire of the spirit but does not impose too much flavour or any colour. All the grappas are distilled from Friuli *vinacce*. There is also a Riserva, a high-strength (50% vol) Teresa Raiz and some other different *classico* styles.

The distillery was founded in 1944 by Giuseppe Tosolini, who is commemorated in the up-market 'Mosto' series of *monovitigno* (varietal or single grape type) eaux de vie presented in hand-blown flasks. Like fully fledged brandies, these are made from grape musts, not pomace, but bottled unaged as young spirits. Refosco and Picolit are the best-known Friuli types.

The Ponte de Bassano across the Po, where Bartolo Nardini set up shop in 1779.

Spain

Windmills look out over the vast vineyard of La Mancha.

DISTILLATION IN WHAT IS NOW SPAIN BEGAN IN THE EIGHTH CENTURY, making it, along with Ireland, the location of the earliest distilling activity in Europe. Today, Spain has two official brandy *appellations*, one large and one, as yet, much smaller.

Brandy de Jerez is made exclusively by the sherry houses in the sherry-producing area in the south of Spain, and Brandy del Penedès is made by just two firms in Cataluña, in north-eastern Spain, where the country's best champagne-method sparkling wines are produced.

Brandy de Jerez

BRANDY DE JEREZ IS ONE OF THE WORLD'S MAJOR SPIRITS CATEGORIES, both in terms of volume and quality. Like armagnac and cognac, its production is carefully prescribed and the regulations specify a brandy that is markedly different from its French counterparts. The style of the brandy is rich, aromatic and generous, a circumstance that can be misunderstood by those who have only cognac as their benchmark. It is aged in casks which have formerly held sherry for fermentation and/or maturation — a circumstance it shares with the best malt whiskies — so there is much flavour and texture for the wood to endow to the spirit; there is, however, also finesse and harmony.

Brandy de Jerez ages in a solera system like that of sherry, which has the effect of accelerating maturation. This 'dynamic ageing' mellows brandy so three or four years of it is equivalent to seven or eight years of 'static', ie passive, ageing that takes place in Cognac and elsewhere. The brandy solera consists of a series of butts, each holding slightly older spirit than the one beside it. When mature spirit is drawn off from the final barrel, it is replenished with the same amount of the next-oldest eau de vie and so on back down the line, with new spirit being introduced at the start. No more than a third of the volume is removed from any butt, the principle being that a lesser volume of a younger spirit (or wine) takes on the characteristics and maturity of a greater volume of an older one. There can be as many as 30 stages in the movement of spirit through a solera scale.

'Brandy de Jerez Solera' must age for six months, 'Reserva' for a year and 'Gran Reserva' for minimum three years; the great Jerez brandies age for much longer, usually 12 to 15 years. Old Reservas and Gran Reservas are sweeter, richer and silkier than the simple Solera style. The brandy used to be made from sherry grapes grown in Jerez but these all go to sherry production now, and the main distillation grape is the Airen, grown in La Mancha and Extremadura. Four kinds of spirit are used to build brandies of very precise structure; pot still once and twice distilled is called *alquitara* and is the best; unique, medium-strength *holandas* (so called because it was first distilled expressly for 'Hollanders' – Dutch traders); and high-strength *destilados*, the latter two from continuous stills. Fruit-derived flavour enhancers and oak essence (*boisé*) are widely (and honourably) used. Brandy de Jerez now has higher sales volume than armagnac.

Bobadilla 103 • One of the top four best-selling brands in the Solera category with Etiqueta Blanca, the white label. The Bobadilla house style for its younger spirits is light, based on a brandy created in the 1930s which was finer and drier than other Spanish brands at the time. As something of a brandy specialist, Bobadilla has its own distillery at Tomelloso in La Mancha. Black-labelled Etiqueta Negra is the Reserva and Gran Capitán, the Gran Reserva.

Top left: The top-selling Cardenal Mendoza ages in a typical Jerez cellar. The brand takes its name from a famous statesman who helped Columbus to procure royal patronage for his voyage to America.

highly painstaking. All distillates are aged statically for several years in American ex-sherry oak, and then the best — up to 17 different eaux de vie — are blended and switched to solera ageing. The result is a brandy with more weight and opulence than any other; there is a sweet edge, some bite and mellow-fruit *rancio*.

The bodega has 15,000 casks covering both the solera and the static-ageing sections. Cardenal Mendoza began over a century ago as a genuine family reserve and at Sanchez Romate (*qv*) the four barrels in which the brandy was first blended and aged are still in place. The brandy takes its name from Cardenal Mendoza, a famous statesman who helped Christopher Columbus obtain royal patronage for his first voyage to America.

Carlos I • Top-end Gran Reserva from Domecq (*qv*), made from 80% pot-still spirit, including a little made from the prestige Palomino grape. Rich and oaky, Carlos I Imperial is 100% pot-still brandy and is, on average, 12 years old, although there is some 17-year-old spirit in the blend. It is rich in aroma, mouth-filling, and has old-gold fruit *rancio* and a dry close.

Luis Caballero • The company's maturation bodegas date from the 1600s, and the Milenario solera from 1795, but the company was established in 1830. The Caballero family in Galicia originally supplied Jerez brandy makers with timber for casks, but eventually moved south and began distilling themselves. In 1925, the first Luis Caballero sailed to Argentina on the maiden voyage of the liner *Infanta Isabel de Borbón* with 3,000 cases of Caballero brandy and ready to do business.

Caballero's range is Decano Solera, which is a 100,000-case brand; Gran Señor, which displaces Chevalier as the Reserva quality; and Milenario, the Gran Reserva. Caballero has its own vineyards and owns the beautiful Moorish castle of San Marcos in Puerto de Santa María. The Caballero brand name, used by González Byass for its amontillado sherry, was originally bought from the Luis Caballero house.

Cardenal Mendoza • The top-selling, top-category Brandy de Jerez, having displaced Lepanto (*qv*) some years ago. It is a 100% *holandas* spirit Gran Reserva, some aged for well over 15 years but with a 12-year average age. The maturation process is unusual and

Carlos III • The second best-selling Reserva on the Spanish market from Domecq (*qv*). It is 50% pot-still spirit and has a touch of dryness.

Conde de Osborne • Top of the Osborne (*qv*) range, Gran Reserva in a crooked bottle designed by Salvador Dalí. It is aged for the equivalent of 18 years.

Domecq • The world's biggest sherry-producer with an enormous brandy operation (and the world's biggest brandy brand, Presidente) in Mexico, and the biggest mature brandy stocks in Jerez. The company was founded in 1730, but by rights it should have been making armagnac down the centuries, since the family's roots are in Gascony. Domecq created the first Spanish brandy brand, Fundador (*qv*) in 1874, and for many people today it is still the first Jerez brandy they encounter. The company has three distilleries in different parts of Spain and the distillates vary according to which soleras they go into. Domecq's range is Tres Cepas (Solera); Fundador (*qv*) and Carlos III (*qv*) (both Reserva); Carlos I and Carlos I Imperial (*qv*) (both Gran Reserva).

Duff Gordon • Solera and Reserva brandies from a famous house now owned by Osborne (*qv*). Sir James Duff, a Scotsman who was British Consul in Cádiz, set up as a sherry and brandy producer in 1768 in partnership with his nephew, Sir William Gordon. Their customers included Queen Victoria, the Russian tsar and many other crowned heads and aristocrats of Europe. Washington Irving, author of *Rip Van Winkle*, who later became US ambassador to Spain, was also a client. The brandies are matured at the bodegas in Puerto de Santa María.

Espléndido • Fifth-best-selling brand in the young Solera category in Spain. Owned by Garvey, which was one of the first bodegas in Jerez, set up in 1780 by an émigré from County Waterford, in Ireland. The company pioneered brandy exports with a cask sent to the UK in 1858, and today has a warrant to supply the Spanish royal family. Espléndido is full and toffeed in style. The company recently launched a new Gran Reserva, called Conde de Garvey.

Fundador • The first-ever Spanish brandy brand, introduced in 1874 by Domecq (*qv*). Historically it has been a rich, rounded Solera brandy with 25% pot-still content, but was recently upgraded to Reserva quality with longer ageing.

González Byass • High-profile sherry house, owner of the Lepanto (*qv*) Gran Reserva, which is one of the top two Jerez brandies in terms of absolute quality. Manuel María González opened in the sherry and brandy business in 1835, in ancient bodegas beside the old Alcázar in Jerez town. Robert Byass, a British wine merchant, was brought in to help on the distribution side. The company was the first to set up a viticultural laboratory in Jerez and establish scientific quality control. An important part of that continuing

Brandy and sherry bodegas have certain similarities, but the products are easily distinguished.

Above: 'La Concha' (the shell) built in 1862 by Eiffel for González Byass to commemorate the visit of Queen Isabel. Each of the 168 casks in this open bodega displays a national crest honouring an export market.

Right: An old Lepanto brandy cellar.

solera which was laid down in the middle of last century. The name was sanctioned in 1949 when the then Duque d'Alba, the Spanish ambassador to London, was asked if his title could be used to name the brand. When he tasted it, he said it was too good for a mere dukedom and that it should be named for his illustrious ancestor, the Grand Duke — hence Gran Duque d'Alba.

Lepanto • Top-ranked Gran Reserva brandy from González Byass (*qv*), made partly with Palomino sherry grapes. Lepanto is 100% *holandas* spirit, has an average of 15 years of ageing and is sold in a hand-painted decanter. A former brand leader in the de luxe category, it is splendidly rich and mellow, pungent, oaky, spicy and earthy.

tradition are the apparently mundane plastic boxes used at vintage time which, in fact, are the company's own creation to prevent grapes fermenting before they reach the winery. González Byass owns 1,800 hectares of vineyards and today's business is still in family hands.

The maturation bodegas next to the Alcázar were redesigned by Gustave Eiffel, famous for his Paris tower, in a dramatic circular layout that echoes a great bullring. Visitors can see the famous mice, which climb a miniature ladder to the rim of a filled glass to lap the sherry it contains. Soberano is the biggest-selling Brandy de Jerez and is Solera quality; Insuperable is a Reserva; and splendid, opulent Gran Reserva Lepanto (*qv*) is the flagship. The company's Tío Pepe brand is the world's best-selling fino sherry. González Byass also produces an XO cognac from vines in the Charentes it has owned since 1929.

Gran Duque d'Alba • One of the very top brands, the company producing only this Gran Reserva quality. It was recently bought by Williams & Humbert (Bols) which, in the past, has not been greatly involved in the brandy business. The entire Bertemati bodega in Jerez is given over to Gran Duque, with more than 4,000 casks in a five-scale

Osborne • The largest producer of Brandy de Jerez and owner of the two top sellers — nutty, fruity Veterano, in the young solera style, and soft, full Magno, in the middle Reserva category. Independencia, Carabela Santa María and Conde de Osborne (*qv*), all Gran Reservas with different stylistic emphases, complete the range. The company adds nut and fruit flavour enhancers to its brandies before they begin solera ageing. Osborne (pronounced Osbornay) is a name particularly noticed by visitors to Spain, due to the advertising hoardings on roadside hillocks everywhere featuring silhouettes of anatomically correct bulls; the company logo is a bull.

Thomas Osborne, from Exeter, in the west of England, founded the company in 1772 and today it produces over three million cases of Jerez brandy across its five brands. Osborne has a specialist brandy complex of four bodegas in Jerez sheltering 40,000 casks in their soleras, and its own distillery at Tomelloso, in La Mancha. A feature of the Jerez dynasties is the extent to which their names display their international pedigrees, none more so than Enrique Osborne MacPherson, chairman of Osborne.

Sanchez Romate • Proprietor of the leading Gran Reserva brand, Cardenal Mendoza (*qv*). The family business goes back to 1781 and has long been distinguished. In its time the family has been warranted supplier to the Spanish royal family, with a past pope and the British Parliament's House of Lords among an intriguing scatter of customers. The company owns several vineyards in the region and has two other brandies, Abolengo and Monseñor.

Valdespino • The oldest distillery and sherry bodega in Jerez; there is documentation showing that Valdespino was distilling in 1516. As a traditional sherry specialist, the firm's brandy making is small in scale but high in quality. Alfonso el Sabio is the main brand and a rare single-vineyard brandy is due for first release from second pressings from its prime

The famous Osborne bulls, sires to the vast herd of black 'hoarding' bulls advertising the company across Spain — now classified as cultural monuments.

Penedès

Macharnudo estate, which is the source of Fino Inocente, the only single-vineyard sherry.

Valdespino is one of the few remaining firms whose brandy is made from Jerez grapes. The Sello Azul 1850 brand commemorates a fine cellar of brandy sold to Valdespino in that year by an expatriate Briton, Daniel Wilson, who decided to return to the UK. At the bodega the firm displays its antique still — nine metres high! — which was last used at the turn of the century, a time when Valdespino called its brandy Ranac in competition with other Spanish firms who produced *coñac*.

PENEDÈS IS THE OTHER DENOMINATED BRANDY *appellation* in Spain but, unlike the Jerez style, there is a conscious association with the specifics of cognac production. At present, just two firms — Torres and Mascaró — produce fine brandies that are richer and more raisiny than cognacs but leaner than the Jerez eaux de vie to the south.

Mascaró • Range of three pot-still brandies made in the broad cognac fashion but varying in details. The Mascaró family has been making brandy since 1945, but in recent years has concentrated on high-quality production. The fine balance achieved by Antonio Mascaró is to make his brandies more succulent and less austere than cognac, at the same time retaining finesse. He uses local grape types, the Tempranillo and the Parellada, the latter high in acidity, like the Ugni Blanc of Cognac. Ageing is static — *ie* traditional non-solera style — in Limousin oak.

Estilo Fine Marivaux (three-year-old) and Narciso Etiqueta Azul (five-year-old) both show bite and roundness with differing oaky rendering; Don Narciso is only eight years old but has spirit and richness merging nicely.

Torres • Innovative producer of high-quality brandies. Torres' brandies are based on the local Parellada and Cognac's Ugni Blanc grapes, both of which yield wine of high acidity. Classic *holandas* spirit from continuous stills and double-distilled spirit from pot stills are used, separately and combined, to create fine building bricks with which a wide range of styles is produced. The options are further extended by ageing distillates both dynamically, in soleras, and statically, in the traditional 'let-it-lie' manner.

The Torres family has owned vineyards in the Vilafranca area of Penedès since the 1600s, but the present business was established when a member of the family returned from Cuba in 1870 to make wines for export to Spanish colonies in the Americas. Torres' recent fame derives from its success with imported vines, the company's 'claret', made from Cabernet Sauvignon, outscoring Château Latour in a celebrated Paris tasting in 1979. In 1928, Miguel Torres I, grandfather of the present Miguel, began distilling a brandy lighter than the conventional Spanish type, due to its not being aged in ex-sherrywood. He used an old cognac still and made the brandy in the broad Charente style.

With the distilling and ageing possibilities at its disposal, the Torres' range is large and interesting. Torres 5 is three years old and Torres 10 is five years old, both of them continuously distilled *holandas* spirit matured in a three-scale solera. The latter is rich and oaky. Miguel Torres Imperial is seven-year-old pot-still brandy aged as in Cognac in French oak; it is graceful, shyly grapey and firm. Miguel I starts off in heavy-toast new oak then moves to older wood, the total time taking 10 years. It is deep, warming and toffeed, ripe with oaky tones. Honorable is 18-year-old Ugni Blanc from Limousin oak, showing opulence, creamy oak and spice. It regularly outdoes cognacs in blind tastings. Miguel I and Honorable are also pot-still brandies.

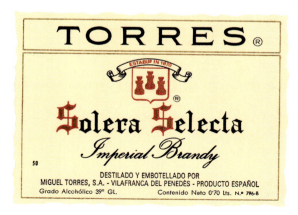

The inspirational, but uncharacteristically suited Miguel A. Torres outside one of his underground ageing cellars near Pacs del Penedès.

United States

Balloonists in northern California's Sonoma Valley drink in the panoramic view of the vineyards.

In 1842, Swiss-Born American Pioneer John Sutter, who founded the city of Sacramento, found time to distil brandy from wild grapes in his fort at the settlement. When the Californian Gold Rush followed, many of those who did not make a strike took advantage of the tax exemptions on new vineyards and soon wine making and brandy distillation were established all over California. The phylloxera aphid, which began destroying European vineyards in the 1870s, was accidentally imported from America but equally it was American scientists Munson and Jaeger who solved the problem by coming up with louse-resistant rootstocks for grafting. A grateful France awarded the men the Légion d'Honneur.

William Thompson's new seedless grape, developed in 1872, became the basis of Californian brandy production and the generic product was good enough to be picking up export orders to Europe by the end of the century. Leland Stanford became the world's biggest brandy distiller and, when he died, the business was left to Stanford University at Palo Alto. California's own phylloxera problems, and then Prohibition, slowed down the development of brandy drinking in the USA but the delays gave the opportunity for a fresh start after the last war. In 1938, due to overproduction, growers were required to distil half of their crops into brandy and store it. During World War II these nicely maturing spirits were assessed by European and US experts and a prototype California brandy was 'designed'. it was lighter than European brandies and different in aroma and flavour.

The present-day California brandy style grew from this and trade leaders like A. K. Morrow, L. K. Marshall and E. B. Brown did most to foster good attitudes towards producing for quality. The main grapes used today are Thompson Seedless, Emperor and Flame Tokay, although small-production distilleries are starting to appear which grow Ugni Blanc, Folle Blanche and Colombard to make California 'cognacs'. The California style of brandy is produced in continuous stills for lightness and smoothness, but pot-still spirit is being blended in by some distillers in search of more particular distillates. Most California brandy is matured for two to 12 years in bourbon or brandy oak and is minimum 40% vol in strength. Fuller-flavoured spirits to be drunk on their own are 'sipping' brandies but the most popular types are the lighter mixing brandies.

Some distillers (eg Korbel) make use of solera-system ageing as practised in both sherry and brandy making in Spain (qv). This 'dynamic ageing' system (as opposed to the static or passive ageing of cognac and most other brandies) does seem to accelerate time and has the effect of creating maturity in spirits beyond given years. It also adds depth of flavour and body.

Christian Brothers • Formerly America's top-selling brandy, it was made by the brothers themselves until 1989, when they withdrew from the business. The operation is still a 1.5 million-case brand and is now owned by the UK group Grand Metropolitan. Four different blending spirits are produced from both pot stills and continuous stills and the final brandy is matured, usually for two years, in 55-gallon white American oak barrels which endow full, fruity aromatics. Christian Brothers is widely drunk with mixers but is rich and complex enough to be sipped.

The XO Rare Reserve has a majority of pot still brandy and is aged for six years; it has grapey, creamy fragrance, good body and a warm mellow length.

Crown Regency • Medium-weight California brandy from an interesting cooperative at Lodi. The group has a number of other brands — including Royal Host and Mission Host — which carry cordial and wine enhancers but Crown Regency is a straight spirit from an old 1930s continuous still. It has done well in the past in blind tastings against several well-known cognac brands and the XOS is a blend of eight-to 20-year-old brandies.

E&J • The story of the Gallo brothers has traditionally been that they learned wine making from a pamphlet found in the local library when they were students during Prohibition. Whether or not this is true, Gallo wine is now the top-selling brand in the UK and Gallo brandy is the top-selling brand in the US (two million cases a year). E&J is made for mixing, not sipping, and, despite the volume turned over, it is carefully made. Distilled in continuous stills which yield more smoothness and lightness than flavour, the majority of the spirit is aged for just three years, although some of it goes on to mature for up to 12 years in charred, seasoned American white oak; no sweetening or flavouring is added and the final brandy is filtered through charcoal to remove any final corners.

Above: The Christian Brothers Winery in Napa Valley, founded by a French Catholic teaching order, finally changed hands in 1989.

Brandy

Germain-Robin • Hubert Germain-Robin and Ansley Coale began producing handmade 'California cognac' in the early 1980s, from an ancient pot still shipped over from Cognac to Mendocino. When it was first released, the brandy received instant recognition and their Reserve was served at a White House gala dinner when the Gorbachevs last visited. The partners use a particularly painstaking Cognac process which has died out there due to the expense and time it needs. Germain-Robin should certainly have inherited a few brandy-making secrets; he is of the Robin dynasty in France, which has been making cognac since 1782. The grapes used are Mendocino-grown Colombard, Pinot Noir and Gamay, a combination that gives a rare complexity to the brandy plus good grapey tone and finesse. Cellaring is in Limousin oak and the premium quality of the vines means that less ageing is needed. The VSOP is about six years old and the Rare has scored better than some extremely illustrious top brands in blind tastings. The company name is Alambic.

Méthode Traditionelle

JEPSON
RARE
BRANDY

A California Alambic Pot Still Brandy

DISTILLED BY JEPSON VINEYARDS, UKIAH, CA
ALCOHOL 40% BY VOLUME. (80 PROOF)

80 PROOF   750 ML

Jepson • 'California cognac' from a partnership between Davis viticulture graduate Rick Jones and Chicago industrialist Robert Jepson. The brandy is double-distilled in an authentic cognac still imported to Ukiah from France. The grapes — exclusively from 50-year-old Colombard vines, one of the minority cognac varieties — are grown and the spirit

Germain-Robin has a highly individual operation with customised barrels all noted in the inventory and quality control records.

distilled on the Russian River estate, so the final brandy is a single-property product. Ageing is in Limousin oak and the actual blend is composed of brandies of six to eight years of age. Jones travelled in Cognac after graduation, having been seduced by the pilot distillery in the department at Davis. Production is around 500 cases a year and experimental distillation with other grape types, including Chenin Blanc and Chardonnay, goes on with a view to finding new blending ideas.

Flavour is soft, ripe, intensely grapey and laced with smoke and vanilla; 40% vol. The brandy was served at the birthday dinner of the then US President George Bush in 1991.

Korbel • Brandy from Colombard, Chenin Blanc and Flame Tokay grapes which matures in a solera system like both the sherries and brandies of Jerez in Spain (see the introduction to Spanish brandies). This adds texture and flavour to Korbel brandy, which is distilled in a continuous still. Its solera has 15 stages and the movement of the spirit is carried out up to six times a year. Korbel brandy is richer than its likely four years of age might suggest, and can be sipped or used for mixing. The Korbels were Czech immigrants and first produced brandy in 1892. The business is now owned by the Heck family, originally from Alsace.

Paul Masson • Easy-to-drink style of brandy principally from continuous stills but containing 15% pot-still spirit. From Colombard grapes and aged for three years in small American oak barrels, the style is mellow and gentle. The cellars are kept humid to promote natural strength loss during ageing and a small amount of sugar syrup is added to soften the style still further.

The Masson family emigrated to the USA from Burgundy when phylloxera destroyed their vineyards in 1878. They produced 'champagne' which both won international awards and qualified as 'medicinal wine' during Prohibition. The beautiful mountain vineyard near Saratoga is now a national monument. Paul Masson brandy is soft, tasty and approachable.

RMS • California pot-still brandy from cognac house Rémy Martin. The distillery is at Calistoga, and was originally a partnership between Rémy and the Davies family at Schramsberg Vineyards, who make distinguished sparkling wines. It has been Rémy's own project since 1986 and part of the operation is to experiment with different grape types for distillation. Colombard, Muscat, Pinot Noir, Chenin Blanc and Palomino are distilled and aged separately for two years before being blended and matured in Limousin oak for a further three or four years. A rich, fragrant, medium-textured brandy.

Grappa

GRAPPA, THE POMACE BRANDY ASSOCIATED WITH ITALY, has a considerable following in America from both Italian-Americans and the fashion conscious. The restaurateur at the Bella Voce in San Francisco has '1-GRAPPA' as the registration plate on his car. Grappa has been a smart-set drink in Europe and the USA for the past decade, and both designer and rustic styles are produced in boutique distilleries in California, Oregon and elsewhere.

The Jörg Rupf distillery makes grappa from Zinfandel and a 'marc' of Gewürztraminer. These German copper stills are specially made to retain intensity of fruit aroma.

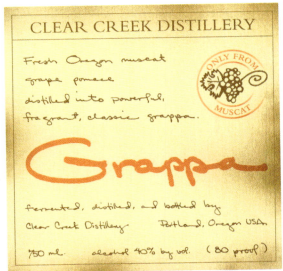

The Bonny Doon mountain vineyards, sheltered in parts by conifer woods, lie near the earthquake zone of the Santa Cruz Mountains.

Bonny Doon • Randall Grahm uses an authentic Italian *bagna-maria* still which heats distillates with steam. The pot still holds only 250 litres, which means lots of work for small amounts of distillate at a time but it is ideally suited for artisanal production. Grahm's grappas are unaged and made from the entire fruit, what is called *ue* in north Italian dialect. Grahm's Grappa di Moscato is soft and elegant with great aroma; mind you, Moscato is always a seductive grape when used in spirits. The Ca' del Solo Grappa di Malvasia, also from the entire grape, is equally intensely perfumed but in its own different way. This is why these grappas are not aged; to do so would subdue them.

Clear Creek • Small distillery in Portland, Oregon, producing grappa from local vineyards' pomace. Stephen McCarthy and his brothers use small, German-made pot stills to produce a range of grappas and fruit brandies based on production methods in Switzerland and the Black Forest. McCarthy takes pomace from David Lett's distinguished vineyard, The Eyrie, and adds a little yeast to get combustive fermentation and intensely aromatic grappa. The Muscat Ottonel grape is naturally spicy and rich but it is remarkable just how much fragrance and flavour McCarthy manages to pull over in the distillation.

Creekside • Distillery in Gordon Valley, Solano County, run by Don Johnson, who makes grappa from Cabernet Sauvignon grapes.

St George Spirits • Jorg Rupf was born in Alsace, France, and, having quit a legal post in the Ministry of Culture in Munich, he went to California. He set up a tiny distillery where he hand produces eaux de vie in the European traditions that his family had been following in the Black Forest for generations.

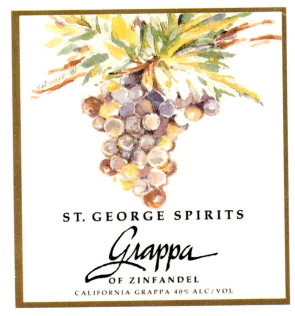

The fruit is crushed at the peak of ripeness and fermented on the lees with cultured yeasts. The German copper stills are small and specially made to retain intensity of fruit aromas. The Marc de Gewürztraminer is aged in oak and, although it is Jorg's tribute to Alsace, his version is made from whole grapes and not the grape pomace. Like the companion Marc de Traminer, it is smooth and floral in character from the grape flesh presented to the yeasts. Zinfandel grapes are regarded as America's contribution to the world vines' Hall of Fame and his Grappa di Zinfandel is, of course, the ultimate American grappa. It is made from wet pomace from Sonoma and Napa Zinfandel, and is smooth, fruity and spicy. All 40% vol.

Applejack

APPLEJACK IS AN APPLE BRANDY that used to be made in winter time in the backwoods by leaving fermented apple juice outside on the window sill to freeze the water and leave behind the apple-flavoured alcohol. (The headache-making elements came with it, unfortunately; no middle cut of the distillation there.) Early settlers in New Jersey and Virginia distilled applejack that was eloquently dubbed 'Jersey Lightning' and it is easy to imagine the cause of the condition called apple palsy that it often brought on. Today, applejack is double-distilled in pot stills and must age for a minimum of two years in oak.

Bonny Doon • Apple eau de vie from Golden Delicious fruit produced as part of Randall Grahm's development programme at his distillery. The Pomme 'Golden' is well scented and authentic in flavour, with a nice musky tail-off.

Clear Creek • Apple brandy from Stephen McCarthy's fine artisanal operation in Oregon that is a mix in style between the muskiness of calvados and the clarion-clear fruit notes of Swiss/German *apfelbrand*. Two years in Limousin oak casks softens some of the 40% vol bite.

CLEAR CREEK

Eau de Vie de Pomme

APPLE BRANDY BARREL-AGED IN LIMOUSIN OAK

DISTILLED AND BOTTLED BY
CLEAR CREEK DISTILLERY PORTLAND, OREGON
ALCOHOL 40% BY VOL. (80 PROOF) 750 ML
PRODUCT OF U.S.A.

Laird • The Laird company is the USA's oldest brandy distillery, established in 1780 by descendants of immigrant Scots who brought their whisky-making skills with them to America in 1698. Their applejack is made from whole, tree-ripened apples from orchards in the Delaware Valley.

Natural fermentation takes up to a month in 20,000-gallon oak vats immediately after the vintage, and the cider is then distilled twice in pot stills. The spirit is reduced to 65% vol and aged over four to eight years in large charred-oak barrels. Applejack is popular in the northern USA and Florida as increasing numbers of northerners head south to retire.

Laird's Bonded 100% Proof (50% vol) is the top of the range and aged up to 10 years; there is also an apple brandy and a blended applejack, made lighter by its being combined with silent spirit.

Left: The fruit washed for applejack moves by conveyor belt to the crusher.

Below: Lairds want you to know that they are over two hundred years old.

South Africa

The Cape has some of the most dramatic vineyard scenery in the world.

THE FIRST CAPE BRANDIES WERE DISTILLED IN 1672, JUST 20 YEARS AFTER JAN VAN RIEBEECK LANDED to found the colony. For a long time they were dreadful — 'gastric terrorism' André Brink called them — being crudely distilled from stalks, skins and anything else that fell into the vat but, as the country opened up, every ox-drawn wagon that headed for the hinterland had its puncheon in the back. It countered snake bite and disinfected wounds, so there were occasions when the taste was less important. Nicknames like *witblits* (white lightning) and 'Cape Smoke' testified vividly to its fieriness although, in fact, *Kaapse-smaak* referred directly to the distinctively awful 'Cape flavour'. *Dop*, meaning brandy, originally came from the word for husk, or pomace brandy.

In the 19th century, improvements were gradually made and in the 1890s a Frenchman, René Santhagen, settled at Oude Molen near Stellenbosch and began distilling brandy in a pair of cognac pot stills he had brought with him. His products were so superior to the local efforts that his methods became the basis of legislation in 1909, which specified healthy wine, pot-still distillation and proper maturation for brandy making. (Santhagen had a bridge built between his top-floor bedroom at Oude Molen and the distillery next door so that he had direct access 24 hours a day during the distilling season.)

Today, brandy is the national drink and it accounts for half the spirit consumption in South Africa. Ugni Blanc and Colombard grapes (as used in cognac production) are augmented by Chenin Blanc, Cinsaut and Palomino in Cape brandy production and the vineyards lie in the Little Karoo, Worcester, Robertson, Olifants River, Orange River and around Stellenbosch and Paarl. To encourage quality production, the government offered tax rebates to growers who made wines specially for distillation and for spirits aged a minimum of three years in oak. These became known as rebate wines and brandies, in fact terms which indicated quality and merit. Both pot stills and continuous stills are used but blended brandy must contain at least 30% matured eau de vie and no more than 70% grape spirit distilled at high strength. Much of the production is light in flavour for mixing. In 1991, the legal minimum strength of South African brandies was reduced from 43% to 38% vol, contributing to the softness of the broad generic style.

In addition to the mainstream large-volume production by the established brands, an increasing number of wine makers are producing small-batch handmade brandies, including several in the traditional style of cognac.

Backsberg • This distinguished wine estate at Paarl imported a pot still from France in the early 1990s and began distilling and 'laying down' spirit with which to market the Cape's first 'cognac' in 1994. Brandy was made on the farm 150 years ago, when the water supply contract required that cooling water used in distilling had to be returned to the stream, and the present owner, Gerrit Lotz, remembers his father distilling spirit to sell as brandy and for fortifying sweet wines.

The wines are from Chenin Blanc vines and prepared as in Cognac. They are unsulphured and distilled on their lees. Chilling the condenser water ensures optimum capture of the more volatile aroma and flavour elements. The separation of the heart of each distillation run is computer-controlled and identical for each batch. The spirit goes into Limousin oak for three years. Lotz is a believer in maximum control for the producer and, although his is the first estate 'cognac', he wants to see many more emerge with the power invested in them by law to oversee everything 'from bud-burst to bottling' on the estate. 'Only this way will both the producer and the consumer be protected,' he says.

Barrydale Cooperative • Brandy is something of a speciality at this cooperative in the Klein Karoo with up to 60% of its grapes going into brandy production. However, it is also the only cooperative so far in South Africa to have produced a champagne-method sparkling wine. The pot-still spirit it distils is sold in bulk to Distillers Corporation and goes into its own blends. Barrydale was set up in 1940 and the vineyards in the Tradouw Valley have a microclimate that gives milder summers and colder winters than elsewhere in the Klein Karoo.

South Africa's *voortrekkers* carried brandy with them as they went inland with the wagon teams. It was a taste inherited from their Dutch forefathers and it travelled better than wine.

Pruning vines by hand is time consuming but this skilled work promotes grape quality. Colombard and Ugni Blanc are the preferred cultivars for brandy.

Olof Bergh • Brand launched in 1988 which is aged in a solera system like the Jerez brandies in Spain. A blend of pot- and continuous-still spirits, it has decent weight and texture.

Boplaas • Small-batch pot-still brandy, the first of its kind in South Africa. Distillation began at Boplaas in the Klein Karoo in 1989 and the first releases were late in 1994. Local advice came from Buks Venter at KWV and Fanie van Niekerk, and several cognac experts, including Robert Léauté of Rémy Martin, paid visits. Only Colombard grapes are used, which are left unsulphured and the wine goes through its malolactic fermentation before distillation. An old Santhagen (cognac-style) still is used, which Carel Nel bought from Gilbey's in Stellenbosch and the brandy ages in Limousin oak for three to five years. The yield is about 500 cases a year, most of it selling at the estate, with a little planned for export.

Carel Nel's great-great-grandfather, Daniel, had made brandy in the 1860s at Boplaas and exported it to London. As a modern wine maker, Nel uses a microlight aircraft to carry out regular inspections of his vineyards.

Clos Cabrière • Vineyard in Franschhoek run by the innovative von Arnims, who produce champagne-method sparkling wines. Their estate pot-still brandy, Fine de Jourdan, is distilled from the third pressing, the final 150 litres of juice per ton of Chardonnay grapes, which has a high proportion of flavour-yielding solids in suspension. (The first two pressings go to making the wines.) Achim von Arnim was keen to produce his spirit in precisely the Champagne manner and researched this with the help of the Customs and Excise, KWV and his contacts in Champagne. The precise details of his method are kept secret.

The pot still, which was donated by a shareholder of the company, is smaller than standard at 400 litres capacity, and an exception was made in the granting of the licence. The wine is unsulphured and the malolactic fermentation is avoided if possible. The spirit comes off the still at 70% vol and so far has been aged for three years, the ratio of new oak to old being limited to 20% to avoid excessive woodiness. The first distillation took place in 1990 (three 300-litre casks) and the best season so far has been the dozen barrels produced in 1994. The brandy is named after the Huguenot who first farmed the site in 1694.

Fine de Jourdan • Estate brandy from Clos Cabrière (*qv*) in Franschhoek.

Fish Eagle • Premium pot-still brand marketed as 100% natural. The brandy is presented as free of preservatives and additives but then, so are other brandies from the Distillers Corporation. All good distilling wines are free of sulphur dioxide to avoid off-aroma and flavour coming over in distillation. The brandy is, nonetheless, soft, smooth and attractive in style with a big, grapey nose. The vines are mainly Ugni Blanc and Colombard. It is pale in colour (no caramel for colouring) and goes into small casks of new French oak seasoned outdoors (not kiln-dried) for nine months, then into old wood.

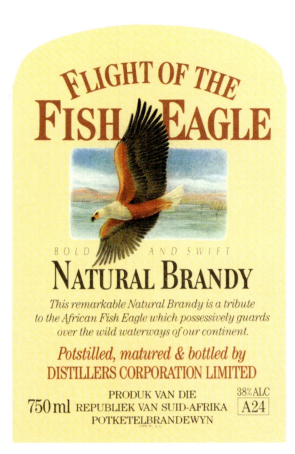

KWV • Prestige pot-still brand with very high profile in recent years. In the early 1990s, KWV brandies caught the attention of the world when they won the Domecq Trophy for Best Brandy in consecutive years — the 20-year-old in 1990 and the 10-year-old in 1991 — in the International Wine & Spirit Competition in London. The KWV wine-farmers cooperative (Kooperatieve Wijnbouwers Vereniging Beperkt) was formed in 1924 to regulate both wine and brandy production, a sometimes controversial circumstance since, in having its own brands, it was both administrator and competitor in the marketplace. The first KWV double-distilled brandy was made in 1926 in pot stills specially made for the company; they are reported to be still in use.

The premium KWV brandies were first marketed in 1984 but their making began in the 1970s, when an assessment was made of the mature stocks in the group's cellars. Of the 10-year-old brandy, a sizeable amount was thought capable of improving further and was left in place; it is this parcel that went on to become KWV 20-year-old. The brandies are slightly sweetened and *bonificateurs* (natural flavour enhancers) are added; the strength is reduced gradually over years of ageing to bottling-strength with distilled water.

These brandies carry rich, spicy, succulent flavour and are round and opulent in texture. Both are complex and silky, while the 20-year-old is more mellowed with fine *rancio*. There is also a five-year-old (caramel and grape flavours, a little fiery) and a three-year-old Three-star.

Bottom: Part of the vast KWV complex, the South African national cooperative, founded in 1924.

as a water bottle for rural horseback riders. For the occasion of its 75th anniversary in 1990 the blend was reformulated to incorporate the present five-year-old content. Producers Stellenbosch Farmers' Winery build their own casks from imported French oak. The nose and flavours of Mellow-Wood are pleasantly toasty, a little spicy, and there is alcoholic snap at the end. The 'exceptional for medicinal use' legend on the label gave way in 1994 to 'rich, warm, smooth and always mellow'.

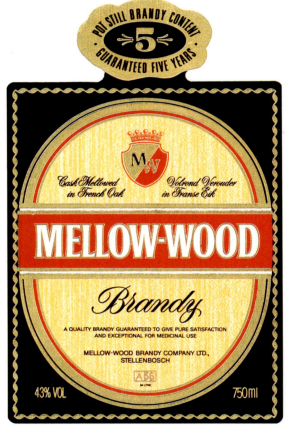

The Mons Ruber estate in the Klein Karoo region, some distance from the Cape wine heartland, is characterised by the extraordinary red hills around the farm.

Mellow-Wood • Brand blended from pot- and continuous-still spirits in three- and five-year-old ranges. The ages refer only to the 30% pot-still content in the blend, which is oak-aged for these periods. The Mellow-Wood brand was introduced in South Africa in 1915 and in its distinctive flask in 1939. The flask was extremely popular because it fitted in coat pockets without showing, did not roll around on car floors and fitted into briefcases and lunch boxes! It also fitted snugly into saddlebags and was reusable

Mons Ruber • Brandy from the Hanepoot (Muscat d'Alexandrie) grape. Mons Ruber is situated in the semi-desert of the Klein Karoo and the name, Latin for Red Hill, refers to the distinctive colour of a nearby range of hills. The farm has produced wines and brandies since the 1850s, and it also reared ostriches for their feathers in the days when these were fashionable. The British royal family visited Mons Ruber in 1947 and the then Princess Elizabeth was shown how to clip ostriches.

The Meyer family at Mons Ruber made *witblits* — white lightning — as well as brandy in the past and, although it had an important role in the social circumstances of the depressed 1930s, it was a rough, raw spirit and production was discouraged.

The Meyers' Cognac-type pot still dates from the 1930s and is wood-fired. Its positioning in the yard is typical of the time and was carefully worked out in advance. It is near trees for the shade they offer: one an orange tree, since its leaves placed in the spout gave an orange flavour to the spirit; one a fig tree which would be in fruit when distillation was being carried out; and a willow tree for shade. The still was always near an irrigation canal so that the condensing coils could be laid in the water, and near the cellar since there was no pumping equipment and distilling wine had to be carried to it by the pailful. In the 1930s, wood to heat the still was brought by cable-car from the Red Hills.

The Hanepoot brandy produced in 1994 by brothers Radie and Erhard Meyers' is the first 'proper' distillation since those extraordinary days 60 years ago, and the spirit is now ageing in small Limousin oak barrels. Some blending of the first few distilling seasons will probably be carried out in order to build a brandy that the Meyers feel is good enough. The law requires three years' minimum ageing, so there is time for them to consider just how the label will look.

Old Château • The brand was established in 1921. The brandy was reformulated in 1989 to incorporate an unspecified proportion of five-year-old oak-aged pot-still spirit. In the category style — soft and grapey with some nip from 43% vol strength.

Oude Meester • Range of pot-still brandies from the country's leading brand. Oude Meester VSOP was launched by the Distillers Corporation in 1948 as a liqueur (*ie* after-dinner) brandy and two years later won Best Brandy award in the Half-Century British Empire Exhibition Wine Competition in London.

Oude Meester VSOP is aged for five to eight

King George VI and Queen Elizabeth examine a Mons Ruber ostrich during the 1947 Royal visit.

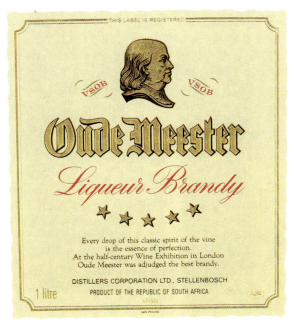

years in imported French oak and keeps its traditional 43% vol strength, leaving it up to stable mate Souverain to fill the 38% vol slot. Souverain is the first South African 12-year-old brandy and was introduced in 1988. It spends the entire 12-year period in the same small 300-litre vats. The house style is round in texture and light in the delivery of flavour.

Paarl Rock • Small-batch 'hand-made' brand produced in Paarl. The Paarl Wine & Brandy Company was founded in 1856 by the de Villiers family, Huguenot refugees from the Charente. The first de Villiers had landed in the Cape from La Rochelle in 1689. The company was one of several who made great efforts to produce for quality with a view to building up export sales. Cecil Rhodes was for a time one of Paarl's shareholders and the company had very grand offices and cellars in the town. The style is subtle and a little austere, but classy with zesty, understated power. In 1991 Paarl Rock released the first South African brandy to be made from a single grape-type, Hanepoot, more widely known as Muscat.

Richelieu • French-style pot-still brand. This was Distillers Corporation's first postwar brandy launch and is consciously produced in what the company calls 'the age-old French tradition'. On the other hand, it has a certain fullness of body and is recommended for mixing.

Royal Oak • This 'Golden Liqueur' brand, used principally for mixing, is subdued in flavour. It has a slight toasty quality and is sweet, soft and grapey.

Ryn • The cellars were built in 1904, to be used as a cooperative by local growers in the hard years that followed the Boer War. Large rocks from the nearby Eerste River were used as building stone. The distillery has been restored and is used as an educational centre for brandy-tastings and seminars, cellar tours and music concerts. There are four John Dore pot stills and a six-column continuous still that stands five storeys high. Van Ryn has its own cooperage. The Rare Cabinet Brandy is aged for up to 20 years in oak. The aroma is forward and grapey, the texture soft and light, the flavour toffeed and sharpish.

Viceroy • Another brandy from the Van Ryn label, Viceroy Old Liqueur has good body, some wood aroma and an alcoholic nip.

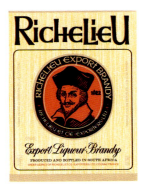

Australia

BRANDY MAKING IN AUSTRALIA GREW FROM THE NEED TO HAVE GRAPE SPIRIT with which to make port. Vines were planted by immigrants from the wine-growing countries of Europe, first of all to provide wines for their own consumption and latterly to be sold as commercial products. The British, Dutch and other settlers of northern European origins were accustomed to fortified wines and to make these you needed brandy to combine with the base wines. However, over-production was also a factor in bringing about the growth of distillation, particularly after the introduction of the seedless Sultana grape to the Murray River area.

The number of distilleries grew throughout the 19th century and in 1901 laws were first drawn up for the regulation of brandy production both to specify a safe product and to set up a taxation structure. Interest in home-produced brandies ebbed and flowed during the 20th century with the rise and fall of the availability of cognac and other imported spirits. Since the 1980s, however, home brandy has thrived, maintaining a 75% share of the market, which has doubled since the end of World War II.

Today brandy is made in South Australia, Victoria and New South Wales. Grapes used are the traditional Doradillo and Sultana, plus more recently the Pedro Ximenez and Palomino (used in sherry making in Jerez) and the White Heritage (the Australian name for Cognac's Ugni Blanc, which in turn is the Trebbiano of Italy). Both pot and continuous stills are used and new spirit must be between 74% and 83% vol (*cf* cognac spirit at 70-72% vol). Maturation in oakwood is mostly between two (the legal minimum) and 20 years. On labels, 'Old' indicates minimum five years' ageing; 'Very Old' minimum 10 years. 'Blended' brandy is a blend of pot- and continuous-still spirit and wine; grape and prune juices, honey and other 'enhancers' are permitted.

The Barossa valley in South Australia is not unlike its namesake in Spain. Early settlers turned to distilling and laid the foundations of an industry.

A 19th century Barossa homestead with the evening sun projecting shadows from the immaculately crafted ironwork.

Black Bottle • Popular brand with unorthodox distillation method from the BRL Hardy Wine Company. The spirit is double-distilled but the second time through a continuous still, rendering good flavour and aroma, as well as finer texture. Thomas Hardy tried cattle droving and prospecting for gold when he arrived from Devon in 1850. When he planted vines in 1853, he spent the four years before they would first produce grapes digging cellars to store the wine. His first still was an old Cornish boiler with a fractionating column mounted on top; the next was a 700-gallon gum-wood vat with the same column fixed in position.

Hardy's better-quality brandy is produced entirely from pot stills at Waikere and matures in small oak casks at McLaren Vale. Most of the total spirit is aged for a short time before going into Black Bottle three-year-old, but a proportion matures longer to maintain stocks for blending the older brandies. Hardy's produces hogshead and puncheon casks for its wines and brandies in its own cooperage at McLaren Vale. The present fifth-generation chair-

man, Sir James Hardy, was a recent America's Cup yacht skipper.

The pot-still VSOP is from Doradillo grapes; it is mellow and dignified from 25 years in oak.

Château Tanunda • Aromatic dry brandies from the giant Seppelt wine company. Château Tanunda was always a distillery, run by a cooperative in the early 1900s. By the time Seppelt bought it, the brandy stocks in the cellars were large and already old.

Château Yaldara • Young but well-flavoured brandy from Lyndoch, in the Barossa Valley. Herman Thumm, an immigrant from Germany in the 1940s, developed his own vacuum-distillation technique, which carries more taste and aroma over into the brandy. He took over an old flour mill and rebuilt it into the battlemented château in place today. The distillery was built in 1974, and the company has about 45 hectares of vineyards. The brandy is three years old and zesty.

made, elegant and well textured. The fine, small range includes a silky Seven-Star XO with 20- to 50-year-old brandies in the blend.

Stock/Penfolds • Brandy sold under the brand name of the Italian Stock company (*qv* Italy) in Australia is distilled to their specifications by Penfolds at Nuriootpa, South Australia. The light, soft style is produced by both pot- and continuous still distillation and the brandy ages for up to eight years in American oak hogsheads.

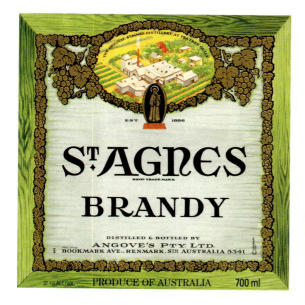

St Agnes • Pot-still brandy named after the patron saint of purity, and aged in small hogshead casks. The business was begun by a Dr Angove, who emigrated to South Australia from Cornwall in Britain in the 1880s. He planted vines at Tea Tree Gully near Adelaide where he set up in general practice and where the first steps in distillation took place. Angove believed in the therapeutic values of wine. In 1910, his sons built the first winery and distillery on the Murray River at Renmark and it was there that St Agnes brandy was first produced.

The Angoves are also important wine makers and they invented the 'wine box' in 1965, the airtight take-away wine containers with press taps now used everywhere. Their early Château Downunda wine label is widely remembered. The brandy is carefully

Top: Dr Angove's two sons started distilling when their new winery outside Adelaide was completed. St Agnes brandy was an immediate success.

Bottom: Vintage time at Angove's eighty years on; the company longevity is the fruit of resourceful and innovative management.

Portugal

Aveleda, a classic Portuguese mansion in the Vinho Verde region.

IN PORTUGAL, THE GENERAL WORD FOR BRANDY (including the high-strength spirit used to fortify port) is *aguardente* and pomace brandy is *bagaço* or *bagaceira*. Brandy in Portugal does not have the same importance or volume that it has in Spain; it is a small adjunct to the wine industry. *Vinho verde* wines, which are high in acidity like those from Ugni Blanc in Cognac, make good brandy. Bairrada, too, yields appropriate styles of wine for distillation.

Aguardente is a little drier and less opulent than its Spanish counterpart, but some full-bodied brandy is produced by ageing in port casks. Both pot and continuous stills are used, so styles can vary from firm and understated to fine and smooth in texture. Natural flavourings, such as nut and prune essences, are often added.

Bagaceira is at least as popular as *aguardente* in Portugal, much of it made from *bagaço*, or pomace, that goes straight from the grape press to the distillery, resulting in delightfully fresh and fragrant spirit. Every wine cooperative makes some but there can be problems with excessive methanol content in those from the remotest back-country distillers, for whom zeal for tradition can remove the will to err on the safe side.

Antiqua • Zesty, spicy, grapey *aguardente* from Caves Aliança, one of the more dynamic, new-generation wine firms in the country famous for its Dão reds and *vinhos verdes*.

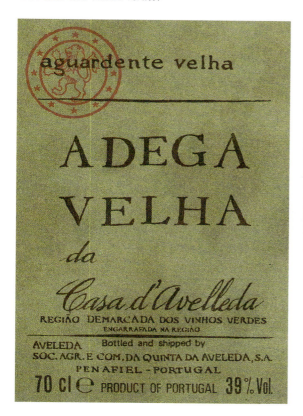

launched Reserva Velha are largely drawn from the 'Mother' stocks and are much more elegant and polished. CR&F also produces a fine, resonant *bagaceira*.

Caves da Porça • Brand name of a Douro cooperative at Murca which produces an authentically fragrant *velha*. Deeply coloured and intensely oaky. Round and quite spirity (45% vol).

The Vinho Verde region in northern Portugal has a cool luscious green landscape producing high acid grapes ideal for brandy.

Aveleda • Leading brand of *vinho verde* in international markets, which has both pot and continuous stills with which to make *aguardente* and *bagaceira*. Both are rounded in texture and aromatic.

Carvalho, Ribeiro & Ferreira • The company, established in 1888, has extensive 'Mother' stocks of old (*velha*) *aguardentes* which it blends with other, already senior spirits to produce mellow, settled brandies of character and grace as well as younger, keener styles. Its brandies are produced in a small pot still with an eight-metre-high fractionating column. CR&F takes its high profile as a wine maker in Portugal seriously. Its '1920' brand is well established and, aged in oak for only a year at most, it is natural with no additives. The Reserva and a recently

Mexico

The Mayan 'Temple of Inscriptions' at Palenque is a symbol of Mexico's ancient culture. The vineyard programme set up by Cortès in the 16th century is by comparison a recent development.

IT WAS CORTÈS HIMSELF WHO FOSTERED THE DEVELOPMENT OF VINEYARDS IN MEXICO. During his time as governor of New Spain in the 1520s, he required that all incoming ships from Europe bring vines, and every recipient of a *repartimiento* land grant had to plant 1,000 vines for every 100 Indians working on the property for at least five consecutive years. Today, Mexican wines can be excellent in quality but 90% of the vineyards' yield goes into brandy production. Brandy is very popular in the country and there are several multi-million case brands, including the world's biggest brandy brand, Presidente (*qv*). After World War I,

when the French persuaded the Mexican government to prohibit use of the term *coñac*, Mexicans liked the ring of the word 'brandy' that replaced it and the category took off.

The generic style is that of the traditional Spanish brandies and Fundador from Spain was the brand leader until imports were restricted. This meant local production was galvanised and grew with the consumer clamour for the product. None of the main brands is more than 40 years old (although some of the actual firms go back hundreds of years). Brandy's growth displaced rum and tequila as traditional Mexican spirits. Both 'mixing' and 'sipping' cultures co-exist with the prestige of the chosen brand important.

The main vineyard areas are in Sonora, Coahuila, Zacatecas and Baja California, where Thomson Seedless, Cariñan, Flame Tokay, Perlette, Bula Dulce, Palomino, Ruby and St Emilion (the Ugni Blanc of Cognac) are the prevailing vines. Distillation is in both pot and continuous stills and the solera system is used for ageing, as in Jerez, Spain (*qv*).

Almacenes Guajuardo • Distillery firm. The Vinícola del Marqués Aguayo is the oldest winery in the Americas, established from a grove of wild vines discovered in 1593 at Parras. Today, the company specialises in the production of brandy.

Casa Madero • Pot-still brandy distiller. The winery at Parras dates from the 1620s, and was bought by an ancestor of the present owning family in 1870. Evaristo Madero travelled in Europe and brought back vine cuttings from the main wine-growing countries. While he was in Cognac he bought a pot still and arranged for technicians to come to Mexico to install it. Francisco Madero, the Mexican president who was assassinated in 1913, was a descendant.

Martel • Brand from the Mexican arm of the French cognac house Martell. It is a pot-still brandy from Ugni Blanc grapes grown at the large vineyards at San Juan del Río. The property was first planted in 1965.

Don Pedro • Premium brand, up-market companion to Presidente (*qv*). Don Pedro, introduced by Domecq in the late 1960s, sells more than three million cases a year (98% within Mexico) and has been one of the world's fastest-growing spirit brands in the early 1990s. Although both Don Pedro and Presidente are matured at Los Reyes, each brandy has its own separate solera and *criaderas* for ageing. Don Pedro takes between eight and 10 years to progress through the solera and emerges with greater softness and mellowness. It is less in the Spanish style, with its own

distinct characteristics. It costs perhaps 30% more than Presidente at retail and is expected to be sipped and savoured rather than mixed.

Presidente • Biggest-selling brandy in the world. Owned by Domecq (*qv* Spain), the sherry and brandy firm, recently bought by Allied Distillers in the U.K., the brand sells over five million cases a year, including a small amount to the USA, but 95% of it domestically. When brandy imports to Mexico were discontinued in the 1950s, Domecq set up supply arrangements with grape growers and brought in European technology to distil the wine they produced. Presidente is aged near Mexico City at Los Reyes in the largest maturation bodegas in Central and South America, where about 400,000 toasted white oak barrels lie mellowing their contents. Presidente goes through a three-stage solera over a period of six years. Sugar syrup and caramel for colouring are added. Quite full and sweet, with some bite — helpful when it comes to mixing.

Presidente uses every opportunity to maintain number one position in world-wide brandy sales, as this mobile advertising on Acapulco beach indicates.

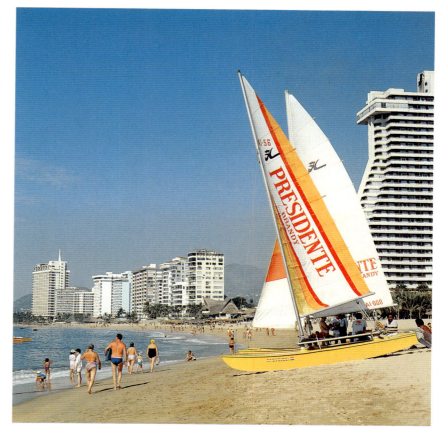

Armenia

Astvatsatsin church in Armenia, built in 1215. Distilling in the region developed out of a monastic tradition.

ARMENIA, ON THE SHORE OF THE BLACK SEA, is where the vine and wine making itself may well have begun. If Mount Ararat is indeed where the Ark grounded after the Great Flood, then this is where Noah planted his vineyard. The beginnings of distillation also disappear back into the mists of time but certainly Armenia has long been associated with brandy making. In 1887, the Armenian capital, Yerevan, became the region's focus of excellence when a distillery was established in the lee of Mount Ararat, which continued the monastic distilling tradition in the area.

The Ararat distillery furnished fine spirits for the Tsar and other noble households and from the start it steadily built up an exclusive cellar, carved into the side of Mount Ararat, of very old distillates which became its 'Golden Reserve'. During the course of this century, Ararat's best brandies were at the disposal of the Russian Communist Party bosses and their visiting guests; Winston Churchill is said to have greatly enjoyed the distillery's brandy, which was on the drinks table throughout the Yalta Conference in 1945.

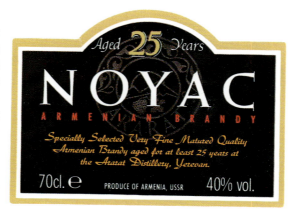

In the final years of the Soviet Union, the distillery concentrated on producing commercial brandies for export to earn hard currency and this has survived the transition to national independence. Local grapes to the fore are the Saperavi, Voskeat and Chilar but Muscadine and two Madeira grapes (Sercial and Verdelho) also figure.

Ararat • Brand name used for the distillery's brandies exported directly to western markets. The centenary of commercial brandy production in Yerevan was in 1987, the distillery being located on the site of the old Sardar Khan fortress. A local specialist who had graduated from the distinguished French viticultural college at Montpellier set up the brandy production in 1892 and began with three imported Charentais pot stills. In 1901, they released their first 'Selected Fine Champagne' brandy. During the last war, a false wall was erected in a warehouse behind which the distillery's most precious old stocks lay hidden from possible plundering; they survived and still contribute to today's blends. New brandy styles were evolved and the still house now has 12 cognac pot stills. The distillery has its own cooperage.

Export brandies are widely available in Three- and Six-Star styles, with each star signifying one year of ageing.

Noyac • A range of old brandies which draws upon the Ararat Golden Reserve cellar and features fine, complex eaux de vie which show some of the flavour tones of the local vines used to make the distilling wines. Noyac means 'Noah's Spring', referring to the water source which feeds the brandy production. The brandy has been double-distilled in cognac pot stills and aged in Limousin or local Armenian oak for up to 40 years. Casks of Noyac were brought out of Yerevan by London-based expatriate Vartan Ouzounian and bottled in a smart new presentation. Previously, only 10% of production used to escape to the west; now Ouzounian is re-exporting it to Russia for sale duty free. The brand is available in Asia-Pacific, the USA and Europe.

There is a chocolate-like richness to these old brandies, the texture becoming richer the older the age. The 10- and 18-year-olds won awards in the 1991 International Wine & Spirit Competition in London. There is also a 25-year-old.

Tasting is a serious business when you match grape flavours with the brandy.

England

It was not lack of imagination that saw brandy distillation in England disappear 300 years ago. William and Mary actually took the trouble to disapprove of it in 1688 and no one had the nerve to complain. Smuggling compensated, and one enthusiastic brandy smuggler was the grandfather of writer Thomas Hardy. It is said that he had a squint built into the famous Hardy cottage near Dorchester so that he could look down the lane for approaching excise men. In the mid-1980s, the late Bertram Bulmer, former head of the large cider firm that still bears his family name, wrested permission from the Customs and Excise to distil cider into apple brandy in his cider museum in Hereford. Next came a stately-home owner and a Somerset cider maker who, after a decade of effort, got a licence to distil at Brympton d'Evercy House near Yeovil. Word of this kind travels fast and now, in the space of a few years, England already has several small-scale producers of apple brandy, wine brandy and wine eau de vie.

King Offa • Cider brandy produced in a tiny distillery attached to the Bulmer Cider Museum in Hereford, England. The late Bertram Bulmer, former chairman of Bulmer's Cider, ended a 300-year proscription of cider brandy-distillation in England in 1984, when he obtained a museum licence to distil. The French tried to stop him using the word 'brandy', claiming it for their own grape spirit, but, enlisting the help of Mrs Thatcher and the UK Ministry of Agriculture, Food and Fisheries, Bulmer saw them off. The Queen was presented with the first bottle produced in 1987 — only fair, perhaps, since she had given Bulmer an oak tree from Windsor Great Park with which to make maturation casks. Ex-bourbon oak barrels with local Hereford oak ends are now the main wood combination.

Nick Bulmer has now taken up from where his father left off and has developed a whole range of devices — feeders, heat sensors, timers *etc* — which enable the pot still to function for long periods without continuous supervision. The tiny still yields perhaps 200 litres in a day. Until recently, each bottling was single-vintage brandy but now, with a respectable number of distilling seasons behind them, blending options are possible. The brandy is full and aromatic with rich, musky intensity.

Lamberhurst • Wine brandy. In 1990, when Lamberhurst vineyard in Kent announced the sale of a small batch of the first wine brandy to be made in England for 300 years, a queue was waiting at the gates at six o' clock on the morning of the sale and the little shop was sold out by seven o' clock. Lamberhurst had bought wines in for the experiment but the following year, 15,000 litres of their own 1990 vintage went down to Julian Temperley's distillery in Somerset for distilling. This pattern continues until Lamberhurst can instal its own still, for which it recently received a licence.

The three-year-old spirit is clean, fresh and pleasantly soft, and wine maker Stephen Donnelly is currently conducting research into the best wood and ageing period for the brandy.

Somerset Royal • Apple brandy. Cider maker Julian Temperley makes his apple/cider brandy in an old creamery beside an abandoned railway line in deepest Somerset. He has two calvados stills called Josephine and Fifi, each with distinct, female personalities, say staff. Josephine is 'solid and reliable'; Fifi is 'very French, small and fast'. Temperley began distilling at Brympton d'Evercy with Charles Clive-Ponsonby-Fane and then financed the setting up of his own operation by taking on founder subscribers — among them John Cleese — who agreed to pay up front and wait for their brandy. The first vintage sold out in advance and a bottle of it brought extra publicity when the British Antarctic Survey took it to the South Pole for New Year 1991-92. Temperley learned to distil, has had to research the best types of oak casks for maturation and also does the distillation for wine producers looking to make wine brandies. He got it right, though, and the brandy was well received.

For the moment, his 'standard' three-year-old brandy is rich, zesty, aromatic and, of necessity, youthful. Once he gets a few more seasons under his belt, Temperley will have the stock to produce a five-year-old, and a 10-year-old is planned for the year 2000.

Wootton • Wine eau de vie. Colin Gillespie is an award-winning wine maker in Somerset, establishing his vineyard at Wootton in 1971, when there were only a score of working vineyards in the country. In 1992, he had a test distillation done by Julian Temperley of some of his Müller-Thurgau and Seyval Blanc wine. Gillespie envisaged making an aged brandy and had consulted his friend Bernard Hine (see Hine, Cognac) on the best wood to use. When his distillate came back it was so delightfully fresh, grapey, soft and appealing that he decided to forget years in oak and bottled it as a young eau de vie. It was absolutely unique in the UK — the only one of its kind and probably the first for centuries. The first year of full production was in 1993 from 100% Seyval grapes and it sold out.

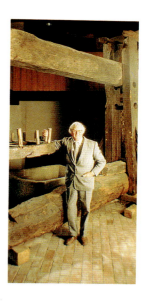

Opposite page: Vineyards at Wootton in the foothills of the Mendips.

Top: Colin Gillespie, pioneer of English eau de vie.

Left: Grape picking at Lamberhurst, Kent.

Israel

in many other countries around the world. The Colombard grape is widely grown for distilling wines, both pot and continuous stills are used and maturation is in Limousin oak barrels.

Askalon • Proprietors of the Grand 41 brandy brand. In 1787, J. Hirsch Segal set up a distillery in the Russian town of Bobroisk; in 1925, the Segal brothers emigrated to Palestine and established the first distillery in the Sarona district of Tel Aviv, now called Hakirya. Today, the Askalon company is run by the sixth and seventh generations of the Segal family. Grand 41 is produced in a continuous still akin to that used in Armagnac and aged for four years in French oak. It is fragrant and gentle in flavour.

Carmel • Brand name of a large wine and spirits cooperative. Carmel are Israel's oldest wine and spirits producers (see above), and today their products are exported to more than 40 countries around the globe, often on their own merits but especially where there are Jewish communities. Their brandies are well regarded and have won top awards in recent years at the International Wine & Spirit Competition in London. The vineyards which produce the distilling wines for Carmel brandy dot the Holy Land but the distillery and century-old cellars are situated at Richon-le-Zion. Richon 777 is six years old and is full-flavoured and rich; Brandy 100 is nine years old and has firm, mellow-fruit flavour and balance; and the 15-year-old is rested, fine and graceful.

Stock 84 • Lighter-styled aperitif brandy made at the Barkan distillery to the specifications of the Italian firm Stock (*qv*). The house style is smooth with a touch of fire and standardised wherever it is made in the world under this kind of licensed production arrangement. The brand is well established on the Israeli market.

Vineyards by the Sea of Galilee, with metal trellising posts for better leaf exposure.

WINE AND SPIRIT PRODUCTION IN ISRAEL, in the wake of pioneering work by Noah, began with the Carmel operation established in 1882 by Baron Edmond de Rothschild. Management of the business was handed over to the farmers in 1906 and it became a cooperative, a status that it retains to this day. Two subsequent prime ministers of Israel worked in the vineyards in the early days.

French influences still show as a follow-on from the Rothschilds having sent out French experts a century ago to establish operating principles in the vineyards. At the same time, the cognaçais precepts in brandy production followed in Israel are now used

Brandy 100
CARMEL

Brandies from Other Countries

Brazil

Macieira • Brazilian brandy from Seagram. Based on the Portuguese style, the Five-Star is 100% grape spirit with some ageing, while the Three-Star is a blend of grape, ginger and other spirits.

While many Brazilians still stick with the traditional *cachaça* — cane spirit — brandy continues to gain in popularity.

Cyprus

WINE MAKING IN CYPRUS GOES BACK TO CLASSICAL TIMES but distillation seems to have been a relatively late development. The Haggipavlu company was the first to begin producing brandy on the island in 1868, when it imported a cognac still from France.

Brandy was so popular that they almost gave up wine making to concentrate on distilling. Brandy is

Traditional grape baskets handed down through the centuries of viticultural history in Cyprus.

part of Cypriot culture now and special low-strength types are often served with meals instead of wine.

Styles are typically smooth and light from high-strength distillation, so fruit peel and walnut extracts are usually added to the brandies for flavour

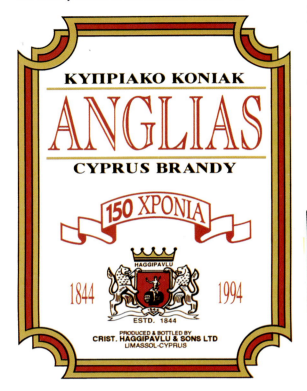

Anglias • Brand from Haggipavlu, which also produces a wide range of spirits and liqueurs. In the 1930s, the company exported a special brandy blend to the UK but it was introduced at home when Cypriots began asking for 'Anglias brandy — that brandy for England'. Christodoulis Haggipavlu began making and transporting wine to the Middle East from Limassol in 1894.

Haggipavlu had the distinction of sharing the Grand Prize for Best Brandy at the 1914 International Exhibition in London with Bisquit Napoléon cognac. The original 1868 pot still is on show at the distillery, still in working order, but now retired. The house style is soft and grapey, and Anglias is the best-selling brand on the island. The range includes 15-year-old Alexander and rises to quality XO.

Czech Republic

Slovignac • Czech brand first established before World War II by the Tauber brothers in Prague. The Slovignac brand name was introduced in 1955 and belongs to the Seliko firm in Olomouc. The brandy content is aged for an unspecified time in oak barrels after distillation. The house style is soft, rounded and grapey and there are two types: the Three-Star is a 50/50 blend of wine distillate and neutral spirit; the Two-Star is sweeter and a 25/75 blend of wine and neutral spirit. Both have raisins, imported rum and other natural enhancers added to improve the flavour; 40% vol. The brand has picked up a number of awards at national and eastern European competitions in recent years.

Greece

Metaxa • Greek brandy flavoured with muscat wine. Opinions vary as to whether Metaxa retains pure brandy status due to this flavour enhancement it undergoes. However it is double-distilled in pot stills from grape wine and aged in oak casks, just as is done with fully fledged brandies elsewhere, many of which are just as openly 'improved'. 40% vol. Metaxa sells over a million cases a year.

*T*doniko Tsipouro • Young wine eau de vie from French-style Domaine Kostas Lazarides in Adriani Drama, in Greek Macedonia.

The spirit is produced in a new German-designed still from Cabernet, Merlot, Sauvignon and Semillon vines grown on the property's 35 hectares. Unaged and grapy, there is also a version flavoured with local anise extract.

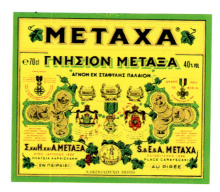

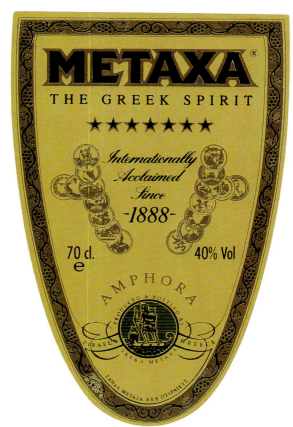

Poland

*P*olmos Winiak Luksusowy • Polish brandy (*winiak* means cognac or brandy) from imported matured wine distillates and rectified neutral spirit.

A little sherry-type wine is added for flavouring. The compounded spirit is aged for several years to marry and improve and when bottled has a good, forward nose and smooth, pleasant flavour; 43% vol.

Slovakia

*M*artignac • Blend of wine brandy and neutral spirit with added flavour-enhancers. The brand is one of the spirits range from the St Nicolaus (*qv*) company in Liptovsky Mikulas.

*S*t Nicolaus • Wood-aged brandy from the St Nicolaus company of Liptovsky Mikulas in Slovakia. St Nicolaus is associated with the establishment of this royal town in 1268.

The Stark family established a distillery in the town in 1868 and by 1907 had diversified to the extent of supplying electricity for Liptovsky Mikulas and the neighbouring village. A state enterprise until 1992, the company produces a wide range of alcoholic drinks and foodstuffs, and distributes Coca-Cola.

Taiwan

*F*ortune • Pot-still brandy from locally produced wines. Following double distillation the spirit is aged for at least five years; 41% vol.

*T*ea Brandy • Sweet, light quaffing brandy. A combination of flavours produced by infusing Taiwanese grape-spirit with fine-quality Wu Lung tea; 25% vol.

Vodka

VODKA IS THE TRADITIONAL SPIRIT PRODUCED IN POLAND, RUSSIA AND OTHER PARTS OF EASTERN EUROPE from fermented grain, potatoes or other plant stuffs. If made in a pot still, it has the gentle and often complex fragrances and savour of the crop from which it was produced. If made in a continuous still, it is usually neutral spirit and devoid of any character.

Modern marketing and technology have created this latter, now dominant, style of international vodka, which is distilled to a very high strength to remove all aroma and flavour and then diluted to bottling strength. They have fostered the public perception that vodka must be neutral and featureless so that you have to add your own flavour; in marketing terms, 'vodka' has a pleasing ring to it that would be lacking in any drinks product bearing the description 'neutral spirit'. Today's mass-produced vodkas have about 30 milligrams of flavouring elements per litre, whereas whiskies and cognacs have up to 2,600.

In truth, this international vodka is stateless, has nothing to do with Poland or Russia and, while customarily claiming the latter's heritage, shows little loyalty to its traditions. Indeed, Smirnoff, former distiller to the Tsar and the world's best-selling vodka brand, was originally marketed in the West as 'white whiskey' and only recently introduced its first vodka actually produced in Russia since the Revolution.

The Poles market a high-strength (96% vol) clear distillate in bottle but they call it Polish Pure Spirit and regard it as a distinct product from the wide range of vodkas they make.

The incidence of high-strength spirits in Poland and Russia originally had much to do with their severe winters, when only strong liquors could be transported by traders; lower-proof alcohols usually froze. When subsequently used for making liqueurs or retailing in bottle, they would be diluted.

Traditional vodkas are still produced and, like malt whisky and cognac, are made in pot stills because these allow the defining aromas and flavours to come over in the distillation. Such vodkas show gentle fragrance and taste as well as clean finish. The majority are clear and dry but others contain natural enhancers like herbs, berries, spices, grasses, fruits, honey and fruit distillates. There are both subtle and full-flavoured styles which hark back to the days when the off tastes of badly made spirit had to be masked. These flavours are not just tacked on but well integrated in the spirit.

Grain, predominantly rye, has long been the traditional raw material associated with vodka making, an initial impetus in 15th-century Russia having been given by the overproduction of cereal. Rye in distillation gave welcome discernible flavour. Today, the use of grain as a raw material indicates aspiration towards a certain quality by the distiller and many grain vodkas, particularly rye, are made in pot stills in order to capture their particularities.

Potatoes are often dismissed, certainly by the Russians, as the material distillers use if they cannot afford grain. However, special varieties have now been developed in relation to soil and climatic conditions which produce fine spirit. Beet has long been used as a subsidiary source material but by far the main substance for mass-produced vodka today is molasses, the rich by-product of sugar refining.

Cereal crops need a heating phase to break down starch in the milled grist to fermentable sugar, whereas molasses comes already rich in sugar.

Opposite page: A landscape of rye fields in Masuria, Poland.

Below: Potatoes have long been a base material for distillation. Recent research has matched specific varieties to suitable climatic conditions.

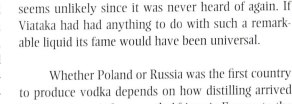

Mashing with hot water produces a sweet liquid called wort and, when yeasts are added, fermentation takes place and a kind of low-strength beer, or wash, is formed. This is double-distilled in a pot still to yield spirit of about 60% vol which retains flavour characteristics. In the past, third and perhaps fourth distillations gave purer, stronger spirit but today, if strong, silent spirit is wanted, a continuous still is used. This separates alcohol and water vapours from a continuous feed of wash and it is possible to distil precisely to a desired alcoholic strength. The distillate is purified further by being filtered through charcoal and then diluted to bottling strength — minimum 37.5% vol in the European Community.

Before distillation was widespread, the only way of producing alcohol stronger than the strongest ales or wines was by freezing. In Poland in the eighth century, it was known that the water in wine or ale left outside in winter would freeze and leave a higher-strength alcohol residue due to water's lower freezing point. There are claims that vodka was being drunk at the Viataka fort in Russia in the 1300s, but this seems unlikely since it was never heard of again. If Viataka had had anything to do with such a remarkable liquid its fame would have been universal.

Whether Poland or Russia was the first country to produce vodka depends on how distilling arrived in Europe: was it from north Africa via Europe to the west, or Persia to the south? It could have been the latter, since there are indications that a clear spirit was made in Persia in the 11th century. But wherever it originated, it was not until the 15th century that distilling knowledge reached eastern Europe and local crops were established as raw materials. Governments, feudal lords and monasteries took distilling monopolies in some areas but in most locations vodka production became a legitimate form of commerce as long as taxes were paid.

To begin with, single distillation would have been the norm, giving only 16% vol alcohol from a low-strength wash or beer, but eventually the idea of redistilling two, three or more times to obtain stronger and cleaner distillate would have occurred to someone. Filtration helped remove impurities; felt and sand, as used by the Romans, made up early filters. In the 18th century, charcoal was found to be highly effective and the standards achieved then are largely those still in effect today.

In Poland and Russia, vodkas were flavoured with the likes of honey, pepper, orange and lemon peel, cherries, rowan berries, walnuts, mint and many other aromatics. Neshinskaya Riabina, made from ash berries, was one of the most popular types produced by the original Smirnoffs in Moscow during the 19th century. Some types, such as Starka and Zubrovka/Zubrówka, which originated within what was previously a single political entity, are produced in now-divergent styles in both Russia and Poland.

A vodka and ginger ale mixed drink called the Moscow Mule was eventually the first catalyst for consumer interest in vodka in America and the latest developments have concerned the successes of Scandinavian vodkas. These have, at least partly, taken things full circle in their encouragements to consumers to make their own fruit and vodka infusions at home instead of just adding mixers.

Traditional dancers in elegant costumes lead the way at a Russian winter festival.

Russia

W**HEN** C**HRISTIANITY WAS INTRODUCED TO** K**IEV IN** 988, it was said to be because the Grand Prince learned that Islam proscribed alcohol. Quite dismayed, he turned to the Christian church and was delighted to discover that wine was actually required for rituals such as communion.

Strong mead was the most powerful drink made in Russia over the following 250 years but, by the 14th century, through contacts with monasteries and foreign merchants, spirit production was known and beginning to be carried out in Russia. Vodka existed long before it acquired its modern name and, to begin with, was called *perevara* (made from mead and beer) and *korchma* (hooch or pot wine).

From the outset, it was made from rye and exports began with quantities sent to Sweden in 1505. In the 1540s, Ivan the Terrible set up the first Russian vodka monopoly, establishing exclusivity for his own inns (called *kabaks)* and stills, and outlawing all others except those sanctioned to the nobles of the country. His treasury should have enjoyed fat profits but, as has happened in nearly every other country where taxation and restriction on alcohol was heavy-handed, illicit distilling became endemic.

In the 17th century, vodka was served at imperial banquets and drunk as part of religious ceremony in church. The study of distillation had advanced and, by the end of the 17th century, experimental quintuple-distillation was occasionally carried out at the laboratory in the Tsar's palace. As in Poland, the earliest use of the word 'vodka' in Russia referred to medicinal potions in the 16th and 17th centuries, before broadening out to embrace flavoured and aromatised vodkas and, finally, in the second half of the 19th century, clear vodkas.

Peter the Great enjoyed his vodka and always took supplies with him when he travelled abroad.

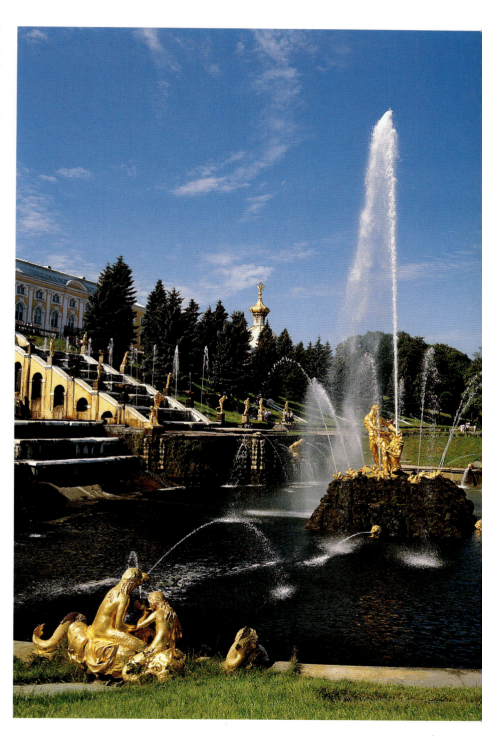

Above: Wealthy Muscovites in this 1816 scene would have enjoyed the highest quality vodka.

Previous page: The Summer Palace fountains in St Petersburg.

Right: The two-headed eagle crest has been associated with Russia since 1472.

Once, during a trip to Versailles in 1717, he ran out of vodka and had to make do with wine and cognac. Despite the fact that it would have been the best available, he grumbled about the privation and even wrote to the Tsarina when he was down to his last bottle, saying he did not know what he would do when it was gone. Not surprisingly, he took an active part in vodka's development and is credited with the invention of a modified still to improve certain production aspects.

Vodka production was entirely in the hands of the privileged classes in the 18th century. It was often of extravagantly high quality, with landowners being able to use crops from their estates and the unpaid labour of the serfs to make it. Vodkas were flavoured with everything from acorns and chicory to horseradish and mint. An important development took place in 1780, when the Tsar commissioned Theodore Lowitz, a chemist, to research ways of purifying vodka and he came up with the first use of charcoal filtration.

Although they produced a native product that had evolved within their boundaries, the Russians were never averse to bringing in the latest foreign equipment to do the required job. Copper stills and pipes were imported from Poland, Germany and Sweden in the 17th century, and Coffey stills from Britain during the 19th century. With time, such plant was adapted to suit local circumstances such as very slow distillation rates and rich, thick mashes. High-quality rye vodka was restricted to the wealthy or exported; everyone else had to make do with poorly

made beet and potato vodka which was sold by the bucketful — an official unit of measure.

Such products were inferior because the technology of the time was not up to the task of purifying them the way it could the traditional rye vodkas. These latter were highly regarded abroad and the wine makers of Málaga and Jerez were among many who used Russian spirit to fortify their wines.

A lot of state-funded research was carried out at the turn of the century to determine the optimum production methods and alcoholic strength for vodka. Under a 1902 law, true Moscow vodka, conventionally taken as the benchmark for Russian vodka, is 40% vol when diluted and ready to drink. According to William Pokhlebkin, of the Moscow Academy of Sciences, the classic Moscow style is clear rye vodka without added flavours, soft 'living' (not distilled) water from local rivers and that 40% vol strength.

Russian vodka lends itself as an accompaniment to rich *zakuska* snack foods — smoked and salted salmon, herring and other fish, assorted pickles, cream and butter pancakes, *pelmeni* (spicy meat balls in dough), sour cabbage with spiced onions and black pepper, and so on.

All distilleries are still owned by the Russian state. The biggest and best known are in Moscow (including the Kristall, now increasingly well known outside Russia), St Petersburg, Samara, Irkutsk, Kaliningrad, Kaluga and Kursk. They are all shareholders in the Russian export agency, Sojuzplodoimport, which is the brand-owner of many — but not all — Russian vodkas. NB: Moskovskaya is a brand, *osobaya* means 'special' and is better or standard quality for export. Local Moskovskaya can be of poor quality.

These 'brand names' which follow are, in reality, a combination of descriptive terms (*krepkaya* means 'strong'), styles (*pertsovka* is pepper vodka), and locations (Moskovskaya — Moscow).

The imposing Dormition Cathedral in the Trinity-Sergius monastery near Moscow was built in the 16th century, the time of the earliest known references to vodka.

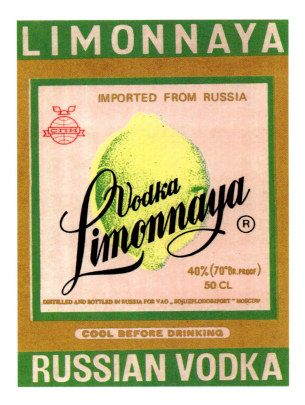

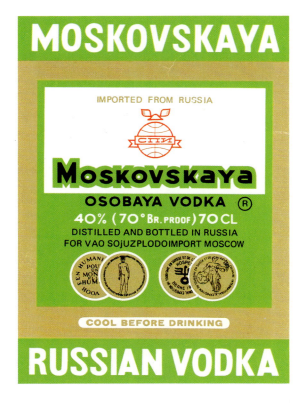

Krepkaya • Clear, strong grain vodka widely used by those who like more powerful cocktails or prefer stronger impact when drinking neat vodka. *Krepkaya* means 'strong' in Russian and it certainly is at 56% vol.

Kubanskaya • Grain vodka flavoured with infusions of dried lemon and Seville-orange peels. The Kuban cossacks of southern Russia used to make this vodka to their own recipe which is very distinct from that of Moscow. Good aroma, slightly bitter edge to its flavour; 40% vol.

Limonnaya • Lemon-flavoured vodka distilled from lemon peel infusions. A little sugar is added before bottling. Full, unctuous lemon flavour with some alcoholic, but not citric, nip in the swallow; 40% vol.

Moskovskaya • The local *osobaya* is the classic product with its own soft rye taste but no other aroma or added flavouring. The export version is essentially the same. There is also a de luxe version, called Cristall, with superior packaging available in duty-free and other prestige outlets. Made from rye and rye malt, it has a creamy texture to the nose, warming, faintly herby taste with some fire; 40% vol.

Okhotnichya • A traditional 'hunter's vodka' which has affinity with gin. Ginger, tormentil, ash-week root, clove, black and red peppers, juniper berries, orange and lemon peels, coffee and anis are macerated in spirit and redistilled. To grain spirit is added some of this infusion together with sugar and white port-style wine, so that the latter makes up about 20% of the final volume. Rich and resonant in flavour; 45% vol.

Pertsovka • Peter the Great is said to have sprinkled black pepper on his vodka regularly and the practice was probably widespread in his time. Pertsovka maintains the tradition but the peppers (both red and

black) and cubeb are now macerated into the spirit before it is bottled.

Yellowish-brown in colour, the style is hot and spicy but not unbearable, and there is a rich, vanilla-like aroma which could catch you pleasingly off guard. You tend not to notice the 35% vol alcohol and it makes an excellent base for a Bloody Mary.

*P*osolskaya • Lesser known, relatively recently introduced brand but one worth watching out for. Similar to the classic Moscow style.

*P*shenichnaya • Good quality vodka made from 100% wheat; 40% vol.

*R*usskaya • Inexpensive clear vodka with small amount of added cinnamon. The brand was introduced in the 1970s and is made from potatoes and distilled, not 'living' water; 40% vol.

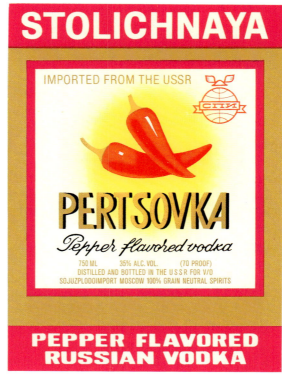

Top: The Summer Palace in St Petersburg was built for Peter the Great, who was famous for his vodka drinking.

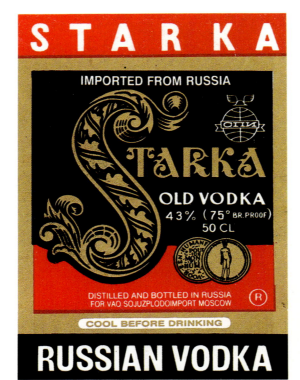

STARKA

IMPORTED FROM RUSSIA

STARKA

OLD VODKA

43% (75° BR.PROOF)

50 CL

DISTILLED AND BOTTLED IN RUSSIA
FOR VAO SOJUZPLODOIMPORT MOSCOW

COOL BEFORE DRINKING

RUSSIAN VODKA

from the Klyazma river. The name means 'Golden Ring', the Russian district famous for its beautiful church architecture.

*Z*ubrovka • The Russian counterpart to Poland's Zubrówka (*qv*). The vodka aromatised with the zubrovka bison grass is traditional to the forest area that spans the borders between the two countries.

The Russian version is yellow-green in colour but does not come with a blade of the grass in each bottle, as does the Polish version. Creamy, caramel nose; silky texture; winey flavour; 40% vol.

*S*tarka • The name means 'old'. Flavoured vodka, light brown in colour, distilled from an infusion of the leaves of Crimean apple and pear trees. Grape spirit and port-style wine are added and the result is a mild, pleasantly fruity drink; 43% vol.

*S*tolichnaya • Along with Moskovskaya (*qv*), the highest-profile authentic Russian vodka, despite the tongue-twister pronunciation (stol-EETCH-n'yah) needed to order one in a bar. (The name means 'capital city'.) It has a small amount of added sugar to lend silk to the texture and is triple-filtered through silver-birch charcoal. Warming, balmy texture to nose but tiny fragrance; gentle malty, rusky flavour, sweet-edged; 40% vol.

*S*tolovays • Clear vodka made from grain with a higher-than-average strength of 50% vol.

*Z*olotoe Koltso • Lesser-known brand that is nonetheless close to the classic Moscow style. Draws water

Poland

Whatever the claims of Russia to the contrary, vodka is claimed as an original Polish spirit by the Poles. The first written references to vodka production in Poland date from the 15th century and several authors, among them Golebiowski and Ostrowska-Szymanska, claim it was in use in the country at least a century earlier.

In 1546, King Jan Olbracht gave every citizen the right to produce and sell liquors, although this was closely followed in the 1560s by a taxation structure for distilling vodka, selling it and buying stills and tubs. Not to be left out, the country's aristocracy lobbied for 'propinatory privilege' and, in 1572, they were given exclusivity to produce liquors, sell them and even the power to force the peasantry to drink in their local squire's inn. The vodka trade then became a major source of income for the landed class and the country's treasury.

If grain was used for distillation, it was predominantly rye, but initially no distinction was made between root, grain or fruit distillate and spirit was called *okowita* (from 'aqua vitae'), *gorzalka, gorzale wino* ('burnt wine' *cf* Brandy) or, in Latin, *vinum crematum* to distinguish it from medicinal distillates. For example, a 1534 medical treatise described an aftershave lotion as 'vodka for washing the chin after shaving'. Medicinal vodkas were usually mixed with herbal infusions, low in strength and taken by the mere spoonful; sometimes they did not even reach the mouth but were rubbed on aching joints and palsied digits. Through time, however, 'vodka' came to indicate beverage spirit.

Kraków was one of the earliest production centres, with stills already active in the 1550s, but Poznan soon overtook it in importance. By 1580, it had 49 working stills and sold to Wroclaw and farther afield. Vodka was a currency and Poznań craftsmen regularly paid for goods supplied from other

cities by buying and despatching to their creditors consignments of equivalent value.

Everyone drank vodka; aristocrats used to carry flasks of it in small cases and sip some in the morning and afternoon wherever they happened to be. Hunters enjoyed it, particularly during winter when the vodka could be chilled in the snow only metres from a blazing fire. In the 17th and 18th centuries, the larger country houses and monasteries had their own stills, recipes were invented and more sophisticated production techniques were developed.

The vodka industry — *ie* producing solely for purposes of trade — emerged at this time and continued to develop during the 19th century, when many vodka and liqueur distilleries were established. Potatoes and sugar beet came to be used more and more as raw materials. In the 18th century, vodka was exported through the Baltic port of Gdansk to a number of different countries and it is a matter of pride for Poles that one of these was Russia. In addition to being a shipping point, Gdansk was also a major production centre.

The Polish alcohol monopoly was formed in 1919 to supervise production and to control the trade in alcohol. After World War II, the spirits-production administrative arm took the name Polmos, which was also used as a brand name for exports.

Opposite page: The old town square in Poznań, west Poland. Once the residence of Polish kings and still a centre of distillation.
Top right: The market square at Kraków. A centre for distillation as early as 1550.

Below: Wooden storage vessels each holding the equivalent of some 35,000 bottles.

Most Polish vodkas — and certainly the best — are produced from rye grain, but some have a potato base. It is customary to use small quantities of fruit spirit to add some nuance of flavour to otherwise-clean spirit. Fruits include cherry, blackcurrant, blackberry and strawberry; walnuts, honey and assorted herbs are similarly used through maceration.

Poland produces more than 53 million cases of vodka a year, 60% of which are clear styles and the rest flavoured in one way or another. There are 25 distilleries and bottling plants around the country which used to be part of the state monopoly but which are now independent profit centres and mutually competitive. All of them have been introducing new brands recently, so there are now several hundred brands of spirit on the Polish market. Established brands, such as Wyborowa, are produced in a number of different distilleries under contract to Agros which, like Polmos, is no longer part of the state but does still own the brand names.

There are three categories of Polish vodka, the higher the purity the better the grading: Standard (*zwykly*), premium (*wyborowy*) and de luxe (*luksusowy*). For those who like an element of flavour or fragrance, premium vodkas are the best and, indeed, Wyborowa vodka is Poland's favourite premium brand in both the domestic and export markets. Water for production is usually taken direct from natural springs.

Baltic • Clear vodka made from rectified potato spirit. The light soils on the Baltic coast yield a high grade of potato whose starches are saccharified with fresh barley malt and fermented with specially developed yeasts. The beers are distilled and rectified in local agricultural distilleries to remove unpleasant fermentation by-products but retain the potato aromas. Reduction in strength and charcoal filtration are then carried out, followed by a short settling period. All batches are tasted by a panel before bottling and there is no addition of enhancers or sugar.

Bielska Extra • New dry brand with a subtle herbal infusion. There were a number of distilleries in the Bielsko-Biala area of Silesia in the early part of the century and the old-style slivovitz plum brandy made there by the forerunner of today's Polmos distillery was famous throughout Poland. The distilleries included names like Stock, Jenkner and Gessler, but these and other companies had to surrender both plant and recipes to the Communist authorities at the end of World War II. Bielska red cap is 38% vol, the blue 40% vol. Gentle, delicate nose, with a touch of oil in flavour.

Bielska Zytnia • Dry-grain kosher brand lightly flavoured with a blend of fruit spirits. There is a tradition of kosher distilling in the area that goes back to the 18th century and, in 1957, with its reputation for plum spirits, 'Branch B of the Silesian Vodka Factory' (as the Polmos distillery at Bielsko-Biala was then known) began production of Passover slivovitz. Its success led to the establishing of a range of kosher vodkas for the state organisation and, with the break-up of Polmos in 1991, new brands are taking their place. Soft in bouquet and flavour; 40% vol.

Cytrynówka • Lemon-flavoured vodka. Both lemon peel and the fragrant leaves of the lemon tree are combined with clear rectified spirit to produce the final distillate. Cytrynówka is full in body but gentle in its lemon impact. It may be drunk on its own, however it does go particularly well with pastry; 40% vol.

Happy • This new kosher dry-grain brand has a distinctive, fresh, zesty fragrance and taste. It is blended using several different citrus spirits and, indeed, it has a 'happy', zingy character; 40% vol.

Vodka

Jarzebiak • Traditional dry, rowan-flavoured vodka. This is a long-established style made by blending spirit distilled directly from fermented rowan berries (*jarzebiak*) picked after the first frost, silent spirit and infusion distillates. Old gold in colour from ageing in oak cask, it has good fruit fragrance and musky concentration. Creamy, spicy/peppery finish with a touch of fire; 40% vol. There is also a de luxe version, with added aged wine distillate and sugar, more suited to the end of a meal.

Karpatia • New grain brand with fetching bouquet from added fruit spirit. It is available at 38% and 42% vol.

Kasztelanska • Oak-aged vodka with mellowed, concentrated complexity. Deep yellow-brown in colour, it is wood and vanilla fragrant, with herby, citrus overlay. It is smooth and there is the warming, spicy edge of nutmeg or cinnamon; 40% vol.

Krakus • Rye vodka. Spirit from specially selected rye varieties is rectified twice and refined to a mellowness of texture that has made this a very popular brand. It is named for Kraków, Poland's ancient capital city; 40% vol.

Lanique • Brand name for vodkas produced at the Lancut distillery, which is one of the oldest and largest in the country. In addition to its versions of established national products like Wyborowa and Zubrówka, Lanique has a range of fruit-flavoured vodkas — orange, lemon, plum and cherry — and kosher vodkas.

A speciality is Rose Petal vodka liqueur, flavoured with attar of roses and described as more expensive, ounce for ounce, than gold; 37.5-40% vol.

Luksusowa • Clear, dry vodka made from potato spirit. Luksusowa means 'de luxe'; 45% vol.

Monopolowa • New clear brand made with spring water, which offers a very pure, clean character with no added enhancers. The red cap is 38% vol, the blue 40% vol.

Perfect • Kosher vodka with authentic grain aroma and flavour, and made with spring water. Available at 40% and 42% vol.

Pieprzówka • Pepper-flavoured vodka. Spirit is rectified twice and then combined with Turkish pepper, black pepper and a number of other enhancers. Spicy and very zesty but with bearable fire; 45% vol.

Polish Pure Spirit • *Spirytus Rektyfikowany*, Polish spirit, is famous and awe-inspiringly strong — up to 96% vol (192 US proof). However, just because it comes in a bottle does not mean it is ready for pouring and drinking with a dash of orange or lime. It is sold in this concentrated form for use in greatly diluted form in making liqueurs, infusions and numerous other drinks recipes. It is high in quality, tasteless and, effectively, pure ethyl-alcohol. Polish Pure Spirit is also available at 57% and 80% vol. In Poland, vodka, diluted to taste, is very often drunk throughout a meal, being particularly suitable as an accompaniment to fish dishes and other oily or spicy foods.

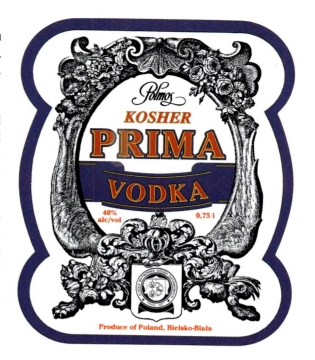

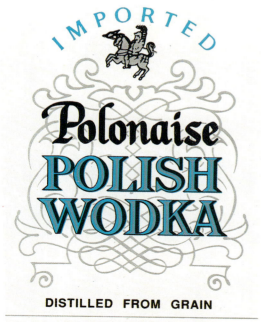

Polonaise • International-style vodka of great cleanness and purity. Just enough rye resonance to lend fleeting soft fragrance. Available at 40% and 50% vol, the latter is fine and silky.

Prima • Dry grain kosher brand with gentle aroma of added fruit spirits; 40% vol.

Rebeka • Small range of clear and flavoured kosher vodkas from the Lancut distillery and marketed under the Lanique label (*qv*); 38-39% vol.

Select • Pure, very clean kosher vodka made from highly rectified potato spirit and spring water. Available at 40% and 42% vol.

Soplica • Centuries-old style of aged vodka, flavoured with aged wine distillate and mature apple spirit, infused with dried fruits. The blend spends a long but unspecified period in oak cask and emerges with deep golden colour. Glyceral vanilla nose; rounded, fruit-edged and mellow in taste and texture; 40% vol. The name is taken from the family of Lithuanian landowners in Mickiewicz's epic poem *Pan Tadeusz*.

Spirytus Rektyfikowany • See Polish Pure Spirit.

Starka • Traditional rye vodka. Starka goes back to the 16th century and was one of the original Polish *gorzalkas*. Today it is still made from best rye and aged in oak. The spirit is made in stills adapted to enhance the rye characteristics and is not subsequently rectified. It goes into small oak casks for 10 years and some Málaga wine is added to the final product. Starka is golden brown in colour, 43% or 50% vol in strength and best drunk chilled. Woody, vanilla-laced, rounded and sweetish. The nose is richer than the winey, rye calm of the taste. There is also a Russian version.

Tatra • Herb-flavoured vodka. This vodka, sometimes called Tatrzanska, originated in the Tatra Mountains and is flavoured with a number of herbs and botanicals, the chief of which is archangelica. It has a freshness of style and is widely used as a summer drink, short or long, chilled or with ice; 45% vol.

Wyborowa • Celebrated international brand made from a single variety of high-grade rye grown in different parts of Poland. The initial distillate is then twice rectified and goes through a secret process to refine it further. The final spirit is clean and clear but it retains notable texture and background flavour. Lovely, insinuating but sustained grain fragrance; slightly grassy and sweet with musky, cachou-like finish. Available at 40% and 45% vol.

Ziolowa Mocna • Dry vodka flavoured with herbs. It is blended from potato spirit and a number of herb distillates to give a full-blooded, spicy, slightly earthy concentration of flavour. Deep, surprisingly mellow bouquet; 44% vol.

Zloty Klos • Clear, clean kosher vodka which is made from grain and natural spring water. Available at 40% and 42% vol.

Zubrówka • Speciality flavoured vodka becoming increasingly visible in international markets. Also known as Bison Brand Vodka, it is rectified twice and blended with an infusion of bison grass (*zubrówka*), a plant endemic to the Bialowieza Forest, where it is grazed by a surviving herd of rare European bison (which are featured on stylish labels of both Polish and Russian brands).

Somerset Maugham wrote lyrically about Zubrówka in *The Razor's Edge*. 'Freshly mown hay… spring flowers… thyme and lavender…' He liked it. 'It's like listening to music by moonlight.' He loved it. The plant lends attractive, botanical aroma and flavour to the spirit and gives it a pale yellow-green colour; 40% and 50% vol. Each bottle contains a sprig of the grass to top up the infusion and attract attention. There is also a Russian version conventionally spelt Zubrovka (*qv*).

Zytnia Extra • A dry vodka made from rye and a small amount of apple spirit and fruit enhancers. This is Poland's favourite brand of vodka. Pale yellow in colour, it is gentle, warming and musky, with glimmers of dried fruit, grainy aroma and velvety texture; 40% vol.

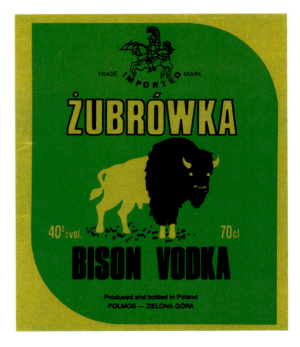

Vodka from Other Countries

Some favourite brands are missing from these listings. More than for any other spirit drinks where detailed recipes, ingredients and production procedures are involved, the making of modern vodkas is mainly a matter of acquiring the right technology to purify spirit, and achieving good distribution. Thus, for the high-volume, high-profile brands like Popov, Gordon's, Kamchatka, Skol, Barton, Vladivar, Gilbey's and others — some of them selling more than three million cases a year and all of them wholesome products — there is no heritage, and hence no story to tell.

A wintry Savonlinna Castle, home to a local opera company, in the province of Saimaa, Finland.

United Kingdom

Smirnoff • The world's top vodka brand, said to sell a case every two seconds somewhere around the globe. Although made in 25 countries, Smirnoff is a British vodka by virtue of ownership of the American company Heublein, which developed the brand, but the spirit itself is distilled in a number of different countries. Smirnoff's 'Russianness' lies mainly in its origins, although in 1994 the company launched its first vodka produced in Russia since the Bolshevik Revolution in 1917.

vodkas were flavoured with raspberries, strawberries, plums, currants and other fruits. During a fair visited by the Tsar in 1886, Piotr Smirnoff got himself noticed by having a real bear in his pavilion and waiters dressed as bears serving vodka. Smirnoff was awarded the warrant to supply the Imperial Court with vodka and other drinks.

In the wake of the October Revolution, Vladimir Smirnoff was detained and led out several times to face a firing squad but each time the deed was postponed. He was eventually rescued by White Russians and fled to Paris, where he managed to open a small distillery, but no one was interested in his vodka. He met Rudolf Kunett, a member of a Russian family who had formerly been grain suppliers to the Smirnoff distilleries. Now domiciled in the USA, Kunett bought Smirnoff's vodka recipe from him and, in 1934, opened a small distillery in Connecticut.

Despite the fact the Prohibition had just been repealed, he could not get sales off the ground; he was managing only 6,000 cases a year and losing money. When, eventually, he could not even raise the price of a licence to trade in liquor, Kunett sold the formula and distillery to Heublein, a local drinks firm. Still in search of a hook to hang the product on, Heublein had a crack at selling it as 'white whiskey', and the 'no taste, no smell' advertising slogan, while it must have seemed absurd to a whiskey drinker, contained the rudiments of the mixed-drink boom to come.

The watershed for Smirnoff was the interest generated by the cocktail, the Moscow Mule, invented in 1946 by a Los Angeles bar owner. His purpose was not to promote vodka but to try and shift an overstock he had of Schweppes ginger ale. At last, Smirnoff became established as a brand. The Russian connection was hastily jettisoned in the USA during the McCarthy era and the fact that the product was made in a Connecticut distillery highlighted — what could be more American? In the more relaxed, affluent years that followed, the product had a role to play in a lifestyle that included mixing drinks like the Bloody Mary and the Screwdriver. From that point on, Heublein was very successful in promoting a vodka mystique and built Smirnoff into the world's

The Smirnoff company dates from the immediate aftermath of Napoleon's retreat from Moscow and, in 1815, the year of the Battle of Waterloo, Ivan Smirnoff leased a fire-scarred warehouse where he began to produce vodka. In those days, Smirnoff's

second-biggest-selling spirit brand. Smirnoff's best-selling Red Label vodka commemorates the Smirnovskaya Vodka No 21, which Piotr Smirnoff supplied to the Tsar's armed forces, and its name is written in Cyrillic script across each bottle's label.

Smirnoff is produced from grain spirits which are redistilled, processed and filtered to give aroma-less, flavourless vodka. With the advent of *glasnost*, a member of the Smirnoff family who had remained in Russia emerged in the early 1990s to claim back the name as a trademark but the Heublein lawyers soon saw him off. Another Smirnoff went to Hamburg to oversee the marketing of Stolichnaya vodka.

Smirnoff's most interesting vodka is also their latest, Black Label, which is made in Moscow from grain in pot stills, just as it was in the days of the Tsars. It has the fragrance and character lacking in the rest of the Smirnoff range but, then, it is made differently and is doing a different job. This is a sipping, not a mixing, vodka and it has something of the silky generic Moscow trademark flavour. Also available as Red Label (37.5% vol); Black Label (40% vol); Silver Label (45.2% vol); Blue Label (45 and 50% vol).

Finland

DISTILLING SKILLS ARE THOUGHT TO HAVE BEEN BROUGHT TO FINLAND IN THE 16TH CENTURY by mercenary soldiers returning from European wars. Beer was the universal drink in the country until distilling capabilities became widespread and, within a century, spirits had completely displaced it. Almost every household had its own copper pot still. In the 18th century, Finland was part of Sweden and many of the distilleries erected during that time were royal properties established in the name of the Swedish Crown.

Commercial distillation in Finland up to the 1880s was limited by the fact that there was only one yeast manufacturer in the country. When a second factory went into production, the Rajamäki distillery was built in 1888 to take advantage of the new supply position and, within a decade, it was the largest of Finland's 27 distilleries.

Finland shadowed the USA with its own period of alcohol prohibition from 1919 to 1932 and

These tethered domesticated reindeer, at Inari in Arctic Finland, are used as draught animals by the native Lapps.

The Finlandia bottling line with the distinctive 'iced' bottle, an important element of their brand image.

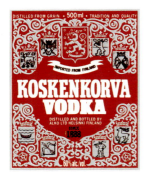

Rajamäki was nationalised in 1920, becoming the State Alcohol Centre. After Finnish prohibition ended, a whole new distilling and production complex was built.

During World War II, Rajamäki went over to producing a different kind of cocktail — 'Molotov cocktails' to combat tanks — and pure alcohol for use as motor fuel.

All Finnish vodka is made from grain and the water used in manufacture is pure enough not to need any special processing treatment.

Finlandia • State-owned premium brand of Finnish vodka, introduced in 1970. Finlandia has played its part in establishing the credibility of Scandinavian vodkas as high-quality products with authentic heritage. Finlandia is a wheat vodka made from spirit rectified to 96% vol and then combined

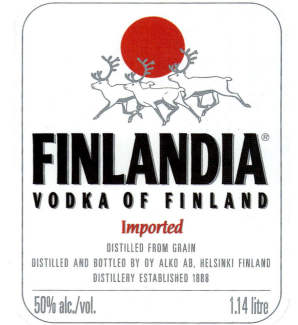

with water from local springs, which are fed by run-off from a glacier. Finlandia is widely exported and also has a strong presence in duty free. Gentle, chemical-free, cereal aroma and silky texture; 40% and 50% vol.

Koskenkorva • Although it is the companion brand to Finlandia, it actually preceded it. Koskenkorva Vilina spirit with three milligrams/litre sugar content to soften the finish was introduced in Finland in 1952. Koskenkorva vodka, without any sugar, is the main domestic vodka and the leading brand in Scandinavia; available at 40%, 50% and 60% vol. Finlandia is the export brand.

Siberia

Sibirskaya • Siberian vodka, from Russia's immense northern region, made from high-quality winter wheat. An evocative touch is the filtration through charcoal made from silver birch trees taken from great Siberian taiga territories; 42-45% vol.

Ukraine

Gorilka • The generic term for the Ukranian clear vodka made from wheat, wheat malt and soft local water flavoured with natural linden. In the past, it was known in Moscow as Cherkassk spirit because of its wheat base (in contrast to Moscow's rye vodkas) and the Cherkassk cossacks who took it to Moscow to sell there and beyond. In those days, it was a poor vodka and was bought by innkeepers as a cheap staple. Gorilka means 'burning,' which could refer either to the fiery spirit it originally was or that it was 'burnt' — *ie* distilled — wine or ale. Distinctive nose typical of the style and mild taste; 40-45% vol.

Ukrainskaya S Pertsem • Pepper vodka from wheat and wheat malt; 40% vol.

A Siberian birch tree, burnt for charcoal and then used for filtration.

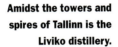

Vodka

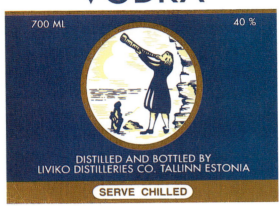

Amidst the towers and spires of Tallinn is the Liviko distillery.

Estonia

Eesti Viin • Recently introduced high-quality grain vodka from the producers of Viru Valge. Eesti Viin is the company's flagship brand; 38% vol.

Viru Valge • Grain vodka from the Liviko distillery in Tallinn. The water is softened and sugar is added to enhance the texture. It is a pleasant, softly styled vodka with an authentic cereal fragrance; 40% vol.

Germany

Gorbatschow • German brand, one of the world's fastest-growing in the early 1990s. The Gorbatschows were among the Russian refugee families arriving in Berlin in the wake of the October Revolution in 1917. They had been official distributors to the Imperial Court of St Petersburg and, in 1921, they

established a distillery in Berlin to make vodka for the émigrés and anyone else interested enough to try their product.

Gorbatschow is the top-selling brand in the German vodka and schnapps sectors and has a market share of about 45%. It is a million-case brand and is exported to the main white-spirit markets of the world. Available at 40%, 50% and 60% vol.

Sweden

SWEDEN'S DISTILLING HERITAGE GOES BACK TO THE 15TH CENTURY, when all spirits were collectively known as *brännvin* (*cf* Dutch *brandewijn*, 'burnt wine'). Sweden's best-known spirit is akvavit (see Schnapps section), which is usually flavoured or spiced in some way, so Swedish vodka could be described as unspiced brännvin. In most European countries the first experience of distillates was as medicinal potions and elixirs; in Sweden, it was also as a constituent in making gunpowder. In the 1460s, a Stockholm ledger recorded payments made to Berend the Powdermaker for '*brännvin* to make gunpowder'. It had also been used as a drink, however, since earlier in the century, when German merchants settling in the country brought with them 'strong waters' that were previously unknown there.

The authorities at the time were highly distrustful of this alternative use of a gunpowder component. At the end of the 15th century, anyone making and selling brännvin other than for gunpowder production was liable to prosecution; people knew where they stood with gunpowder, at least. It was something with which they had to come to terms, however, and in 1498 the first licence 'to keep and serve *brännvin*' was issued although the holder was also required to supply the powdermakers with as much spirit as they needed.

Brännvin was expensive and thus an exclusive drink while it remained a wine-based product in non-wine-producing Sweden but, in the 17th century, it became accessible to the general population when grain mashes were introduced. Sweden grew cereals

Whether winter merriment or summer festivities, there is always a call for a drink.

The Swedish monopoly distillery where Absolut vodka is produced.

two or more visitors they shared a single glass, taking turns to drink from it.

Home distillation diminished as larger-scale production developed in the 1830s. Consumption was prodigious — well over 100 million litres a year — and was three times as much as the Swedish Monopoly sells now to a population that was just over a third of today's eight million people.

Unspiced *brännvin*, or vodka, has maintained its place alongside the akvavits and liqueurs that have been produced by the Swedish state since 1855. The Monopoly also makes 'cover' versions of famous spirit brands from other countries which are so good that they often beat the real thing in blind tastings. However, in the early years of this century, it imported a pot still from Scotland and began a project to make 'Scotch' whisky. It was a failure and the pot still is now displayed in the excellent Spirits Museum in Stockholm.

and spirit production began to spread beyond the scattered stills located in country houses and on wealthy landowners' estates. Household production was permitted and *brännvin* became part of the daily diet of the population. Its status as an agricultural 'foodstuff' is indicated by the practice at the time of consuming it from special *brännvin* bowls with a spoon. *Brännvin* became a 'sup', *ie* soup. Distilling taxes in cities and sales taxes for innkeepers were introduced but home production was allowed to continue.

In 1756, when a period of prohibition was introduced, 180,000 household stills were confiscated, the surrender points being the tithe sheds beside the Lutheran churches throughout the country, which took on the appearance of scrap-metal yards. Later successive crop failures prompted a royal monopoly on production in 1775, and about 60 Crown distilleries were established. King Gustav III was very interested in the product and had his own distillery at the Royal Palace in Stockholm. Home distilling and importing of spirits were banned. The new regime did not work because people began illicit distillation and eventually household production was reinstated. By 1830, there were once again 175,000 small stills in place around the country.

In the 19th century, most homes kept a vodka bottle and two small glasses on a cabinet so that a visitor could be offered some hospitality. If there were

Absolut • Brand from Vin & Sprit monopoly. Lars Olsson Smith was a 19th-century distiller who had a distillery on the island of Reimersholme, in Stockholm. He spoke seven languages and made two fortunes in his lifetime — ultimately losing both of them. His distillery was the largest in Europe and, in 1879, he introduced the means of producing a very pure form of spirit from potatoes, whereas in the south, where high-grade cereals grew, alcohol production remained primitive and undeveloped.

Today, Absolut vodka essentially applies Smith's system to mashes made from grain instead of potatoes. Smith described his spirit as absolutely pure — in Swedish *absolut rent* — and this is where the brand-name comes from.

Absolut was conceived to be a pure product with its own Swedish persona and was targeted at the USA, which constitutes 60% of the world vodka market. The distinctive design of the bottle is based on an old medicine bottle found in a Stockholm antique shop. In duplicating it, the glass had to be 'absolutely' clear in order to emphasise the vodka's purity, so a special type of sand was used to avoid the greenish tinge that transparent glass often has. The modern bottle is manufactured in the Limmared glassworks, founded in 1741, where the original bottle on which it is based was made.

The brand was introduced in 1979 — the centenary of Smith's innovation — and sold 10,000 cases in its first year; by 1987, it was selling 1.4 million cases a year and, in 1993, reached the 4.5 million-case mark. It is the second-top-selling vodka and the 11th-ranked spirit brand in the world, and now exports to 60 countries.

The advertising did much to set the personality of Absolut in the marketplace. It was, and still is, clever, witty, distinctive and sophisticated. It was also original and technologically advanced — to wit the magazine ads which played Christmas greetings to readers and the liquid panels with 'snow' falling around a photograph of the Absolut bottle.

The vodka is made from wheat grown in the fields around the pretty red and white brick-built distillery of Åhus in southern Sweden. The fermented mash is distilled and rectified before being reduced with water from the distillery's own spring. Absolut is now available in both clear and flavoured versions, lemon and (jalapeño) pepper being high profile among the latter. Available at strengths of 40% and 50% vol.

USA

Wolfschmidt • Made in the USA. Wolfschmidt, distillers since 1847, were the first to introduce vodka to the USA, around the turn of the century. The family were suppliers of vodka to the Russian Tsars Nicolai I and Alexander III and their base was Riga, in Latvia. Later, Wolfschmidt's Riga style was produced in Holland for a period but the Wolfschmidt name is now owned by the Jim Beam company and the vodka produced in the USA. It sells just more than a million cases a year; 40% vol.

Left: Design classic — The meteoric rise of Absolut in the world spirit market is as much a tribute to their marketing department as it is to their distillers.

Genever & Gin

G IN IS JUNIPER-FLAVOURED GRAIN SPIRIT AND ORIGINATED IN HOLLAND. The English language name is a shortened version of genever, the Dutch word for the juniper berries from which it is made. Alternate renderings are jenever and geneva (no connection with Geneva, Switzerland) and in Britain it was also known as 'Hollands' and as 'Schiedam', the town where many of the distillers were based.

In Holland, more genever is drunk than any other spirit. A form of it was around in 1585, when the Earl of Leicester led his English expedition to Holland to help the Dutch repel the forces of Philip II of Spain in the Dutch Revolt. The English soldiers told afterwards of the local spirit they got into the habit of drinking — their 'Dutch courage'— before going into battle.

However, gin may actually have started out as a medicine, since the first specific association of juniper berries with distillate was in the diuretic potions developed by Dr Franciscus de la Boë at the University of Leiden in the 1600s.

The drink crossed to England and, in the 1660s, the diarist Samuel Pepys wrote of treating his colic with 'strong water made with juniper'. When William of Orange became king of England, French brandy was proscribed and every encouragement given to produce 'corn brandy', as grain spirit was often known at the time. The English were delighted to show how patriotic they could be but it was a dissolute period. One house in four in London produced gin and, in the 1720s, the majority of the population was permanently drunk. The death rate in the city was higher than the birth rate for more than a decade. Fagin's one-liner in the movie *Oliver* when he snaps at a child, 'Shut up and drink your gin!' had a basis in historical reality.

Controls were eventually reimposed and in the 18th century a number of distillers emerged in London keen to produce high-quality gin rather than mere stupefier. British styles of gin were taken around the world in the days of Empire and some interest in it built up in the USA. Paul Revere and George Washington were among the more celebrated gin drinkers there, and it was usual for Quakers to drink hot gin toddies after funerals. The biggest boost to the US market was from the British gin that was delivered there during Prohibition in the 1920s, and today the leading brands are in the London mould.

The original genever styles are produced in the northern European countries of Holland, Belgium and Germany, while the London style of gin, which is a matter of convention and not controlled in any official way, is the basis of the gins popular in the UK, the USA, Spain and Australia.

Opposite page: *Juniperus communis*, part of the cypress family. Its aromatic berries produce an oil used to flavour gin.

Below: The Juniper harvest in Umbria.

Holland

Amsterdam café life, where genever is the favoured chaser for beer.

THE ORIGINAL DUTCH GENEVER HAS BEEN EXPORTED FOR MORE THAN 200 YEARS and today reaches about 60 countries worldwide. In the 16th century, grain spirits were popular in Flanders because, unlike grape brandy, they escaped taxes. At the time, refugee artisans, including distillers, settled in Amsterdam and Rotterdam to escape the religious persecution to the south.

They were the basis of the genever industry in Holland, an industry that created many auxiliary professions, some of them very strange. Stone-jar 'empties' used to be returned to the genever bottling factories for refilling and companies employed jar sniffers who

checked the empties for, let's say, unacceptable pollution. Jar sniffing was a respectable, well-paid and, understandably, most important profession and a sensitive nose was essential; today, those people would probably be company wine buyers or spirit blenders.

A noticeable feature among genever producers is the number of long-established companies with origins going back to the 17th century and earlier — *eg* Bols (1575), Wenneker (1693) and de Kuyper (1695). The port of Rotterdam was the centre of the world spice trade at the time, and so was the best location for obtaining raw materials and new sources for flavours, hence its sustained dominance as a distilling centre.

There are three categories of genever, all of which have malt wine and juniper content. Malt wine is in fact a distillate made in very similar fashion to malt whisky from a cereal mix of wheat, maize, rye and barley. Since distillation is carried out in pot stills, flavour elements come over just as in malt whisky production. The distillation strength is low — under 60% vol — so comparisons may also be made, in terms of flavour impact, with armagnac which was traditionally distilled to 55-57% vol. Genever is distilled several times with a final distillation to incorporate the juniper berries and other botanicals, the exact combinations of which vary according to each company's secret recipe. One or two producers still distil directly from fermented junipers but this is now very rare.

Old (*oude*) is the original genever style and young (*jonge*) the 20th-century version — the words have nothing to do with the age of the spirit in the bottle and usually both are unaged spirits. Old genever is straw-coloured, sweet and aromatic compared to its young counterpart. The latter is the higher-selling style. *Korenwijn* (corn wine) is a kind of de luxe genever with a higher malt wine content and it is aged in oak casks for three years. It has a pale golden colour and is sold in traditional stone jars. Genever is best served neat and straight from the fridge.

Bols • Brand and company. Bols is one of the world's oldest commercial companies, able to trace its lineage back to 1575, when Lucas Bols distilled from a wooden shed by a stream outside Amsterdam (he was banned from distilling within the city walls because of the fire risk). Ingredients were stored in the shed and Bols's copper pot still was erected outside in the open air. At the time, Dutch merchant ships brought exotic spices and fruits to Amsterdam from all around the world, so Bols's first creations were what have come down to us as liqueurs.

Bols was exporting genever as early as 1691, when orders first went out to Argentina; a special-recipe old genever is still supplied to that market today. The shed is long gone and in 1970, when new premises were formally opened by the Queen of the Netherlands, the company was permitted to add the epithet 'Royal' to its business name.

Corenwyn • Special type of genever from Bols. Corenwyn is an alternative spelling of the generic *korenwijn*, the high-malt genever speciality. Only Bols is permitted use of Corenwyn as a brand name because it was Lucas Bols himself who created the drink back in 1575. It is distilled in copper pot stills in a four-stage process, the last of which has the spirit pass over juniper berries to extract flavour and aroma. Three years' ageing in oak casks endows a pale gold colour and a mellow nut and fruit flavour. It is sold in handmade stone jars.

Left: The handmade Corenwyn stone jars are wheeled into the kiln for firing.

Centre: A distinctive finished product, both in taste and looks. Corenwyn was first distilled by Lucas Bols in 1575.

G oblet • Brand of young genever from the Wenneker company (*qv*). Mild and silky in flavour.

Bottom centre: Hooghoudt distillery in the north of Holland is situated in a picturesque cereal dominated landscape.

De K uyper • Brand and company. Johannes de Kuyper founded his distillery in 1695, and today the business remains in the family's hands. De Kuyper concentrated on export markets, particularly those of the old British Empire, and it was only in 1930 that the firm began to sell in Holland. This is the firm that produces the 'broken' zig-zag green novelty bottle of young genever with the heart-shaped label that every visitor to Holland remembers.

H ooghoudt • Brand and company based in Groningen, in northern Holland. The area is a cereal-growing area, hence the location of the distillery, built by Jan Hooghoudt in 1888. On the occasion of

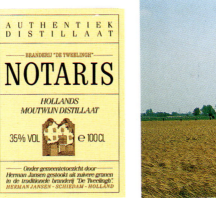

its centenary, Queen Beatrix awarded the company the right to bear the royal coat of arms. Hooghoudt maintains the tradition of steeping the botanicals in large, picturesque earthenware pots and its jenever (with a 'j') is double-distilled in pot stills. There is a soft-flavoured *korenwijn* in the range, as well as a sweet, blackcurrant jenever.

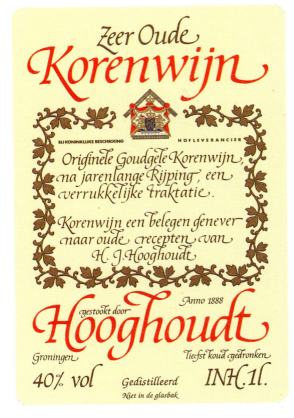

N otaris • Premium geneva (*sic*). Pieter Hansen opened his distillery in 1777 and in later years his grandson added a glassworks because of extortionate pricing for bottles. Making a continuing point to the industry, he called the factory Uit Tegenweer Opgericht, Dutch for 'founded out of protest'. The present company is known by the initials UTO.

The distillery, De Tweelingh, at Schiedam, is very traditional and is the last plant of several which held seals issued by the city council early this century attesting to the high quality of its production. Rye, maize and malted barley are held in a restored mill next door to the distillery prior to grinding. The spirit is made in pot stills and is then used to prepare separate parts of the recipe. Some is redistilled with juniper berries; some with other botanicals; some is left as it is. When all are blended together, a proportion of the resulting mixture is matured in oak vats.

Notaris is a fine malt spirit and the Very Old version is aged for three years in wood. There is a specially shaped glass for drinking it; it has a narrow top to retain the aromas and should be held in the hand like a cognac glass to warm the spirit slightly before drinking; 35% vol. The company also produces Gorter, Sonnema and Vlek genevers.

Royal Dark • Young genever introduced in 1992 by the Bokma company to appeal to a wider range of consumers. It was Bokma's first real innovation, a young grain spirit aged for a year in Limousin oak casks. Smooth and mellow in style.

genever idea by Bokma, following blind-taste consumer research. This had revealed that the flavour of genever has appeal for younger drinkers but that the generic image had become too dated. The substantial extra malt-wine content gives a rounder, more vivid, malty flavour and firm body.

Wenneker • Both brand and company name. Wenneker was founded in 1693, and carries a standard range of genevers — young (the brand name is Goblet), old and *korenwijn*. The old is matured in American oak casks and has a particularly mild taste.

Top: Founded in 1693, the Wenneker & Co. distillery has developed an interesting genever range matured in oak casks.

Below: The De Tweelingh distillery at Schiedam, and its high quality brand, have changed very little since production began in 1777.

Vijf Jaren • Aged genever from Bokma. This is a new idea in genever, an aged product to compete with fine cognacs and whiskies both as aperitif and digestif. The malt wine, grain spirit and botanicals spirit are aged separately for five years (the translation of the brand name) in small Limousin oak casks before being blended and then rested 'to marry'.

Volmout • Young genever with a high malt content. This is one of a number of new renderings of the

United Kingdom

William of Orange encouraged distillation of gin, when he became king in 1689, as a counter measure to the smuggling of French brandy.

FTER THE UNBRIDLED DEBAUCHERY OF THE 1720s in England, when restrictions on production and consumption of gin were non-existent, control was eventually reimposed and, by the end of the century, the first of a number of entrepreneurs had begun producing a better quality of gin in the expectation that there would be a market for it. In 1830, it was the turn of ale to be unfettered by an ineptly judged Act of Parliament and ale houses mushroomed — 100,000 of them, one for every 150 people in England and Wales. Gin palaces — garish, brightly lit and lavishly furnished drinking halls — enabled gin to compete and ultimately coexist. A tiptoe rehabilitation occurred, helped along by gin's popularity among upper-crust officers in the armed services and even recipes using gin in Mrs Beeton's influential and massively respectable *Book of Household Management*.

Gin got an increasingly competition-free run at the UK market during the World War I when a law was suddenly introduced requiring whiskey and brandy to be at least three years old. Both became scarce as young spirit put in the extra ageing time and, in the interim, gin was winning converts.

'Distilled gin' is made by macerating juniper and other botanicals in neutral spirit and distilling it in a pot still. The spirit obtained is the final gin, which is reduced to bottling strength with water. All the well-known brands are made this way. 'Gin' is less expensive and easier to make by 'cold compounding', *ie* mixing, juniper and other flavour essences into neutral spirit and bottling the blend.

London Dry is the dominant style of gin in the UK but the name is not restricted by any kind of legislation as to where it may be made. So-called 'British gin' produced elsewhere in the world is based on this style, which was only dry in comparison to the decidedly sweet Old Tom gin widely sold in London in the first half of the 19th century. Up until then, all spirits were produced in pot stills over open fires and off flavours were disguised by sweetening them up. With the advent of the continuous still, purer spirit that did not need 'doctoring' could be more readily produced, hence the expansion of the 'dry' London style. Today it has fresh, fruity, citric fragrance and flavour.

Plymouth gin, the other recognised UK style, is more intense and 'rooty' in character; in bygone days it was much more pungent, too. This gin must be produced in the town of Plymouth; indeed, the 'appellation' is also something of a trademark since only the Coates company that produces it may do so.

Usually, two distillations are involved: the first in a continuous still to obtain neutral spirit, the final in a pot still to obtain flavoured spirit. A distiller may well only carry out the second if he chooses to buy in neutral alcohol instead of making it himself. Botanicals are macerated in the alcohol and then the flavour-enriched spirit is redistilled in the pot still.

Gin distillers in the UK are permitted access to the spirit running off the still in order to nose it for typicality and authenticity of style. (Scotch whisky distillers are not permitted to do so and must operate by sight only, with the distillate kept locked away within a glass and brass spirit safe. The underlying implication about the integrity of the whisky maker is not very flattering.) The beginning and end of the run-off (the heads and tails or foreshots and feints) are rejected and the distiller's skill lies in detecting the flow points between which it is wholesome; he collects this 'heart' of around 85% vol alcohol, which is subsequently diluted to bottling strength somewhere between 37.5% vol and 57% vol according to brand.

Broadly speaking, the more botanicals in a gin

the higher its quality. An inexpensive gin can get by with, say, four, but a top-quality brand will have up to a dozen. The main botanicals used are juniper berries, coriander, angelica, lemon and orange peels, ginger, cardamom, cassia, cinnamon, orrisroot, liquorice, caraway, calamus, cubeb and grains of paradise.

The recipes of successful brands are secret and occasionally attempts are made to discover them. One insider recipe spy analysed the volumes of all botanicals bought in for a brand and averaged them out over an extended period; it did not work because the buying patterns were deliberately arrhythmic. The owners of Gordon's gin have to 'spike' any pomace they throw out with pomace specially brought in from elsewhere. This distorts the ingredient mix in the pomace to protect against samples being stolen from the dump site for analysis.

The classic mixing of gin with tonic came about as a counter to the risk of malaria. In colonial India, a measure of quinine mixed with aerated water, which gave protection against the disease, became known as Indian tonic water and it was not long before it joined soda water as a gin mixer in the British army messes. Gin and lime originated in the navy, since both ratings and officers drank lime to ward off scurvy during long voyages. Pink gin is gin mixed with a few drops of Angostura bitters. Sloe gin is a liqueur made by macerating sloe berries in gin.

Quinine water was essential for good health in outposts of the Empire. This group in India, around 1897, had discovered the delights of drinking it with gin.

Beefeater • London dry brand from James Burrough. Beefeater is the only remaining international London dry gin still distilled in London, the distillery being located in a quiet back street in Kennington. James Burrough, a chemist, emigrated to Canada in the early years of the 19th century, but returned to London after six years and established a distillery in Chelsea. Exports began to the USA in 1917 and, by 1963, Burrough was the largest exporter of gin from the UK. Beefeater's recipe, which, unusually, includes almonds in its botanicals, is known to only six people. It is the gin brand associated with the original Singapore Sling cocktail, first created at the Raffles Hotel in 1914.

Right: An old diagram showing the thirteen stages of the unique Bombay Sapphire distillation process.

Beefeater has made much of its staying at the conventional strength of 40% vol when rivals dropped to 37.5% vol, the minimum permissible strength, in the early 1990s. The stance paid off with Beefeater's sales rising by 20%.

THE UNIQUE BOMBAY SAPPHIRE DISTILLATION PROCESS

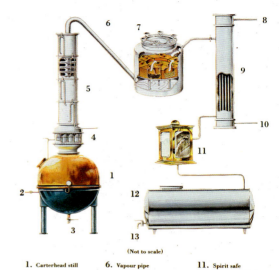

(Not to scale)

1. Carterhead still	6. Vapour pipe	11. Spirit safe
2. Steam inlet	7. Copper botanicals basket	12. Receiving tank
3. Steam outlet	8. Water outlet	13. Bottling line feed
4. Feints chamber	9. Water condenser	
5. Rectifying column	10. Water inlet	

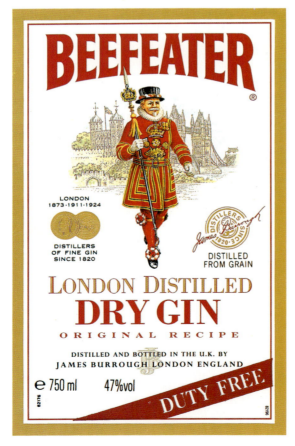

Bombay • London dry brand. Bombay is a well-established gin brand but Bombay Sapphire was the first gin to be promoted as a super-premium product in terms similar to de luxe whiskies and cognacs. Launched in the early 1990s, it is produced from a 1761 recipe and uses 10 different flavouring botanicals (not many British gins use more than six).

The grain spirit is double-distilled before its final day-long distillation in a unique trio of pot stills which incorporate a 130-year-old copper still basket. The botanicals are packed in the basket and during distillation the vapour passes through as if it were a giant tea bag. This 'infusion' technique, used for all Bombay brands, is said to even out the flavouring of the botanicals in the gin, allowing none to become too dominant.

Bombay Sapphire is what they pour you on Concorde if you ask for a gin.

Gin

182

ooth's • Brand and company. One of the early Booths was imprisoned in the Tower of London for having royalist sympathies but the first Booth's gin will have been distilled soon after the family opened a wine-merchanting business in the city in 1740. By the early 19th century Booth's was the largest distilling concern in the UK and was under the control of Felix Booth, the man who literally put Booth's name on the map — of Canada. He sponsored voyages around the northern waters of the country by John and James Ross, who were seeking a north-west sailing passage linking the Atlantic and the Pacific. They did not find one but the Gulf of Boothia and the Boothia Peninsula were among a clutch of waterways and land masses they named. John Ross did, however, find the location of the Magnetic North Pole and had a glass of Booth's gin on the very spot to celebrate.

Booth's main brand is labelled as a dry gin — no mention of London. Its High and Dry brand, now a curiosity, which is pale brown in colour from time spent in ex-sherry casks, is a London dry. The company holds the royal warrant to supply the Queen.

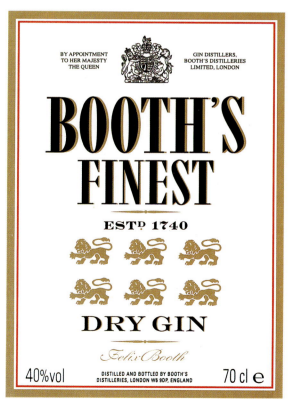

oates • Company which produces Plymouth gin (*qv*) in the town of the same name in Devon. The company was founded in 1793, but the distillery is much older. It was originally the old Black Friars monastery, built in 1425, and when Henry VIII dissolved the country's monasteries it became the town's debtors' prison. Some of the Pilgrim Fathers had their final meeting in the building and slept there overnight immediately prior to *The Mayflower*'s voyage to America in 1620. Later, it was a refuge for Huguenots who had fled persecution in France.

In 1793, the Coates family converted it into a distillery and began producing gin in a style that was fuller-flavoured and more pungent than its London counterparts. Plymouth was a naval dockyard and Coates supplied the Navy with gin for issue to the officers' mess. (The ratings' issue was rum, not gin.) Shipboard grog was always high in strength so as to save storage space.

Gin was produced in many of the towns in the west of England, Bristol and Barnstaple, in Devon, among them. Plymouth probably had a number of distilleries over the years but the Black Friars is the only one remaining.

'Plymouth Gin' today is a combination of *appellation contrôlée* and trademark because by law it may only be produced in the town of Plymouth and in the Black Friars distillery that belongs to Coates. Exclusivity of the generic Plymouth name was won in the courts in the 1880s, when Coates sued a London distillery that had begun to make its own Plymouth gin. No other company can make Plymouth gin in the town — but, ironically, Coates could make London gin there if it chose to.

Plymouth gin has more juniper and fewer citrics than London gin and, while it incorporates many of the other fruit characteristics, Plymouth's botanicals mix shows an emphasis on root flavours. The style is more assertive than the citrus-led London style. Plymouth is vervy, a little earthy, fruity and smooth.

The gin is made by redistilling neutral spirit for high rectification, macerating the botanicals in it and

carrying out a final pot-still distillation. The pot still at Coates is more than 100 years old, and Plymouth is the only gin in Britain still being made in its original distillery.

For the 200th anniversary in 1993, Coates bottled a limited-edition gin at the same strength as the traditional navy issue. If you come across any, beware! Since 100 British Proof is 57% vol, do go heavy with the tonic.

Crown Jewel • High-strength super-premium brand from the makers of Beefeater (qv). Crown Jewel was launched in 1993 as a brand in its own right rather than just a de luxe version of Beefeater. It is rich as well as citric in flavour and aroma, the high strength (50% vol) making it an apt brand for duty free at which it is mainly targeted. At a presentation for the press, bottles of Crown Jewel were taken from the freezer encased in solid blocks of ice — something you dare not do with lower-strength spirits in case the bottle shatters. 'Warm martinis are like minestrone,' sneered the barman as he chipped at the ice. The brand is triple-distilled and has a clean but intense dry flavour.

Gordon's • The world's biggest-selling brand of gin and sixth-biggest-selling spirit. Gordon's sells more in Britain than all the other gins put together but it also sells well in the USA — more than a quarter of the brand's annual turnover of 5.8 million cases.

Alexander Gordon was a Scot domiciled in London who opened a distillery in Southwark, London, in 1769, with the express intention of manufacturing not just another gin but one whose excellence would attract attention — and, of course, sales. In those days of pot stills and open fires, alcohol purity could be a problem and spirit had to be very well made not to need added sugar to mask scorch flavours. Gordon and other distillers who were able to produce clean spirit thus created a London dry style distinct from the flawed and sweetened-up Old Tom gins.

Gordon's business prospered and throughout the 19th century the gin was both exported to the colonies and carried for officers' use on board ships that visited them. Once, a thirsty group of miners settled in a remote part of Australia paid for an order in advance with gold dust to make sure it was delivered. In 1898, the company formed a partnership with another like-minded gin distiller, Charles Tanqueray (qv), to develop both brands' international trade. As a result, Gordon's expanded further in global markets and Tanqueray grew steadily in the USA.

Gordon's gin created controversy in the early 1990s, when it was reduced in strength to 37.5% vol. The company insisted that the flavour was unimpaired but other brands which remained at 40-57% vol made much advertising and promotional capital out of the change. (The version of Gordon's with the yellow label that is exported beyond the European Community is still 40% vol.)

The company holds royal warrants to supply both the Queen and the Queen Mother. The boar's-head symbol on the label is lifted from the escutcheon of the Clan Gordon. A sign of the times: even Gordon's, the quintessential London dry gin, is no longer produced in London but out in the open Essex countryside at Laindon.

Alexander Gordon probably would not have approved of reducing the strength of his gin.

of Reverends Tanqueray to follow his own very special calling. Like Alexander Gordon (*qv*), he wanted to produce a fine gin with a distinctive character and he spent a long time researching his 'recipe'. When he finally began production, his brand thrived and the first 'exports' were made by Britons returning to the colonies, after leave in the UK, with supplies of Tanqueray in their luggage. After the merger with Gordon's in 1898, the Tanqueray brand concentrated on the US market and in the 1950s and 1960s it achieved a high profile by being popular with political and show-business personalities on the West Coast. President Kennedy, Bob Hope and Frank Sinatra were among those known to drink it regularly. Almost 90% of its 1.4 million annual case sales are in the USA, where its market share is over 50%.

The bottle shape is based on the 19th-century London fire hydrants and, like Coca-Cola and Haig Dimple, is protected by worldwide design patents. It is claimed that the secret recipe really is contained in a large black ledger with three locks, the keys to which are held by different people. One of the stills used in the production of the gin dates from the era of Charles Tanqueray himself. The 'Old Tom' pot still is 150 years old and continues to produce the second-distillation spirit. No Tanqueray gin is produced under licence; it is all distilled in England at Laindon in Essex. Strictly speaking it is not in the London dry style, regarding itself as having a style all its own.

Left: The sampling of juniper berries, the principal ingredient in gin, is just one of the steps in quality control.

High & Dry • London dry gin from Booth's (*qv*), which is coloured due to its being aged for a period in oak casks.

Plymouth • The only style of UK gin that is legally tied to a specific geographic location — that of the Devon town of Plymouth. See Coates for details.

Tanqueray • Premium dry brand. Charles Tanqueray set up his distillery at Finsbury, in north London, where he had access to high-quality spring-water. The year was 1830 and Aeneas Coffey had just introduced his version of a continuous still which produced purer, cheaper spirit more easily than pot stills. Huguenot Tanquerays had moved from France to England in 1701, and one had been silversmith to King George II. Charles the gin distiller was something of a contrast to his immediate forebears since he interrupted a succession of three generations

Belgium

In Belgium they spell jenever with a 'J' but otherwise the traditions and history of production, which first took shape in the 1600s, are essentially the same as those of Holland. There is even some evidence that jenever originated here in Flanders (Vlaanderen), in the north of the country, which was originally part of the Netherlands in the time when its territory extended as far as Calais. The Flemish language — similar to Dutch — is the link and is still spoken as far to the south west as northern France.

The first distillers used glass flasks suspended over open fires, which they tended and prodded constantly in order to make the heat as uniform as possible. One of the reasons the juniper berry was introduced as an ingredient was because its strong taste and aroma could mask the unpleasant burnt taste that the spirit often picked up during the distilling process.

Following Austrian, then French, rule in the early part of the 19th century, there was famine and, under Dutch rule, Flemish jenever production was run down. It revived but, during World War I, many of the distilleries' stills were confiscated by the occupying Germans, who needed the copper to manufacture shells. Firms survived by importing alcohol until they could re-establish their own distilleries. Things got even more difficult in 1919, when the Vandervelde Law banned the sale of alcohol in inns and hotels and many distilleries finally failed. Today, there are about a score of jenever producers in Belgium making 150 different spirits, in both old and young styles.

Distilleries had their effect on the landscape, too. There were concentrations of them in the farm land around Eeklo, which was divided into small parcels or *meetjes*; the district that is now called Meetjesland.

Filliers • Small brand and family-owned distillery at Deinze. In 1880, Kamiel Filliers obtained a licence to build a distillery, thereby taking up again the family vocation of jenever production, which had been interrupted when the previous *graanstokerij* (distillery) burned down in 1863. A century ago, there were about two dozen small distilleries like Filliers' in the district, all of them working farms which distilled their own grain and sold their jenever in cask to local pubs and inns. Filliers is one of only two that remain today. The grain mix is wheat, rye and malt and the production methods are unchanged since the 1800s. Two distillations are carried out — the first in a Coffey continuous still, the second in a pot still. The spirit ages in oak casks and the company markets both a five- and an eight-year-old — unique, apparently, in the entire Belgian, Dutch and German jenever industries. Filliers' house style is drawn from the rye content in its cereal mix; the jenever is rich, fragrant and well mellowed.

Hoorebeke • Belgium's oldest jenever brand and company. Van Hoorebeke was founded in 1740, at the time when jenever was starting to be made to a more-or-less fixed routine. The Van Hoorebeke family was originally from Oudenarde, in East Flanders, and since 1400, its business had been first brewing, then distilling. Jan Frans Van Hoorebeke supported the 1789 rebellion against Austrian rule but the distillery at Eeklo was eventually burned to the ground in the aftermath of Waterloo. Another distillery was built, and another, and today the business continues. Van Hoorebeke is the only

Belgian jenever distilled directly from juniper berries and comes off the still at 53% vol — very low as distilling strengths go, but good for creating vivid, rounded flavour. The style is old jenever and carries pale colour from its ageing period in oak. There is also an eight-year-old version. The distillery has a visitors' centre with an audiovisual presentation.

Meyboom • Brand from the Fourcroy firm. Meyboom is one of the new-generation young jenevers designed to target younger, image-conscious consumers. The traditional presentation is replaced by clean, modern packaging and a refreshing, full-flavoured style of spirit.

Peket De Houyeu • Premium brand from the Bouillon company. This is an old jenever, produced since the turn of the century, with colour from oak ageing, not caramel. It is the firm's flagship brand and the stoneware jugs can also be set in pewter as high-quality gifts. Peket de Chevremont and Bastognard are the other jenevers in the range.

Smeets • Brand and distillery. Jenever has been produced in the Hasselt district of Belgium since the 17th century but, although the tradition is there, the Smeets distillery has only been there since 1947. Extra Smeets is a staple young jenever; however, the company's Belegen Hasseltse in stone crock jars is aged five years in oak.

Gin from Other Countries

Lithuania

Nemunas • Lithuanian gin which has recently been introduced and named after the largest river in the country. Gin and schnapps-like spirits are often referred to as brandies in central and northern Europe as the Nemunas label demonstrates. In addition to juniper berries, it is also flavoured with lime blossom, hops and honey and is strong at 60% vol. Very floral in aroma and taste, it is drunk during meals in Lithuania, with both meat and fish dishes, and with (or in) coffee.

Spain

Larios • Brand leader in the country with the highest per capita consumption of gin in the world, some 60% of which is drunk with cola. Larios sells more than all the other Spanish gin producers put together and its 3.2 million cases a year make it the third-largest gin brand in the world. The style is London Dry and any doubts there might be that a Spanish company can produce a good London Dry will be assuaged by the recent tasting of a dozen leading brands by their respective managers and directors for

Wine and Spirit International magazine in London; Larios came top and, what's more, a supermarket own-label beat several of the established international brands.

At the turn of the century, the Larios family bought a Málaga wine firm and, in 1933, began to make gin. Larios had been involved in the construction of the Málaga-Córdoba railway and other great engineering projects — the main street in Málaga itself had been built by Larios — for which Martín Larios y Herrero had been made a marquis by the Spanish Crown. The company's La Mancha distillery is completely given over to state-of-the-art production of the gin; everything else in the Larios portfolio is made at Málaga. 40% vol.

Rives Pitman • Specialist white spirits company in the Osborne drinks group and pioneer of gin in Spain. Rives Pitman uses a master spirit double-distilled to 96.5% vol strength and spirits distilled after maceration of the botanical mixes appropriate to each brand. The still-columns are more than 20 metres high and are said to yield super-fine spirit. There are separate Rives and Pitman brands. Rives Oro is very dry and Rives Special is triple-distilled, while Pitman's is English-style dry gin in a green bottle.

United States

THE USA IS THE WORLD'S BIGGEST GIN MARKET — 12-13 million cases each year — but the majority of the popular brands are those which originated in the UK, such as Gordon's, Tanqueray and Gilbey's, all of them million-case products. The largest seller is, however, locally produced Seagram's.

Seagram's • The best-selling gin in the USA. The brand was introduced in 1939 as a dry gin, but it was golden in colour due to its being aged for up to a year in charred ex-whiskey oak barrels. The hue was deep enough to register 30 points on the Klett scale, by which such tinting is measured. At the time, Seagram's was the only gin brand on the market to be

aged, a process that made it smoother and, to an extent, drier than other brands.

Over the years, the Klett rating has been reduced as gin came to be perceived by consumers as a clear white spirit, but the gin still spends 90 days in the same type of barrel. The brand took over the number-one gin spot in 1981 and, indeed, is the third-best-selling spirit of any kind in the United States. Current sales are around the 4-million-cases-a-year mark.

Having the best-selling gin in the USA, means Seagram's must stock their base ingredients, in this case grain, on a massive scale.

Rum & Cane Spirit

RUM IS MADE FROM THE NATURAL BY-PRODUCTS OF SUGAR PRODUCTION and it could be said that the Caribbean rum industry was established, albeit indirectly, by Christopher Columbus. After his initial voyage across the Atlantic, Columbus was back again in the West Indies in 1493 and this time he took with him sugar cane cuttings from the Canary Islands and planted them in Hispaniola, the island Haiti shares with the Dominican Republic. Sugar making quickly spread around the Caribbean islands but it generated enormous amounts of molasses syrup for which no good use could be found to begin with. In the production of sugar, the cane is crushed to extract the juice, which crystallizes into blocks of sugar when heated. A substantial part of the liquid remains unsolidified and this waste material was called *melazas* due to its honey-like sweetness (in Spanish, *miel* means honey); in English, this became molasses.

It was eventually noticed that this sticky syrup fermented when left in the sun and by the 1650s mixtures of molasses, cane juice and water were being distilled. From its capacity to 'mount up unto the head', this early rum was called 'kill-devil' on Barbados, where English colonists had settled. The French on neighbouring islands rendered this as *guildhive* and a rum distillery was a *guildhiverie*. The modern English word 'rum' is thought to be short for *rumbullion* (although the meaning of this is obscure) and was in use in its shortened form by the 1670s; the French call it *rhum*, which is made in a *rhumerie*, and Spanish-speakers *ron*, made in a *ronería*.

Rum became very big in the British colonies on the east coast of America. At first, rum was traded for pine logs and dried fish but eventually stabilised concentrated molasses was shipped there for the colonists to make their own. In fact, taxes that London wanted to impose on the colonists' rum played their part in the discontent that led to the Boston Tea Party in 1773. Rum even displaced gin as the preferred spirit in England in the 18th century and rum punch became very popular. There were 300 punch houses in London alone and every genteel sitting room had a punch bowl on the credenza.

Rum was the drink of the buccaneers on the Spanish Main; many of them were commissioned by their governments to attack shipping in return for 10 per cent of the plunder.

The Royal Navy issued rum rations as far back as 1655 as a shipboard substitute for water and beer, which went bad within weeks. Unfortunately, too many men were falling out of the rigging due to the influence of the daily half-pint of 80% vol/160 US proof rum allowance that was standard by 1731. It was subsequently mixed with an equal amount of water to mitigate the effect and the rum ration remained part of navy routine until it was phased out in 1969.

During Prohibition, smugglers were described as rum runners but it was mostly whiskey that they handled. Bill McCoy delivered vast quantities of genuine branded spirits — hence the 'real McCoy'

Opposite page: Sugar cane is brought to market at the port of Salvador in Bahia, Brazil, a province rich in the resource.

Below: Burning off the cane after harvesting.

caramel, *ie* burnt sugar. What could be more natural as an additive to rum?

Bottled rums from single distilleries — called single marks — exist but they are very rare. Like cognac, most rums are blended and there are four basic types of rum which are used as building blocks by the blenders. White has very little taste and is charcoal-filtered to minimise flavour and aroma content; light has gentle flavour; medium has good flavour content from the distillation process and oak-cask ageing; and heavy has the greatest flavour from distillation, ageing in oak and often highly flavoured additives.

These are used to create both light and full-bodied styles. Light rums are fermented with cultured yeasts and rapidly distilled to high strength in continuous stills which remove flavour and texture. Maturation time, if any is given, is very short. Full-bodied rums are fermented with natural yeasts and double-distilled more slowly in pot stills; they go on to much longer ageing in casks than light rums. Both types have dunder added at the fermentation stage to give consistency of house style from one production batch to the next. This is similar in function to the sour-mash process in Bourbon and Tennessee whiskey production (*qv*).

Once rums are bottled and reach the shelves classification is by colour:

White Most are light in body (although there are heavy white rums) and subtle in flavour; meant for mixing, eg Bacardi.

Golden Amber or golden rums are medium in flavour and body. All spend some years ageing in oak (*eg* Lemon Hart) but some go on for eight or more years to achieve elegant mellowed balance, *eg* Lamb's eight-year-old Reserve.

Dark This is the traditional, full-bodied, flavoursome 'burnt-sugar' rum that was around from early days and associated with the Royal Navy. It is robust and fruity with the solidity and taste pot stills endow. Fine tuning may be achieved by combining both pot and continuous still spirits, *eg* Lamb's Navy.

epithet — from Nassau in the Bahamas (where the Bacardi company is now based), yet he never broke a law; the Bahamas, where he quite legally bought his supplies, were British territory, and he sold his cargoes on in the Rum Row channel, off the US coast, which was in international waters.

Most rum is made from molasses, fermentation of which takes from 24 hours for light rums to a couple of weeks for heavy styles. Just over half of molasses' bulk is fermentable sugar but there are also trace elements which contribute to the final flavours of the rum. Finer rum with a naturally smoother texture is also made from the actual juice of the sugar-cane in Haiti and Martinique. The lighter styles are more highly rectified and produced in continuous stills after which they are charcoal-filtered and sometimes briefly aged in plain oak casks to add smoothness. Heavier distillates with more congenerics, hence flavours, come from traditional pot stills and go on to become golden or dark rums, ageing for longer periods in charred oak casks for anything from 12 to 20 years. If rum is aged any longer, it starts to lose flavour. Casks are often re-used numerous times, so oak chips are customarily used to perk up the wood aromas in the final spirit.

As is now done with some armagnac production, blends of precise density and texture may be created by combining spirit from both pot and continuous stills. All distillates run off the still as clear, colourless liquids and final colouring comes to a small extent from the cask but principally from added

The Caribbean

In the Caribbean, each island has its traditions of production which, in turn, decide whether their rums can be described as light, medium or heavy. Modern blending, particularly for brands with very large sales volumes, tends to take in the production of several islands and it is not uncommon for spirit from three or four islands — made to a set specification — to be used in a single brand's blend. These will normally be indicated on the label.

Barbados

Lightish, sweetish golden rums manufactured in both pot and continuous stills, (*qqv* Cockspur and Mount Gay, the oldest estate in the Caribbean). Barbados can, perhaps, claim to be the birthplace of rum because it was to the island that Dutchman Pieter Blower first took sugar cane in 1637 and very soon after sugar

Harmony Hall, a classic two-storey Jamaican plantation house.

production got under way, skimmings from the copper kettles were being distilled into 'kill-devil'. By 1650 almost a million litres a year of the fiery stuff was being produced from the pot stills located beside the wind-driven sugar mills.

Cuba

Similar to the rums produced in Puerto Rico, *ie* very light in style from continuous stills.

Above: Kingston, Jamaica is literally a garden city, with the Blue Mountains providing a retreat from the heat.

Right: The bars are always well stocked.

Guyana

Demerara rums are produced here in both pot and continuous stills and named for the Demerara River, which flows through the sugar plantations.

Demerara rums have great ageing potential. Guyana rums are particularly favoured for blending.

Haiti

Heavier, French-style rums which are fermented with natural yeasts, double-distilled in pot stills and aged in casks to give a full-bodied flavour.

Jamaica

The Jamaica style is rich, pungent and heavy from pot-still distillation. Jamaica is to rum what Islay is to malt whisky. Jamaican is the only Caribbean rum with official classifications: six types from light to very full-flavoured. The heavier types evolved as a rum concentrate exported to Germany and Austria when duties on volume of liquid there were particularly heavy. Five per cent of the concentrated rum was (and still is) mixed with 95 per cent neutral spirit to make German *rum verschnitt* and Austrian *inlander rum*. Jamaican rum aromas are rich and vanilla/buttery.

Martinique

French traditions, as here, also yield full-bodied, richly flavoured rums similar in broad style to those of Jamaica. Double-distilled in pot stills.

Puerto Rico

Very light, dry rums manufactured by continuous still; and very high levels of production.

Trinidad

Mainly light rums from continuous stills but there are a few with medium characteristics. Trinidad rums make excellent blending rums.

Appleton's Estate • Jamaican rum brand. The estate was established in the Nassau Valley in the 1740s by the Dickinson brothers, grandsons of one of the first settlers. Francis Dickinson had taken part in the capture of Jamaica from the Spanish in 1655 and parts of the estate go back to the original land grant made by the Crown to Dickinson's sons in 1687.

The rums are distilled in old copper pot stills on the estate and aged in the oak casks that are kept there. There is a staple range of Classic white, golden and dark. The white is aged in charred oak longer than most to attain greater smoothness and is then charcoal-filtered to remove the colour it picks up in the process. The golden is a blend of light and heavy rums and the dark is full-flavoured and resonant in the traditional Jamaica style. These are 40% vol. The Extra is a 12 years old and 43% vol.

Bacardi • The world's biggest rum brand and biggest spirit brand, selling more than 20 million cases a year worldwide. Bacardi was established in Cuba in 1862 by Don Facundo Bacardí y Masó, an émigré

Angostura White label • Trinidad brand. When the Angostura company moved from Venezuela to Trinidad at the turn of the century (see Bitters section for earlier history), it set up in the rum business, buying bulk rum and blending to its own recipe. It continued to operate in this way until the 1940s when, under the initiatives of Robert Siegert, great-grandson of the founder, the company began to distil its own rum. In 1958, when a Canadian firm attempted to take over the firm, the government of Trinidad and Tobago stepped in with a higher bid, bought the company and later sold it back to Siegert Holdings, an *ad hoc* company formed to bid for ownership and whose shareholders were directors and employees of Angostura. White Label epitomises the company's house style — very light and delicate of flavour; 43% vol.

Catalán whose family had arrived in Cuba in 1830. He went into business as a wine merchant and set about trying to improve the quality of the local rum. He bought a small distillery and put his ideas about producing rum in a new, lighter style into practice.

The fruit bats which festooned the ceiling of Don Facundo's distillery shed are thought by many to be the origin of the bat motif on Bacardi rum bottles; others say that it signified family loyalty. Bacardi's son Emilio was an active member of the Cuban underground trying to bring about independence for the island from Spanish rule. Despite his being imprisoned for sedition, the company was appointed supplier to the Spanish royal family, an honour partly brought about by the reported effectiveness of Bacardi rum as a cure for an extended bout of influenza suffered by King Alfonso XIII.

After the brief Spanish-American War in 1898 and the presence on the island of the American military, Coca-Cola started to appear in Cuban bars. One evening, a US serviceman is said to have mixed together Cuban rum and American cola and toasted free Cuba, 'Cuba Libre' — the first rum and Coke! In 1960 the Bacardi plant at Santiago de Cuba was confiscated by the Cuban government and the owners of the company had to move out, but they were careful to take with them all the documentation they needed to show ownership of the brand. The Cubans maintained production at the plant and also tried to use the Bacardi brand name for exports, claiming that it was made where Bacardi rum had always been made. Bacardi challenged this action in the courts and won, so Cuban rum produced at Santiago was renamed Havana Club.

After Castro took over the Bacardi plant in Cuba, the parent company hung out its sign in the Bahamas and built a new (ie additional) distillery. The building site was a swamp and they had to build roads and bring in electricity and telephone lines. Water was conjured out of the landscape by desalination, reverse osmosis and simple catchment but sugar cane was not a Bahamanian crop so molasses had to be brought in by tanker from Trinidad and Guyana. To this day, the Nassau facility supplies the core requirement for the British market.

Previous page, bottom left: Cane crafts by the shore at Runaway Bay, Jamaica — by-products designed to catch the eye of the well lubricated tourist.

Black Label • Trinidadian golden blend of light and heavy rums from Fernandes, but with a higher proportion of the former to give smooth, light body and colour; 43% vol.

Captain Morgan • The largest-selling dark rum in the world. It is named for Captain Henry Morgan, the Welsh pirate who was knighted and appointed lieutenant-governor of Jamaica in 1674 by King Charles II of England for limiting his pillage and mayhem to non-English ships. It is thought that Morgan grew sugar cane and made rum on his estate in Jamaica when he retired from buccaneering. Traditionally, Captain Morgan is a Jamaican rum but its owners, Seagram, have evolved the brand towards a lighter, less specific Caribbean style, using spirit from other islands and distilling it in continuous as well as pot stills. Core rums are from Jamaica for richness and flavour, Guyana Demerara for finesse and spice and Barbados for continuous-still lightness and balance. The Black Label is a blend of Jamaican and Fijian rums and ages in wood for up to four years. It is rich and aromatic in character and available at 37% and 57.2% vol. The White Label is light in body and meant for mixing. Morgan Mellow Spiced is variously two-year-old Jamaican or year-old Puerto Rican golden rum with added spices like vanilla, apricot, fig and tincture of cassia. Light but mellow; quite silky; 35% vol.

Caroni Puncheon • Strong, light rum from Trinidad. The Caroni distillery set up in business in 1918 with the installation of a cast-iron still. A succession of new and second-hand stills (the latter from the takeover of the Esperanza distillery on the island) have followed over the decades, gradually improving the capacity of the plant and the quality of the rums. The present pot and continuous stills date from 1984. The company uses sugar cane from its own estates and all ageing is in charred oak barrels. Caroni has a range of eight light rums and holds large stocks of aged rums of up to 20 years old.

Puncheon is an old, traditional, strong but light style that goes back to the early days of the plantations and is much in demand for blending. It is an extraordinary 75% vol/150 US proof in strength. Caroni ages its light styles for a minimum of three years; its heavy styles (used mainly for blending) for at least six years,

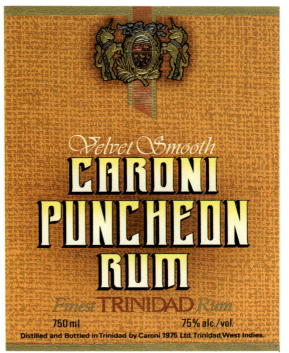

Cockspur • Golden rum brand produced at the larger of the two remaining distilleries on Barbados. The Cockspur brand was founded by a Dane, Valdemar Hanschell, who moved to the island and set up a ship's chandlery and liquor store in 1884. The West India Rum Refinery, where the rum is made, is built of coral stone and it has its own spring that guarantees a continuous water supply. The spirit is produced from pot stills and a yeast strain that is regarded as particularly important to the character of the house style is kept under lock and key with limited access — just like the secret formulae of the great liqueurs; 37.5% vol.

Coruba • Full, richly flavoured dark rum in the old Jamaican tradition and targeted at younger adults with colourful labelling and all-round performance as a mixer or a sipping rum; 40% vol.

Dillon • Martinique distillery and brand. The plantation with its sugar-refinery was founded in 1690 by the Girardin de Montgeralde family; in later years, a neighbour and cousin, Joséphine de Beauharnais, became mistress and then wife of Napoleon. The distillery is named after Arthur Dillon, an Irish Jacobite

stood near St Pierre and in 1900 was taken down and reassembled in its present position. The first column (*ie* continuous) still was installed in 1920 and the hurricane-proof buildings of the present distillery were built of reinforced concrete in 1928. At that time, there were 134 distilleries on Martinique. Dillon is now owned by the Bardinet company in Bordeaux and the main ranges are Negrita and Old Nick, which are shipped to France for any oak-ageing they undergo; Dillon rums are aged in small barrels of Quercy oak at the distillery warehouses. The Très Vieux indicates the year of distillation on the label and is usually about 15 years old when it is bottled and marketed; 45% vol.

E*l Dorado* • Brand name of Demerara Distillers, sole producer of the famed rums of Demerara county in Guyana. The company can produce just about any style of rum from its extraordinary range of still types. It has the latest in modern equipment but has also hung on

soldier who is fondly remembered in Martinique for having helped 'kick the English out of several Caribbean islands', as the Dillon distillery brochure puts it. The Dillon regiment was based at the Girardin estate when in Martinique in 1779, and Dillon later married into the Girardin family. In 1857, the plantation passed into the hands of M. Herve, the mayor of St Pierre, who built a distillery there. He also restored a 17th-century canal that carried water from the local river and it is still in use today.

The present estate residence replaced the old house destroyed in the 1891 hurricane. It formerly

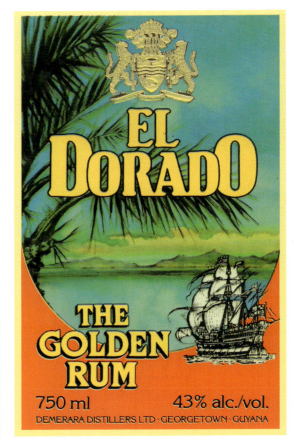

to old-style Demerara pot stills and other patent rum stills. The last fully operational rectangular wooden Coffey still in the Western world is lovingly clung to and used to produce special one-off rums. There is warehousing for over 50,000 casks.

The El Dorado range includes Superior White, Golden and the rich, particular Dark. Special Reserve, aged for 15 years in oak casks, is the company's premium product — very fine, silky and fragrant, with good flavour and lengthy finish.

Félicité Gold • Mellow, light golden style from Trinidad. The particular blend originated on the Félicité estate, which the company now owns, back in 1820. Good core flavour, generous fragrance and very stylish close; 43% vol.

Ferdi's premium • Trinidad golden style from a blend of well-matured light and heavy types. It is classified as a medium rum with notably mellow texture and a bit more weight than other similar brands such as Vat 19 and White Star (*qqv*). The rich colour comes from both the cask and rum caramel; 43% vol.

Lamb's • Company and brand name dating back to 1849, when Alfred Lamb introduced his rums to the UK. Lamb imported casks of new rum to age them in cellars that ran beneath the River Thames, instead of in the Caribbean heat. The cool humidity gave his rums an appealing particularity that brought him great success. Lamb's Reserve is a blend of pot- and continuous-still rums, the youngest of which is eight years old. Rich, toffee fragrance, plus smoke, oak and a touch of spice. The Pale Gold is also rich in weight but has a fruity, light caramel edge and chocolate smokiness. Both 40% vol.

Mount Gay • Barbados golden rum. Dating back to 1660, Mount Gay is one of the oldest estates in the Caribbean and certainly the oldest in Barbados. It was owned at that time by a Dr William Gay, thought to be a cousin of John Gay who wrote *The Beggar's Opera*. There is evidence that there was distilling equipment *in situ* in 1663, so rum has probably been in production ever since. There were hundreds of distilleries on the island in the early 1800s and rum was referred to as 'Barbados water'.

Opposite page, top left: The Empress Joséphine, wife of Napoléon, was a cousin and neighbour to the founding family of the Dillon distillery in Martinique.

Production was originally all from a pair of pot stills but there is now only one of these left and successive continuous stills have been installed over the past decades. Double-distilled spirit for bottling continues to be made in the pot still but it is also blended with distillate from the other still, and sherry-type and prune wines are added according to formula. The rums are made from local Barbadian molasses fermented in oak vats. The blend from the two spirit types is aged in ex-bourbon casks to give a distinctive smoky, elegant taste and mellowed finish.

created by an American ex-marine. Chuck Tobias built a blending and bottling facility in the British Virgin Islands and imported pot-still spirit from Trinidad and elsewhere in the Caribbean. 'Pusser' is a slang rendering of purser, the officer on board any ship who, as the person in charge of victuals and supplies, was responsible for the meting out of the rum ration. Tobias bought an authentic naval recipe from the British Admiralty and even obtained their permission to incorporate the Royal Ensign in the design of the bottle label.

Today, the rum is blended from six rums produced in Guyana and Trinidad; 54.5% vol. In the USA, Pusser's Gold is 40% vol/80 US proof and Admiral's Reserve is 47.75% vol/95.5 US proof.

Old Cask • Mellow, aged rum blend from Trinidad. It is blended from different 10-year-old rums to produce a soft, silky, well-merged finish; 43% vol.

Old Oak • Branded Trinidad range from the Angostura firm. It is a leading brand in Trinidad and Tobago and across the Caribbean, and comes in white and gold styles. There is also a splendidly kitsch 'Limbo Drummer' flask in the shape of a medallioned musician in enormous colourful epaulettes drumming on a rum tub between his knees; 43% vol.

Pusser's • British brand. This brand of apparently impeccable British and naval pedigree was in fact

Royal Oak • Angostura brand of de luxe golden rum from Trinidad. A blend of aged rums showing gentle mellowness and attractive balance; 43% vol.

Stallion Puncheon • Very strong light rum from Trinidad. Puncheon rum is of this type — highly alcoholic, but misleadingly elegant in texture and weight in the mouth. Stallion is the strongest rum produced in Trinidad and Tobago (at least for local consumption) at 78% vol/156 US proof and has a somewhat vodka-like clean-as-a-whistle taste. It must yield a worthwhile saving in the duty-free shop, too.

Vat 19 • Blend of light and heavy types of rum from Trinidad which is subsequently classified as a light golden rum; 43% vol.

Superb
WHITE MAGIC LIGHT
Finest TRINIDAD *Rum*

750 ML   43% alc. / vol.

Distilled and Bottled in Trinidad by Caroni 1975 Ltd. Trinidad, West Indies.

Wray & Nephew is the brand owner of both the Wray and Appleton Estate rums. The company is the oldest in Jamaica, having been founded in 1825, and comprises three large estates — Appleton, Holland and New Yarmouth. Wray's top rums come from the Appleton Estate, which is open to the public for visits to the distillery.

The blenders have stocks of rums of up to 30 years old normally at their disposal and there are some exceptional 50-year-olds still in place. John Wray was a wheelwright by trade but he set up a tavern in Kingston's main square beside the theatre. He also eventually became a successful rum merchant. The company thrived to such an extent that it was able to loan money to the government to help it finance the 1891 Jamaica Exhibition held on the island. The company lost heavily in the great earthquake and fire of 1907 — two employees were killed, records were lost, the head office was flattened and 30 shops destroyed. The theatre in the main square was also lost and Wray's paid for its reconstruction, presenting it to the city and the people of Kingston. Today, there is still a bar operated by Wray's on the site of the old tavern in the square beside the theatre.

The company also produces C. J. Wray, claimed as the world's first dry rum and named after the founder of the business. It is a dry white blend popular as a mixing rum; 40% vol.

White Magic Light • Light white Trinidad rum from Caroni; 43% vol.

White Star • Light-bodied golden rum from Trinidad. Blended from both light and heavy types, it has a proportion of rum caramel to enhance the gentle colour it takes from the time in wood; 43% vol.

Wray's Overproof • Unaged white Jamaica rum blended from light and full-flavoured types. Diverging from the customary local practice, the blending rums used are not aged in oak casks and give distinctive aroma and flavour. The 'overproof/full strength' description usually indicates rums in excess of 60% vol. Wray's, known as 'Whites', is the biggest-selling rum in Jamaica and is widely used in the making of rum punches.

Cargo ships at anchor off Kingston in 1865.

Rum from Other Countries

Australia

Sugar cane has been cultivated in Queensland since 1860.

'NOBODY WANTS TO DIE WHEN THERE'S RUM IN THE BOTTLE,' playwright Douglas Stewart imagines Ned Kelly saying as the final showdown approaches in his play about the Australian outlaw. Rum is, to an extent, unsung in Australia, despite its being the country's second drink to beer. The leading brand, Bundaberg, outsells Johnnie Walker, the world's best-selling Scotch whisky, by two to one.

Sugar plantations were established in Queensland, Australia in the 1860s and rum production got under way in 1888 at the town of Bundaberg, 250 miles to the north of Brisbane.

Bundaberg • Best-selling Australian brand. Bundaberg, or 'Bundy', is extremely popular throughout Australia and is the country's best-selling spirit brand, with almost 10 per cent of the spirits market and 90 per cent of the dark rum sector. Over half of the volume is sold in the brand's home state of Queensland but it has a high profile throughout Australia. Bundy tended to be favoured over beer in the heat of outback because it did not go sour and needed no refrigeration.

While the rum is of excellent quality, it is a brand that does not like to take itself too seriously, advertising its best attributes as being 'genuine, down-to-earth and no bullshit'. Nonetheless, Bundy is claimed to be in the same league of famed Australian brand names as Qantas, Vegemite and Foster's. It has a distinctive square bottle and three-part yellow label, livery that was designed in the early 1960s by Sam McMahon, brother of the Australian prime minister in 1971-72. The polar bear logo on the label symbolises the assertion that Bundy can 'keep out the wickedest cold'.

The rum is made by double-distillation, first in a continuous still and then in a pot still, the spirit

coming over at 78% vol. Bundy ages for two years in American white oak, but this takes place in great 60,000-litre vats instead of barrels. There are more than 150 of these giants, each made from six tonnes of wood, in bond stores around the site. Single style at 37.1% vol.

Venezuela

Pampero • High-quality range from company that pioneered the idea of ageing rum in Venezuela. The company, founded by Alejandro Hernandez, began in the 1930s by making tropical fruit wines and progressed to blending young rums. In 1941, it introduced a pre-mix of cane spirit and cola concentrate, calling it Patria Libre — a salute to the democracy that was burgeoning in Venezuela at the time, as well as to the original rum-and-cola Cuba Libre.

In 1942, the company began ageing rum in small 500-litre oak barrels for six-month periods, an idea they developed until, in 1951, 400 oak casks were filled and documented to become the first legally aged rums in Venezuela. After two years' maturation, they were bottled and launched as Pampero Ron Anejo (Aged Rum). Subsequently, two-, three- and four-year-old rums were introduced, something unique in the country at the time.

One of the magnificent waterfalls at Canaima, Venezuela.

A policy of frequent new product launches was carried forward in the 1960s, a difficult thing to sustain since the competition carried only one or two lines. In 1962, Tresanejo and Dorado headed the quality end of the market; in 1963, Aniversario (the company's 25th) was one of the best rums in the world; in 1964, Anejo Estelar was introduced and went on to pick up many awards. The launch of Light Dry and Golden Dry in 1968 brought to an end the period of creating regular new rums and Pampero settled down with eight rums on the market.

The burden of carrying such a range of different rums, when the main competitor had only one to foster, eventually told and in the 1970s the range was wound down and all efforts went into the Anejo Especial. The move worked: 1977 was the best in the company's history and within two years Pampero regained the domestic brand-leader position.

In the 1980s, Pampero began to tackle export markets, with North America and Spain/Portugal the main focuses of its efforts — a programme still being pursued at present, with Anejo Especial and Aniversario (both 40% vol) the key brands.

The company has always taken a lead in employee welfare, building workers' villages with schools, clinics and creches. The Pampero Foundation is notable for its arts and its cultural sponsorship.

South Africa

INDIAN LABOURERS IN SOUTH AFRICA, MAINLY NATAL, enjoyed sugar-cane spirits but these never had a great image and were usually drunk informally in the kitchen rather than with friends. In the 1950s, cane spirit began to be supplied to on-premises at high strength in large glass containers for the publican to reduce to normal commercial strength. Tots were served from great enamel jars with taps which sat on canteen counters.

Take-home trade developed and the Mainstay brand was introduced to meet the demand. Interest then spread to the Transvaal as holidaymakers returning there from Natal took bottles home with them. When a brandy firm in the Cape launched a brand in 1967, cane spirit had taken on the status of a national spirit.

Mainstay • Cane-spirit brand from Stellenbosch Farmers Winery which became South Africa's biggest spirit brand. It is still the country's top cane spirit, with around 35% market share. Mainstay is a blend of spirits made in South Africa and, under licence in Mauritius, from sugar-cane molasses.

From modest beginnings of 1,500 cases a year in 1954, Mainstay was selling 7,000 cases by 1960 and by the end of the decade had reached half-a-million cases a year. The brand was advertised with lifestyle themes similar to those of Smirnoff and Bacardi, most consistently with a nautical content, no doubt due to the close, perhaps almost subliminal, link with rum. Advertising featured both blacks and whites in the same ads in the 1980s and at the time Mainstay was selling nearly 1.7 million cases a year.

Brazil

Cane spirit in Brazil is called *aguardente de cana* or *cachaça* and, like rum, is produced from molasses, cane juice or a mixture of the two; it is usually unaged. Cachaça is extremely popular and is a multi-million-case seller in its domestic market. Exports go to other South American countries, the USA and Japan. In Europe, Germany, Italy and Portugal take modest quantities.

John Gunther, author of the *Inside* series of books which included Brazil, called it 'this sinister but enlivening fluid' and to begin with it was the poor man's rum. More recently, however, it has taken on an improved image with some of the production going into oak for ageing.

Cana Rio • Brand founded in 1827 in Rio, produced by the Fazenda Soledade distillery. Soledade use copper pot stills instead of continuous stills in the production of the spirit.

Dreher • Ginger-flavoured spirit brand. The Dreher family, originally from Germany, set up a wine business in Bento Goncalves in Rio Grande do Sul, Brazil's southernmost state. In the 1950s, there were practically no domestic drink brands and only the very wealthy had access to imported products.

In 1955, Conhaque Dreher was launched to fill the gap, at least in part, and was immediately successful. The *conhaque* was a simple brandy and

has subsequently evolved into a cane-spirit base flavoured with ginger.

The new formulation gave the drink something extra compared with the cachaça brands it competes with and it has gone on to register annual sales of more than four million cases. It is in the top dozen spirit brands in the world, despite being sold only in Brazil.

Pirassununga • Brand from the Hiram Walker stable, which has about 30 per cent share of the home market. It sells particularly well in São Paulo and Brasília. Sugar syrup is added to the cane spirit and the strength is cut to 39% vol with de-mineralised water.

São Francisco • Seagram brand which has sold as many as 70 million cases a year despite its being aged in oak casks. Where do they get the space to age this kind of volume? The brand is made from cane juice rather than molasses.

Ypióca • Aged cachaça. The brand grew from a sugar refinery bought by the Telles family in Fortaleza in 1846. Two types are made in a modified variation of a Portuguese pot still: *empalhada*, aged for two years, and *conta-gotas*, for four years.

Left: Carnival time in Rio de Janeiro, an intoxicating blend of costume and music with, no doubt, a little cane spirit as catalyst.

Tequila, Akvavit & Schnapps

Tequila/Mezcal

Mexico

YOU NEED TO KNOW YOUR BOTANY TO FULLY UNDERSTAND the lineage of tequila. It is made from an agave plant with blue leaves that grows only in Jalisco province in Mexico where, crouched under an old volcano, the town of Tequila gives its name to the plant-variety as well as to the drink. The agave is a type of mezcal which in turn is part of the lily family. It is also known as the century plant, the maguey or the argarth and looks like a giant pineapple. Despite the mythology, it is not the same plant as the mescal cactus, or peyote, found in the US.

The Aztecs are thought to have made fermented drinks from mezcal as early as the third century BC. They produced a 'wine' called pulque made from its heart and when the Spanish Conquistadores colonised the area they tried distilling it but disliked the results. The first primitive mezcal spirits were made by the Spanish settlers experimenting with different types of agave in their localities; the town of Tequila is named after the local Ticuilas Indians and the mezcal produced in the neighbourhood would naturally make use of the name. The origin of the name 'Mexico' is claimed to derive from 'mezcal'.

It was in the 18th and 19th centuries that the quality of the mezcal made around Tequila began to be perceived as better than most, a credit latterly attributed to the single variety of agave with which it was made.

The agave takes up to 12 years to mature. The heart, the pina, which can weigh up to 60 kilos, is harvested and cooked to create a sugar-rich liquor. Once this has fermented, the best types are double-distilled in pot stills although continuous stills are also used for the standard style. Tequila's early 'killer' image came from the custom followed until comparatively recently of single-distilling rustic tequila in pot stills to give an extracty, smelly and headache-giving potion complete with fusel oils.

Opposite page: Mezcal plants in Jalisco province, near Tequila, grown for their pinas or giant pineapple-like core, spread out to the Sierra Madre horizon.

Top: The first step is to cut away the tall leaves. The remaining pina can weigh anything from 80 to 150 lb.

Bottom: The headquarters of the House of Sauza, founded in 1873.

Good tequila is herby/spicy in aroma and flavour, and a little oily in texture.

There are several categories. Silver is the standard quality and is unaged; Reposado 'rests' for several months in oak; Gold is matured for varying periods in oak (and often coloured with caramel by some firms to cut a corner or two); and Anejo is aged longest, typically for one to three years. The latter can rival the quality (and price) of cognac and de luxe whiskey but there are no very old tequilas because spirits aged more than 10 years turn bitter.

There is an appellation, the 'Denominacion de Origen', which delimits production areas and specifies ingredient-content but it is loosely interpreted by some producers and laxly enforced by the authorities. Compliance with the agave-content regulation (from 51% minimum to 100% in high-grade spirit) is said not to be universal so that variation in quality from one brand to another can be marked. The core producer companies are law-abiding and proud of their products but there are also a number of less responsible catch-penny firms on the periphery of the industry. Brands which adhere to the production regulations carry an NOM number (Norma Oficial Mexicana de Calidad) on their labels.

An agreement exists between Mexico and the USA that tequila and bourbon are respectively Mexican and American products and that neither will allow manufacture of the other's product within its

boundaries. Bulk export and bottling in the destination country is, however, widely practised.

Similarly-produced spirit made outside the delimited Tequila zone is simply called mezcal. It has gained notoriety as the drink with the worm in the bottle — an agave root grub which adds no flavour but does attract attention. It is thought to have originally served the same purpose as gunpowder in determining 'proof' of a spirit's strength. Above a particular alcohol minimum the grub would remain intact; in low-strength spirit it would disintegrate.

Jose Cuervo • The world's best-selling brand, accounting for 4.5 million cases a year. A Spanish colonist, Don Jose Antonio de Cuervo, received a land-grant in Tequila from the Spanish king in 1758 to grow blue agaves, and in 1795 the family set up a company to distil tequila spirit commercially. Cuervo's first exports to the USA were in 1873 when three barrels of tequila were sent to El Paso in Texas.

Cuervo makes its Silver spirit in stainless steel stills and double-distils the Gold and Anejo qualities

Top left: Two or three years barrel ageing gives Tequila a quality which can rival cognac and whisky.

in pairs of pot stills. The house style is light and elegant. Especial is a premium Gold and '1800' is a blend of aged tequilas; 40% vol.

Herradura • Family firm producing exclusively highest grade 100% agave spirit. The brand name means 'horseshoe' and recalls the morning in

Herradura use only blue agave for all of their tequilas and naturally occurring yeasts effect all fermentations. They use exclusively agaves grown on plantations owned and leased by themselves and tended by their own workforce; other producers tend to buy on the commodity market. No pesticides or colourants are used and maturation is in untreated oak casks. Herradura distil and bottle their tequila on the hacienda, the only producer to do so.

They are experimenting with closed fermentation tanks and ex- cognac oak for ageing. Barrels have customarily been made from American and French oak and with the Mexican heat, the 'angels' share' evaporation of spirit in cask can reach 30 per cent loss a year.

Herradura Silver spends two months and Reposado Gold nine months in oak barrels; Gold is aged for 18 months, is well regarded in terms of quality and sells at the same price as Johnnie Walker Black Label Scotch in Mexico. Anejo spends up to three years in oak. Herradura Reposado is a premium label.

Mariachi • Brand from the Seagram firm. Mariachi is double-distilled from blue agave plants and available as Blanco and Oro Especial qualities; 40% vol.

Olmeca • Companion brand to Mariachi (*qv*). Olmeca is double-distilled and available as Blanco and Anejo qualities; 40% vol.

1861 when Feliciano Romo was prospecting on his estate for a site to build his distillery and found a wild agave plant that had grown from underneath a discarded horseshoe and lifted it with its leaves as it grew. The distillery began production in 1870 and is now run by the fifth generation of the Romo family. They change as little that is organic as possible at their distillery at Amatitan, not even cutting down trees in case they influence the formation of the site's natural yeasts.

The old distillery, dating from almost two centuries ago, is still in place with its hole-in-the-ground fermentation pits and the mule-drawn crusher, however these days it is preserved as a museum. The modern distillery in Spanish-Mexican style is very hi-tech where appropriate but the great clay ovens in which the pinas are cooked are based on a design of 1800.

Top: The pinas are compressed and steamed in cylindrical ovens before shredding and pressing. The juice extracted is mixed with sugar and some of the pulp ready for distillation, with each pina yielding 6 gallons of spirit.

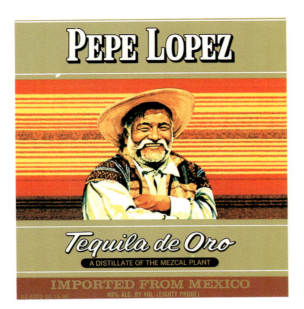

Pepe Lopez • Popular-price brand from the Orendain family. Pepe Lopez began as a hand-crafted tequila in 1857 and is today the fifth-best-selling tequila in the USA. The juice fermented to make Pepe Lopez has the legal minimum 51% blue agave content and the liquor is double-distilled. Available in Silver and Gold qualities; 40% vol.

Sauza • The second-best-selling brand in the world with case sales of over two million a year. The distillery was founded in 1873 by Don Cenobio Sauza. He went to Tequila in 1858 to work in the industry. Distribution was non-existent so he bought five stage-coaches and began distributing tequila all round the state of Jalisco. In 1870 he rented the Antigua Cruz distillery to begin distilling for himself and in 1873 bought it. The old distillery still stands as part of the Sauza complex and the bullet-holes in the smoke-stack bear witness to the attacks from bandidos and revolutionaries it has undergone. Sauza was the first tequila to be exported to the USA, a consignment of three barrels and six jugs being despatched to New Mexico in the same year that Cenobio Sauza bought the distillery. Additional lines, including Anejo, were introduced in the early years of this century.

At Sauza, all young tequila spirits spend a minimum of four months in stainless steel or wooden vats while they are assessed as future Reposado or Anejo qualities.

Sauza produce both Silver and Gold qualities. Hornitos is a Reposado from 100% agave. There are

Don Cenobio Sauza, the bearded founder, and first man to export tequila to the USA, looks on to the contemporary range of Sauza products.

two Anejos — Conmemorativo, aged for two years in white American oak, and top-of-the-range Tres Generaciones, aged for four years in oak and for sipping only. The house style is full and vivid in flavour.

Sierra • German-owned brand that does not take itself too seriously with bottle-caps shaped like little Mexican hats. The range is standard with Silver, Gold and Antiguo (which is an Anejo).

Top left: Sixteen of these wooden 'pipon' vats hold over 850,000 bottles before the angels take their share.

Top right: The Sauza coat of arms.

Left: An unmistakable Mexican icon: the silhouette of the agave tequilana, source of the finest tequila.

but in the distant past it was the poor man's drink.

In production these days, flavouring agents are macerated with spirit and water and then distilled into extracts. To make the final distillate, spirit, water and the extracts are blended in large vats and then stored for a settling period before bottling.

Although akvavit stands on its own as a drink, it is traditionally used as an accompaniment to the seafood and cold-table foods of Denmark and elsewhere in Scandinavia.

Aalborg Taffel • Danish brand. The town of Aalborg gives its name to the best-known brand of Danish akvavit produced by Danish Distillers. It was first made in 1846 by Isidor Henius, a precocious young distiller, not out of his teens, who arrived in Aalborg with his own ideas about how akvavit should be made and a formula to prove it. His recipe is the best-known today and Aalborg Taffel is made with high-strength neutral grain spirit which has caraway (Kummel) flavouring added and is redistilled; 45% vol.

Akvavit

Scandinavia

AKVAVIT PRODUCTION IN DENMARK EMERGED IN THE 15TH CENTURY at about the time distillation skills were being established throughout the rest of Europe. There was reasonable freedom to distil until the 1840s, when the Danish government cracked down and took control. Even so there were over 2,000 legal distilleries in operation and the town of Aalborg (Ålborg) became the centre of production.

Historically, both potatoes and grain were used as raw materials but often the grain could be very poor, and was stretched with pretty well anything botanical, including weeds. Every potato yields the means to make a single small glass of akvavit

Top: Sankt Peder Strade, Copenhagen. As in centuries past akvavit is the spirit of Denmark.

Brondum Kummen • Domestic Danish brand. Anton Brondum was a small distiller of schnapps in Copenhagen who lived during the first three-quarters of the 19th century. He had a number of fine recipes in his books, however, and in 1893 his Kummel (caraway) akvavit with a zesty cinnamon flavour was introduced and became successful. His well-textured 'Snaps' is still used as a base for people who like to add their own herbal mixes.

Harald Jensen • Domestic Danish brand. Fine aromatic mainstream akvavit that has been a consistent seller since its introduction in 1883; 45% vol.

Jubilaeums • Jubilee edition of Aalborg akvavit (qv) issued in 1946 to commemorate the company's centenary. It has a pale golden colour from caraway, coriander and dill flavouring; 42% and 45% vol.

Lysholm Linie • Norwegian brand of aquavit (the spelling the Norwegians prefer). The generic product has been made from local potatoes for more than 200 years, with final flavouring from caraway and other herbs.

The 'line' in the brand-name is the Equator. In what has become a tradition like that of Madeira wine, the spirit is matured in the course of an *ad hoc* voyage by ship to the southern hemisphere and back entailing two crossings of the Equator. A particularity of maturation results from the continuous movement of the ship working the spirit into the fibres of the oak casks in which it travels, together with the range of temperatures encountered *en voyage*.

The routine began over a century ago when it was noticed that aquavit that made the full journey to Australia and back in the cargo clippers of the day took on exceptional smoothness and mellowness. Ships of the Wilhelmsen Line were henceforth contracted to carry batches of the aquavit on their round trips to Australia. Since 1985, the spirit goes even farther, completing round-the-world voyages but still

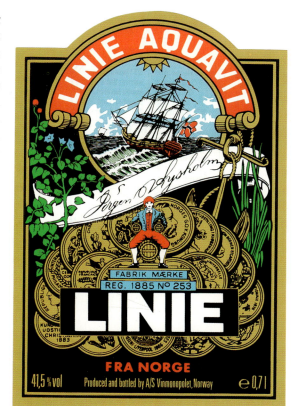

via Australia. The pale gold colour is picked up from the time in cask. The name of the ship in which each batch of Linie aquavit has matured is indicated on the bottle label. The brand achieves some exports to the USA and within Europe, particularly in duty-free. Fragrant and attractive in style; 41.5% vol.

Loiten Export • Companion brand of aquavit to Lysholm Linie (qv). Loiten, like its more famous stablemate, is also matured in oak during a round-the-world ocean voyage, but is made to a different recipe. A distillate of botanicals is made separately before being blended with neutral spirit and put into oakwood; 40% vol.

Schnapps

SCHNAPPS IS A CATCH-ALL TERM FOR THE RANGE OF WHITE AND FLAVOURED SPIRITS produced in the northern hemisphere in Germany, Holland and Scandinavia. Some, like akvavit (from Latin *aqua vitae*) in Denmark, are national drinks in these countries but have not developed sufficiently beyond their home boundaries to become international drinks. Schnapps may be made from grain, potato or molasses and as such most could qualify as vodkas but for their owners' wish to retain their products' individuality and identity.

Germany

GERMAN KORNBRANNTWEIN, LITERALLY 'CORN BRANDY', has the characteristics of a simple, light whiskey when 'natural'. Doppelkorn is stronger, customarily ranging from 38% to 45% vol. Korn (32% vol) and Doppelkorn (38% vol) have been recognised as quite distinct products since as long ago as the 16th century and purity laws have been in force to protect the generic product since 1909.

The term schnapps is also used for lower-strength drinks made from spirit and fruit flavourings. In Germany Apfelkorn — korn spirit flavoured with apple — is particularly popular. There are many Apfelkorn brands available and the best-known is probably Berentzen. International fruit-schnapps brands, like Archer's Peach County, are also experiencing a growth in demand. All of these are usually 20-22% vol.

Alter Koerner • Mild korn schnapps from the Stonsdorfer company. 32% vol.

Berentzen Appel • Mild apfel-korn, *ie* apple, schnapps. Berentzen was founded in 1758 and is now the second-top German spirit company with 10% of the market.

In the 1980s Berentzen were first on the European market with the idea for a fruity, light apple schnapps for export; there was none on any of the European markets, although research had shown that light fruit combined with light grain spirit was well received by consumers. Sales have reached over 300,000 cases in exports alone and Berentzen has three-quarters of the German domestic Apfelkorn market share. The company's Doppelkorn also has a high profile.

Doornkat • German korn schnapps. The brand is made from malted grain and is triple-distilled to include some flavouring content. The final spirit has something of the character of a very light whiskey; 38% vol.

Kornelius • Full-strength korn speciality. This Doppelkorn is distilled in-house from wheat grown in the north of Germany; 38% vol.

Lithuanian national dress. Schnapps could qualify as a vodka, but drinks, like costume, are often a strong source of national identity.

Lithuania

Suktinis • Highly flavoured unique flavoured schnapps known as Lithuanian Balsam. It is literally a distillation of the flavours and aromas of the Lithuanian countryside having macerated with or fermented a cocktail of ingredients. Honey, juniper berries and peppermint are almost run-of-the-mill botanicals compared to the cinnamon, dill seeds, bay leaves, clove blossoms, poplar buds and acorns that also go into it. Once assembled and distilled, Suktinis matures in oak barrels for 22 years and is enormously aromatic, opulent and mouthfilling in taste. By volume, 11% is extract and strength is 50% vol.

Zalgiris • Strong, delicately flavoured schnapps made from mead with added flavouring from cranberry juice and other ingredients. It is bottled at distillation strength of 75% vol (*ie* 150% US proof)! Mead — and honey-based spirits and fortified drinks are popular in Lithuania.

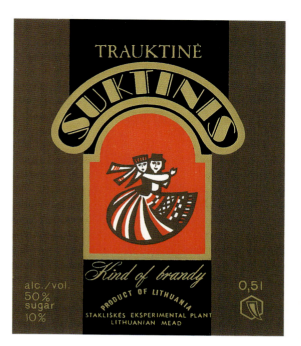

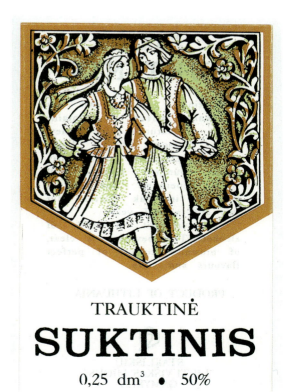

TRAUKTINĖ
SUKTINIS
0,25 dm³ • 50%

Strong, inimitable Lithuanian schnapps would have been the suitable refreshment for guests at Trakai castle in years gone by.

Anise & Bitters

Anise

ANISEED-FLAVOURED SPIRITS HAVE DIFFERENT CULTURES depending on the country in which they are produced. They may be sweet or dry, modest or very high in strength. They are made both by distillation of the fermented aniseeds and any other botanicals in the formula, or macerated in neutral spirit; the perception is that the former represents a higher quality of product.

In English the plant and the drink are called anise but the French word — *anis* — is also in general use; pastis is a French anise-flavoured spirit and anisette is a sweet liqueur. Aniseeds are the anise plant's seeds.

France

DESPITE RESTRICTED GEOGRAPHICAL DISTRIBUTION, the highest-profile anise products are French with two of the Pernod Ricard firm's brands selling 10 million cases worldwide in the anise/pastis category. The sector in France began as absinthe (see Pernod overleaf) and, after a ban during World War I, re-established itself in its present form.

Anis

Anis (in the form of Pernod) is distilled and, with a fair number of other botanicals in its make-up, aspires to some complexity of aroma and flavour.

Pastis

Pastis is made by maceration. With fewer flavouring elements than anis, it is a more straightforward drink.

Some principal brands are listed overleaf.

Opposite page: Star Anise, on sale at Lanzhou free market, Ganzhou. The fruit comes from a small tree, belonging to the magnolia family, that grows wild in south-west China.

Below: Maison Piccini had a regular clientele for their advertised bitters.

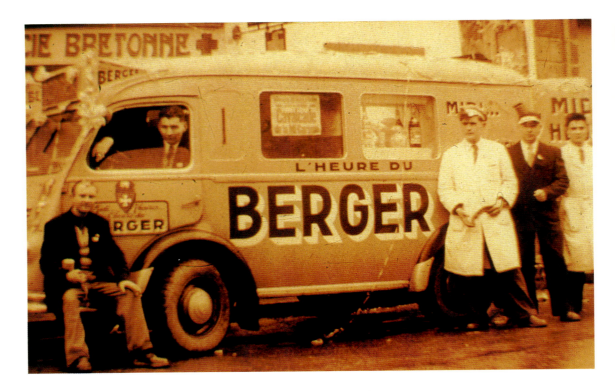

Berger • Brand name for two products: a traditional pastis and Berger Blanc, an unusual white 'pastis' flavoured exclusively with anise and with no other herbs in the blend. Both are 45% vol. Berger were originally Swiss, having taken over, in 1870, an absinthe-distilling business at Neuchatel that had been in operation since 1830. Berger moved their company base to Marseille in 1923 soon after the French law banning production of anise-based drinks was revoked, to begin pastis production.

Pastis 51 • Pastis brand from the Pernod company. The product was launched in 1951 as Pernod 51, all told not a good choice of name since people confused it with Pernod anise and thought the '51' indicated its alcoholic strength. The brand was renamed and in fact it is 45% vol. It is made by macerating powdered liquorice root in a mixture of anise extract, spirit, water and sugar. The anise extract is obtained both from star anise and fennel distillates. After filtration, the blend is bottled. Liquorice, as one of only two main flavourings, dominates the aroma and taste. The brand sells 2.5 million cases a year — 99 per cent of it in western Europe.

Pernod • Anise brand first created as an absinthe substitute. In 1805 Henri-Louis Pernod began producing absinthe at Pontarlier to a recipe obtained by his father-in-law from two Swiss sisters. Absinthe, green aniseed, fennel and hyssop were the sole botanicals and wine-spirit was used as the base. Pernod's absinthe became so popular that catch-penny imitations from firms with names like Perenod, Pernaud and Pernot cashed in merrily. Later in the century other branches of the Pernod family set up competing distilling businesses so that latterly the market was almost literally awash with different Pernod absinthe products.

In the early 20th century absinthe was perceived to be the cause of much mental and physical illness. In Switzerland, a dreadful triple murder, committed by a farmer crazed by absinthe, had the drink banned in 1910 and the proscription written into the Swiss constitution. The French followed suit just five years later and the Pernods, real and counterfeit, closed their doors.

In 1920 production of aniseed drinks was again sanctioned but the absinthe plant — *Artemisia*

absinthium or wormwood, also the basis for vermouth — remained outlawed. Common sense might have made people realise that the high strength of good-quality absinthe spirit — up to 75% vol/150 US proof — was what caused the main health problems and that the brains of writers and artists like de Maupassant, Verlaine and Toulouse-Lautrec had rotted because they were dying of chronic syphilis. There is now talk of withdrawing the ban on absinthe.

A merger of three Pernod distillery firms took place in 1928 and the Pernod anise brand was introduced. The aniseed flavouring comes from the star or Chinese anise tree which grows only in Vietnam and China, and fennel (green aniseed). Distillates from them are combined with spirits made from the 15 secret ingredients in the formula, liquorice extract, softened water, sugar and neutral spirit.

Pernod is different from pastis like Ricard and Pastis 51 (*qqv*) in that it is distilled and has only minor liquorice content in what is claimed to be a more complex flavour. The taste is typically dry, aniseedy and minty with liquorice. Pernod sells just under a million cases a year; 40 and 45% vol.

Ricard • Pastis brand that is the world's third-best-selling spirit. Introduced in 1932 by the Paul Ricard firm, it is made from anise, fennel (green anise), liquorice and other Provençal herbs. These are macerated in silent spirit to produce full-flavoured, classic pastis. Ricard sells 7.5 million cases a year.

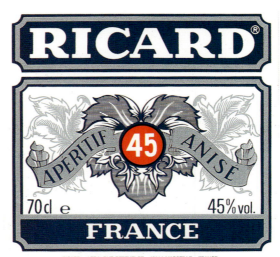

The soldiers' daily absinthe ration in the 1847 Algerian campaign established the habit, and marble tables, water and absinthe became features immortalised by the artists of Bohemian café society later in the century.

Italy

Sambuca

Sambuca is a distillate but has a high sugar content — around 350 grammes per litre — since it is a liqueur and not an aperitif. Essential oil of fennel (green anise), which has been rectified to a lower degree and which retains good natural fragrance, is often blended in to lend aroma to the product. References to anise drinks in Italian settings have been found in a number of Latin texts and anise cordials were used medicinally on board ships. In the first century AD, Pliny the Elder in Rome wrote at length about anise and the Moors took anise drinks with them when they invaded Sicily in 1,000 AD. A non-alcoholic anise drink called zammu was made at the time and when alcohol was added it became zambur. Eventually the drink's preparation and name evolved into 'sambuca'.

The convention of serving sambuca with three coffee beans on the surface is known as *con mosca* — 'with flies'. Some leading brands are listed here.

Ramazzotti • Brand from a company perhaps better known for its amaro bitters. Ramazzotti's sambuca is based on distillates from star anise combined with silent spirit. It has a fine, dry, refreshing house style with a minty overlay; 40% vol.

Romana • Brand produced in Rome and one of the first sambucas to be marketed. The Pallini family who developed it had been liqueurists since 1875. Romana is the best-selling export sambuca brand; 42% vol.

Vaccari • This brand was formerly marketed as Galliano sambuca but has been renamed in tribute to Arturo Vaccari, the pioneer Italian distiller who was the originator of the Galliano liqueur. Vaccari uses both star anise and fennel from the Mediterranean. The star type is infused in spirit for four days, the fennel for two days, and then both are redistilled. The two distillates are blended and essential oils added, after which the final blend 'marries' for two months; 38% and 42% vol.

A silently striking contrast between nature's abundance and man's industry at this northern Italian distillery.

Greece

Ouzo

Ouzo is a water-white distillate. It is dryish, with less than 50 grammes per litre sugar-content and must also, by law, have a minimum strength of 37.5% vol, although purists say that good-quality ouzo needs to be minimum 46% vol. It is drunk much as pastis (which is usually 45% vol) is taken in France, *ie* as an aperitif or café drink with water. The tendency or otherwise to turn cloudy when water is added is an indicator of the concentration in the spirit of anise or fennel, and, hence, of quality.

Ouzo is what used to be called raki and has a close cousin called tsipouro. Raki is the name of the pomace left behind after pressing grapes as well as the grappa-like distillate produced from it. It was usually flavoured with aniseed, fennel, mastic and herbs and began to be known as ouzo when consignments of raki bound for Marseille were marked with the Italian phrase '*Uso Massalia*' ('For commercial use, Marseille').

Tsipouro

Tsipouro, like ouzo, is a kind of grappa made from the pomace (raki) left after grape-pressing. It is made all over Greece in small alambics for private use but some specialist distillers are now making limited commercial quantities.

Some leading brands are listed below.

Idoniko • Small-batch tsipouro brand from the distillery on the Domaine Lazaridi wine estate at Adriani Drama. Constantin Lazaridi has a gleaming, impeccable little still room with copper pot stills and rectifiers, and stainless steel pipes and silos. Distillation takes about three hours and the 'heart' of each run amounts to just over half of the total volume of wash.

The spirit comes off the still at about 84% vol and, after reduction to about 40% vol, Macedonian anise is added and the spirit is then redistilled. This final distillate is cut to Idoniko's bottling strength of 46% vol.

Ouzo 12 • Large ouzo brand, possibly the world's top-selling ouzo. It was first produced by the Kaloyannis brothers in 1880 and when put on sale it was the blend in cask number 12 that was agreed upon as the house style — hence the brand name.

In 1988, the business was bought by Metaxa. The brand's high profile in recent years has made it a target for counterfeiters and imitators. The most bare-faced example was a brand called Ouzo 21 with an otherwise identical bottle label.

Other widely distributed brands include Metaxa, Tsantali, Sans Rival, Achaia Clauss, and Boutari.

ζωγραφική   Ι. Νάνος

ΤΣΙΠΟΥΡΟ ΜΕ ΓΛΥΚΑΝΙΣΟ TSIPOURO ANISE

Η απόσταξη και η εμφιάλωση έγινε στο κτήμα μας στην Αδριανή Δράμας από την ΠΟΤΟΠΟΙΪΑ ΚΩΣΤΑ ΛΑΖΑΡΙΔΗ Distilled & Bottled by DISTILLERY CONSTANTIN LAZARIDI ADRIANI DRAMA

e200 ml   46 % vol.

ΕΛΛΗΝΙΚΟ ΠΡΟΪΟΝ PRODUCT OF GREECE L. 3340

Much like pastis, ouzo is a café drink, taken with water and a little sunshine, in streets and marketplaces throughout Greece.

Spain

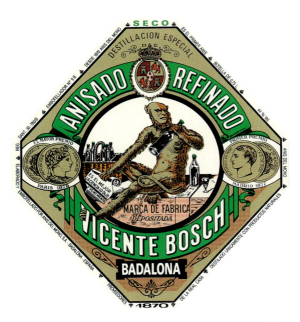

THE ANISE PLANT WIDELY USED IN ANISE-PRODUCTION in Spain is called *matalauva*. Anise spirits, both sweet and dry, are very popular and there are many brands available. There is a tradition, as elsewhere in Europe, of high-strength distillates representing the best quality. Sweet anise was introduced in 1920 when a sugar syrup was added to the water with which anise spirit is reduced to bottling strength.

Two important brands follow.

Alcholera de Chinchón • Brand of particularly high-grade anise. Chinchón is 50 kilometres from Madrid and in 1777 its mayor and wine growers were contracted to supply the Spanish royal household with a 100,000-litre order for anise liqueur. This extraordinary order was filled by the joint production of the countless small stills in the area and this artisanal set-up remained in operation until a new law in 1904 closed them down. A growers' consortium later took their place and, although it became a private company, it kept alive the tradition in the area for producing anise.

This was the Alcoholera de Chinchón, founded as a cooperative in 1911 and privatised in 1945. It produces a particular quality of anise from a variety of aniseed which is difficult to grow and which is har-

vested by hand from a single annual crop. Also, all of the company's products are distilled.

The present distillery is very modern and in front of it there is a monument to the town's anis production heritage consisting of the rectification tower from the first distillery set up in 1912.

The sweet style (Dulce) is 38% vol and has over 260 grams per litre of sugar; the dry (Seco) is 48% vol/96 US proof and unsugared. An outstanding product is the Seco Especial which is 74% vol/148 US proof and required royal consent to bottle at this high strength.

Anis del Mono • Brand founded in Badalona at the tail-end of last century by Catalan entrepreneur Vicente Bosch. All three of the customary anise plants are used to make the company's products and they are distilled into essential oils for blending. It takes 100 grammes of aniseed to yield two grammes of these oils. Other botanicals in essence form are added to the blend.

The company was the first to use an illuminated publicity sign in Spain and the brand's diamond-patterned bottle is based on a perfume bottle Bosch bought in Paris as a gift for his wife. The two styles are Dulce (sweet) which has a red label, Seco (dry) a green.

Bitters

BITTERS ARE CLOSER TO THE ORIGINAL MEDIEVAL APOTHECARIES' POTIONS even than modern liqueurs since the austere flavours are often an acquired taste and the reason for drinking them is at least vaguely medicinal, *ie* to stimulate the metabolism or as a hangover cure. These are therapeutic drinks converted to leisure status.

Bitters (*amaro* in Italian brands) tend to have herbs, roots and other botanicals but less fruit and sugar; the emphasis in the content is different. So different, in fact, that for many the likes of Angostura and Underberg are as much health products as drinks products.

Angostura • Brand of concentrated aromatic bitters. Dr J.G.B. Siegert was an army surgeon who served in the Prussian army and saw action at the Battle of Waterloo. He went to Venezuela and served in a similar capacity in Simon Bolivar's army, which ousted the Spanish from the country. He was made surgeon-general at a military hospital which enabled him to study the medicinal properties of the tropical herbs in his adopted country. From these four years of researches came the formula for a product that was successfully used in the hospital and the doctor's private practice as a stomachic and pick-me-up.

He eventually marketed the mix and, despite encyclopedia entries to the contrary, Siegert's bitters is not named for angostura bark in the formula. He named it after Angostura, the city where he lived and which is now called Ciudad Bolivar; and, in fact, Angostura bitters contains no angostura bark.

Siegert died in 1870 and, with Venezuela becoming very unstable, in 1875 his sons moved house and business to Trinidad — not at all far in geographic terms since it sits just off the coast of Venezuela, but a world away in political equilibrium. Today Angostura bitters is still made there on a rum base by the same family. Its main ingredient is gentian root and, of course, the others — even their number — are secret; 44.7% volume.

The golden petals of the gentian plant, which needs twenty years to mature. While remaining a mystery to scientists, its root provides infusions and distillates for liquoristes.

CAMPARI *Soda* Si

Top: An example of the classic tradition of advertising established by Davide Campari.

Right: Gaspare Campari who founded the company in 1860.

Campari • Italian brand. Gaspare Campari was a restaurateur, owning a succession of café-bars in Turin and Novara. He introduced his bitters drink to patrons of his new café in Milan in 1862 and later in his Camparino restaurant located in the majestic glass-roofed galleria that runs between the Duomo and La Scala. Ernest Hemingway and the Prince of Wales are among the numerous celebrities who have lunched or dined regularly at the restaurant in subsequent decades. Reconstructions of Campari's cafés have been made in the beautiful villa, the Casa Alta, that is now the Campari headquarters. Campari is the world's best-selling bitters with 2.8 million cases a year; 25% vol.

Echt Stonsdorfer • German brand. The company was formed in 1810 in Stonsdorf near the source of the River Elbe in Silesia. Today, the business is run from Hamburg, at the other end of the river. Christian Koerner was an experienced distiller and when he took over a brewery in Stonsdorf he was already studying a number of curative herbal drinks produced informally in the locale. Echt Stonsdorfer was his creation based on what he had learned from those

around him. The formula for the drink is unusual in that it is based on fruit-juice (from wood-blueberries), which comprises about 10% of the mix. There are 43 ingredients in all which yield a full-bodied, bitter-fruit flavour; 32% vol.

Fernet-Branca • Brand name of the Fratelli Branca distillery firm. Fernet-Branca was founded in Milan in 1845 as a commercial enterprise, although the bitters itself was available as a local herborist's preparation from the early years of the century. The product found export sales from the outset and the company logo of an eagle hovering above the earth is said to symbolise the Branca brothers' commercial farsightedness.

There are 30 roots and herbs in the recipe which is secret but does include gentian, rhubarb, camomile and saffron. The mix is made by a combination of hot and cold infusions in alcohol and it ages in 100-hectolitre vats of Slavonian oak for a year. Oak-influence has a particular role to play in Fernet-Branca's final character, so the vat bottoms are renewed periodically to sustain the wood's overall contribution to the product. All the extract is produced from the original recipe at two plants in Milan

and Chiasso, Switzerland, and sent out to licensees who make up the final product in other countries in Europe, as well as in the USA and Argentina. There is also a mint-flavoured 'summertime' version of the brand, Brancamenta. Both are 40% vol.

Gammel Dansk Bitter Dram • Danish brand, the largest-selling spirit in Denmark. The brand was launched in the late 1960s after three years of experiments with different old recipes and up to 100 herbs and spices. Finally a formula of 29 ingredients that gave a fine overall taste with no one dominant flavour was decided upon. Once blended, the mixture spends three months 'marrying'. Gentian-root is an important ingredient for its bitter-sweet taste and rowanberries are also used. Children in the area around Roskilde where Gammel Dansk is made know they can make pocket-money by gathering rowanberries. They take them to the plant and are paid 'cash on delivery'.

Many consumers buy it unashamedly as a hangover cure but there is also the general feeling that it is probably a healthy drink. Only two people know the formula and they are said to be immune to bribery and truth serum. Gammel Dansk is also perceived to be a warming drink, and the company has

Rhubarb (*Rheum palmatum*). One of the thirty roots and herbs in the Fernet Branca recipe.

used shivering naturists in its advertising to make that point; 38% vol.

Jägermeister • German brand. The Jägermeister company was established in 1878 but the drink associated with it was not introduced until 1935. The name means 'master of the hunt' and the brand logo of the deer with the cross between its antlers recalls a vision in the life of St Hubert, the patron saint of hunters.

There are 56 botanicals in the drink, including citrus peel, aniseed, liquorice, poppy seeds, saffron, ginger, juniper berries and ginseng. These macerate in spirit for up to six weeks and then mature for a year in seasoned oak casks before blending. Jägermeister sells 2.6 million cases a year, which

makes it the world's number two brand of bitters; 35% vol.

Punt e Mes • Italian bitter-sweet aperitif. The Carpano company was established in Turin in 1786, producing a range of drinks products and running their own Carpano Bar in the city. One day in 1870 a stockbroker, deep in conversation about business on the Stock Exchange, ordered an aperitif. In those days wines and bitters were mixed on the spot and he absent-mindedly ordered his drink with one-and-a-half 'points' — *punt e mes* in the Piedmontese dialect — of bitters in it, although he was clearly thinking of movement of stocks and shares. His instruction was taken to mean measures and the drink delivered accordingly. The mixture turned out to be delicious and was eventually bottled with Punt e Mes as its brand name.

Ramazzotti • Italian brand. In 1815 Milan herbalist Ausano Ramazzotti made a bitter drink made from 33 herbs and roots macerated in alcohol. It was the time when the café fashion was catching on in Milan and he opened his own café near La Scala opera house where he served his Amaro instead of coffee. It caught on and soon he was employing more than 100 people to manufacture it. The formula

The beautiful northern Italian countryside provides a profusion of herbs and roots for Italian bitters.

includes gentian, orange peel, cinchona bark, angelica, zedoary, masterwort, anise and iris. The strong taste starts sweet, becoming dry and bitter; 30% vol.

Riga Balsam / Melnais Balzams • Latvian bitters that is more or less the national drink. Almost every house in the country keeps some and it serves equally well for social or medicinal drinking.

An 18th-century Riga pharmacist, Abraham Kunze, first produced the latter-day Riga Black Balsam but the origin of the preparation is thought to go much further back in time. In the 1840s it was made by the Wolfschmidt firm whose name lives on in an American brand of vodka. President de Gaulle of France and Queen Elizabeth II of Great Britain are both known to have enjoyed Black Balsam offered to them in the past.

There are 16 ingredients, including a number of natural balsams or resins known to have healing

or soothing qualities. Raspberry, honey, mint, wormwood(!), lime-tree blossom and many other plants and roots are among the exotic components merged with neutral alcohol.

The flavour is rich and rooty, complex and bitter-sweet at the finish. The balsam is sold in a shiny ceramic bottle similar to those in which the druggists of old Riga kept their medicines.

Suze • French bitters distilled from gentian root and drunk as an aperitif. Gentian is grown commercially in the Auvergne and the Jura regions and is a large, originally wild flower with golden petals. It takes 20 years to reach full maturity but its system of germination is still unknown to science. Only the roots are used for medicinal purposes and are dug up — with great difficulty — with a double-pronged tool called a Devil's Fork. Both distillates and infusions are made from the roots and these, together with a number of herbs and other botanicals, are blended to make the final Suze mixture.

The brand first appeared in 1889 and was immediately successful — so much so that there have been over 200 imitation products produced in tall bottles with a ribbon down the side over the past century. And the company have an example of every one of them in its archives. Over the past two decades, Pernod Ricard, who own the brand, have researched means of farming gentian to limit the amount of wild gentian being picked. The taste of Suze is slightly bitter; 16% vol.

Top right: Suze, *'l'amie de l'estomac'*, needs a strong arm to unearth the gentian root with the Devil's fork. Below: Multi-packs for the dedicated user.

Underberg • Bitters designed to aid digestion in the way cognacs and other spirits do in a more general sense. 'After a good meal' it says on the bottle, and the tiny dose-size phials, encased in twists of brown paper, are a familiar sight in restaurants around the world. The elixir is made from unspecified aromatic herbs collected from 43 countries and, once blended, is 'married' for several months in oak barrels before bottling. Part of its effectiveness is claimed to be its capacity to stimulate digestion without hyperacidity.

Hubert Underberg was a busy man one June day in 1846: he founded his company at the town hall in Rheinberg and he also got married. He had formulated his product after some years of research and the business is today run by the fifth generation of the family. Christiane, wife of the present head of the firm, Emil Underberg, was the model and inspiration for the Underberg Girl who figures in the brand's publicity material. The product has been marketed solely in the two-centilitre bottle-size since the 1940s; 44% vol.

Bitters

230

Zwack Unicum • Hungarian brand. Jozsef Zwack was court physician to the Austro-Hungarian emperor who was a compliant consumer of the restorative herbal drink Zwack had created in 1790. This was Unicum and, armed with the recipe, a descendant Zwack, also named Jozsef and only 20 years of age, opened his Budapest liqueur factory in 1840. Perhaps not surprisingly he became official supplier to the Habsburgs' Austro-Hungarian court. Unicum was the core product and it was practically the national drink of Hungary. The company lost its assets — buildings, plant and stocks — in the wake of the Communist take-over of Hungary after the last war and Peter Zwack and his father went into exile in the USA. They still had the formula, however, and during the years of exile, Unicum was produced in Italy.

With the improved political situation, Peter Zwack went back to Hungary in 1990 after 42 years of exile and bought back what was in fact his own family property confiscated in 1948. 'I left at the last and returned at the first possible moment,' he says. The original Zwack Unicum is once again produced in Hungary and available in its shops. The formula comprises 40 botanicals and the final blend is mellowed in oak for six months before being bottled; 42% vol.

The tranquil Danube flows past Hungary's parliament building in contrast to the turbulent history of Zwack Unicum.

Liqueurs

ost liqueurs seem to follow the same script: a secret and very old recipe handed down from the past that is now known to two or three people who never travel on the same plane together. It also helps to have connections with monasticism, romantic historical figures or exotic locations.

The very ingredients of liqueurs should provide the feel of the latter but in the global village of today we unfortunately take it for granted that spices derive from the farthest corners of the planet. Just a century ago, oranges were a rare novelty in Europe, so that when a French distiller called Cointreau introduced a liqueur made with the 'new' orange fruit from the Dutch colony of Curaçao in the Caribbean it was a sensation. 'Curaçao' is now the category name for orange liqueurs and the 'triple sec' production technique still used to make them in the water-white, double-distilled style.

Liqueurs are sweet but the Italian word *liquori* is more general and includes dry spirits and fortifieds. Liqueurs to Americans are cordials. Conventional usage means that liqueurs like cherry brandy, apricot brandy *et al* are misnamed, since they are not real brandies, *ie* unsweetened grape distillates. Fruit brandies, like kirsch (cherry) and slivovic (plum), are correctly named but dry in style.

Liqueurs' antecedents were the apothecaries' potions and medicines of the Middle Ages, and because they tended to taste unpleasant, herb, plant and fruit essences came to be added to mask the off-flavours. The first documented liqueur was the caraway (*Kummel*) preparation distilled in 1575 by Lucas Bols just outside Amsterdam. He used caraway because it was known to be an effective aid to diges-

tion and, since alcohol has anaesthetic properties, Bols may well have created the first effective digestif.

The religious orders throughout Europe did much of the research regarding distillation and the properties of the herbs and berries that grew around their abbeys and monasteries. Benedictine is documented as far back as 1510 at the abbey near Fécamp in northern France and Chartreuse was made for the brothers at Voiron long before it came to be produced for sale in the outside world in 1848.

Liqueurs divide mainly according to their ingredient types, *ie* herb and spice mixes, fruits, nuts, creams and so on. Whatever the flavouring substance, the highest quality is achieved by distillation, either of the fermented materials or spirit in which they have been infused. Many liqueurs are based on cognac, brandy, whisk(e)y, rum and other finished spirits. Maceration of flavourings in neutral spirit works well and is used for many high-volume liqueur brands, but wine-based liqueurs lack flavour impact and vividness.

Crèmes and creams are not the same thing. crème (*de menthe, de noix etc*) indicates a liqueur with a solus flavour while 'cream' liqueur combines alcohol and dairy cream in the style successfully pioneered by Bailey's Irish Cream.

Opposite page: Cherries were originally used to mask an apothecaries' potion with a more pleasant flavour.

Left: Nuts also offer a profusion of flavourings for the liqueur.

Amaretto Di Saronno • Italian almond and apricot liqueur. Amaretto is a generic term but the Saronno brand produced in the town by the I.L.L.V.A. firm is a registered trademark and was the original product of this type. The company has sought to emphasise this by now referring to the liqueur as Disaronno Amaretto.

The drink is said to have been first made up by the model for the Madonna depicted in the *Adoration of the Magi* fresco in the Santa Maria delle Grazie sanctuary in Saronno. It was painted by a pupil of da Vinci, Bernardino Luini, in 1525 and when the widow who ran the inn at which Luini was lodging modelled for him she showed her appreciation of the honour by preparing the liqueur for him from the contents of her garden. The bitter almond and apricot flavours dovetail, since both are from the same fruit genus, Prunus. (Bitter almonds are the kernels of the *Prunus amygdalus amara*, from which *amaretto* — 'slightly bitter' — comes.) Commercial production of the recipe was begun in the 18th century by the Reina family in their apothecary shop in the main piazza of Saronno. There are 17 ingredients in all. Di Saronno sells 1.8 million cases a year; 28% vol.

Below: *Angelica baccifera* with compound leaves and clusters of small white/greenish flowers provides aromatic flavourings.

Aurum • Italian orange liqueur. In contrast to the high-powered marketing culture that governs commercial brands today, Aurum has the distinction of having had its brand name chosen by a famous poet — Gabriele d'Annunzio. Distiller Amedeo Pomilio invited d'Annunzio to name his new orange liqueur and after first thinking of *aurantium*, Latin for orange (*ie* 'golden fruit'), the word for gold itself, 'aurum', was decided upon. The original production plant, in a pine wood near Pescara, was modelled on a Roman amphitheatre. The liqueur is distilled from a particular type of orange from the Abruzzi and then combined with 10-year-old brandy. The blend of the two spirits is further matured in oak barrels. The bottle is based on a wine flask excavated at Pompei; 40% vol.

Baileys Irish Cream • The original Irish cream (as opposed to crème - — see introduction) liqueur. Made from Irish whiskey and dairy cream, the brand was introduced in the 1970s and was an immediate success. Its rise was meteoric and it quickly claimed a quarter of the world liqueurs market share. Much technical research went into the formulation to avoid the cream curdling when it came in contact with the alcohol, and also to give the product an acceptable shelf life. The problems were overcome and there are now many imitators.

Bénédictine D.O.M. • French herb liqueur based on an elixir produced in 1510 by a monk at the Benedictine Abbey of Fécamp on the coast of Normandy. The recipe of Don Bernardo Vincelli was said to have restored listless brothers and countered

is taken by miners for rheumatism and expectant mothers as a tonic. The initials on the label stand for *Deo Optimo Maximo* — 'To God, most good, most great'. Heathery, zesty flavour; 40% vol. The distillery also produces B&B, which is a brandy-and-Bénédictine pre-mix. It is less sweet due to the brandy content.

Bols • One of Holland's most distinguished liqueur and spirits houses, and surely the world's oldest. Lucas Bols founded his business in 1575 outside Amsterdam, because the fire-conscious town councillors would not sanction his still inside the town walls. At the time, Dutch merchants travelled far and wide and brought back wonderful spices and flavouring plants to Amsterdam. These became the basis of the Dutch liqueur industry with cinnamon, citrus fruits, cloves, vanilla, peels, rose oil, coffee and numerous others appearing in the marketplace in Amsterdam.

Bols' range today comprises 34 liqueurs, including 'standards' like cherry and apricot 'brandies', advocaat and *crème de bananes*, and high-profile specialities like Blue Curaçao, Pisang Ambon and Teardrop crème de menthe. Red Orange, Coconut and Kiwi are recent innovations and Bols Premier, introduced in the early 1990s, is the company's flagship premium liqueur. It is made from botanicals, cognac and old-style genever.

Top left: Bénédictine originated as an exclusivity for the religious brotherhood before circulating on elegant social tables.

epidemics of the time but the abbey was razed during the French Revolution and the order dispersed. Documents and papers from the abbey had been lodged with an official and in 1863 a descendant, Alexandre Le Grand, unearthed the recipe from their midst during a rummage. He re-created the elixir, named it and commissioned the design and construction of the riotously neo-Gothic, neo-Renaissance distillery-cum-museum in place today.

The liqueur is made from 27 herbs and spices, among them nutmeg, hyssop, angelica, thyme, cardamom, cinnamon, coriander and… tea. These are assembled into four different combinations which are macerated in spirit, redistilled in copper pot stills and matured separately in oak barrels for three months. The final liqueur is made by assembling a blend of these four distillates in the correct proportions and putting it back into casks to marry for a further eight months. There are 30,000 barrels of mellowing Bénédictine couched in the distillery cellars at any given time.

Interestingly, the therapeutic function of Don Bernardo's elixir continues. In the Far East, Bénédictine

Cointreau • French orange liqueur. Cointreau is a triple-sec Curaçao (see introduction above) that sells more than a million cases a year worldwide. In the 1850s, Edouard Cointreau, the son of a liqueur producer in Angers in France, stopped off at the Dutch island colony of Curaçao in the Caribbean during a sales trip. He came across a native bitter orange that grew there and had quantities of its peel dried and sent to Angers. After tests and tryouts with sweet oranges and other ingredients, the liqueur was successfully introduced in France and, in the 1870s, farther afield. Cointreau marketed it simply as the triple-sec liqueur that it was, but the style was so widely copied by other firms that eventually the company's own name was used as the brand-name.

Top & Bottom: The snow-covered monastery of La Grande Chartreuse in the French Alps where Chartreuse is still made in the calm of the cloisters by Carthusian monks.

Chartreuse • French herb liqueur made by Carthusian monks at Voiron, near Grenoble, in the French Alps. The recipe was said to have been given to the fathers in 1605 by an officer in the army of Henri IV, but it was not marketed as a commercial product until 1848. It caught on very quickly and a new distillery was built to cope with the demand. During the Carthusians' exile from France between 1903 and 1931, the liqueurs (for there are two styles) were produced in Tarragona in Spain.

The shopping list is lengthy, a total of 130 ingredients' being involved. Green Chartreuse is the original recipe and strong at 55% vol; yellow Chartreuse is a variation and 40-43% vol. Some say the two types are meant to be mixed and drunk as a blend. The hard-to-find V.E.P. version is aged longer — a dozen years — in cask and the link with medicinal potions continues with the Elixir Végétal, a devastatingly effective 80% vol (160 US proof) cold-cure that is classified as a pharmaceutical product.

Cocoribe • American coconut and rum liqueur. The connection between the two is thought to have been established by traditional marriage ceremonial in the Caribbean in which a bridegroom presented a rum-filled coconut to his bride to signify that he would provide for her.

Cuarenta Y Tres • Spanish herb liqueur also known as Licor 43. *Cuarenta y tres* means 43 in Spanish and this is the number of ingredients that make up the liqueur's formula.

236

Drambuie • Scottish herbs and whisky liqueur. Bonnie Prince Charlie, fleetingly a claimant to the British throne in the 1740s, is said to have given the recipe to one Mackinnon of Strathaird on Skye in return for having helped him escape government soldiers in the wake of the Battle of Culloden. It must have seemed a trite, if not bizarre, bestowal, when all over the Highlands houses were being torched and people shot for harbouring him, but it came good, as they say, in 1906 when descendants began producing the liqueur commercially. From the early days of making a mere 12 bottles a fortnight, the MacKinnons saw Drambuie eventually go to the Houses of Parliament, Buckingham Palace and to expatriate Scots and regiments all over the world. Today it is served on the QE2, Concorde and the Orient Express.

Honey and herbs go into the making of a secret syrup which is taken in measured quantities from padlocked containers and added to a malt and grain whisky blend. The name is a phonetic version of *an dram buidheach*, 'the drink that satisfies'.

Galliano • Italian herb liqueur that sells in the distinctive slim bottle that is always the tallest on any shelf. The liqueur was created in 1896 by Armando Vaccari in tribute to Giuseppe Galliano, the heroic Italian soldier who, in the same year, had defended a fort for 44 days during the Italian invasion of Abyssinia. The fort of Enda Jesus is depicted on the bottle's label. Instant export beginnings were created for Vaccari, since Livorno in Tuscany, where Galliano was first made, was the embarkation port for emigrants to the USA and nearly everyone took a bottle away as a souvenir of *la patria*.

The liqueur is made near Milan from 40 herbs and other botanicals, the most important of which are vanilla and anise. Seven infusions, seven distillations, two blending stages and six months' 'marrying' are involved in the production process. The brand has been high profile for the past two decades due to the Harvey Wallbanger cocktail. Harvey was a Californian surfer who drank too much after losing an important contest. His favourite drink was a Screwdriver with added Galliano, so that when he left the bar bouncing off walls the mixture was dubbed 'Harvey's Wallbanger'; 35% vol.

Glayva • Scottish herbs and whisky liqueur. The name is a phonetic rendering of the Gaelic *Gle mhath!* ('very good'), said to be the spontaneous comment of one of the tasters when different formulations were being tried in the creation of the brand. It was introduced in 1947.

Grand Marnier • French orange liqueur. Although it is technically a Curaçao (see introduction above), it is distinctive in its having a cognac spirit base instead of less characterful grape distillate or neutral spirit. The ageing of the cognac takes place at the company's beautiful Château de Bourg in the Charente region but the liqueur is produced at Neauphle-le-Château.

The Lapostolle family were liqueur producers in the town in the early 19th century. They bought into a cognac distillery in the 1870s and experimented with blends of cognac spirit and bitter oranges from Haiti, finally introducing Grand Marnier liqueur in 1880. Today, a bottle is sold every two seconds somewhere in the world — that means 1.3 million cases a year. At the warehouses north of Paris, railway wagons run right into the loading bays.

The orange peel is macerated in spirit and then redistillation takes place to lock in the aromas. This distillate is in turn blended with cognac and sugar syrup to make the final liqueur. After a 'marrying' period and filtration, it is bottled.

The standard product is Cordon Rouge (40% vol) and the Cuvée du Centenaire, which celebrates the 1927 centenary of the company, is made with 10-year-old cognac (40% vol). Other liqueurs from the company are Cherry Marnier (24% vol), from Dalmatian cherries and brandy (not cognac), and Grande Passion (24% vol) from passion fruit and armagnac.

Heering • Danish cherry liqueur that figured in the creation of the original Singapore Sling cocktail in 1915 at the Raffles Hotel in Singapore. What used to be called Cherry Heering was first made in 1818 in Denmark when Peter Heering opened a grocer's shop in Copenhagen. He acquired a recipe for a cherry cordial which he decided to make commercially. The Stevns cherries used to make the liqueur are a native Danish type which grow in the south of the country and Heering located his distillery there.

The cherries are crushed and, together with some botanicals, are macerated in spirit in large wooden vats for several months. Once the liqueur is blended, it ages for a full three years in oak. Part of the blending process involves mixing old and new production, much as sherries are combined in a solera system. The company left the Heering family after five generations of ownership when it was sold to Danish Distillers in 1990; 25% vol.

Irish Velvet • Irish coffee and whiskey liqueur. The whiskey content is Jameson's (*qv*) and although the liqueur can stand on its own it is also intended as a mix for making Irish coffee.

Izarra • Basque liqueur made from Pyrenean flowers and plants and armagnac. There is an air of mystery to this fine liqueur from the mountains at the core of the Basque homeland which straddles the border between France and Spain but which, politically, does not exist. Izarra means 'star' in the Basque language, Euskara (which is remarkable in that it is related to no other linguistic group).

The liqueur is made in Bayonne, the Basque town in south-west France that gave its name to the bayonet. Izarra has been made since the 1830s.

Right: Stevns cherries, each one perfectly ripe, mature slowly in Denmark where the cold climate creates wonderful aromatic qualities.

Krupnik • Polish honey liqueur. The recipe is from south-east Poland where honey liqueurs are long-established traditional drinks. Natural honey from wild bees in forest areas is harvested and spices are added to give a rich, honeyed flavour and spicy edge. Krupnik is often drunk hot, particularly by hunters in winter, and at normal temperature goes well with coffee or cake; 40% vol.

De **K**uyper • Dutch liqueurs house established in 1695. The combined sales of De Kuyper liqueurs made under a permanent licensing agreement with Jim Beam Brands in the USA amount to almost four million cases a year and make it the world's largest-selling liqueur brand. De Kuyper produces the usual core range as well as specialities like crème de cacao, white triple-sec, blackberry brandy, cherry whisky, curaçaos, and their single brands, Peachtree and low-strength Kwai Feh, made from lychees.

Kahlúa • Coffee liqueur. Kahlúa is known as a Mexican product that features the country's coffee, but the little figure on the brand's original label wore not a sombrero and poncho, as he does today, but a turban. Was the brand originally Turkish or Moroccan? Both countries produce coffee and that archway in the picture looks pretty Moorish.

Whatever the detailed pedigree, Kahlúa was first imported to the USA on the repeal of Prohibition, became American-owned and changed hands several times before being promoted as a mixer base in the 1950s. The Kahlúa and milk cocktail, the Sombrero, first concocted in Boston, Massachusetts, made it a national brand and it is now drunk with milk in every country to which it is exported.

It is richly flavoured and full-bodied in style and is the world's second-top-selling single brand of liqueur. Kahlúa is made from cane spirit, Mexican coffee and vanilla. The liqueur is made in Mexico and elsewhere under licence.

Mandarine Napoléon • Belgian tangerine and cognac liqueur. The brand was introduced in 1892 and said to have been based on a drink given by Napoléon to Madame Mars, the actress, in an attempt to seduce her. Fresh tangerine peels are steeped in spirit, redistilled and matured for a time. To make the final liqueur, it is blended with Napoléon-quality cognac, cold-filtered and reduced to 38% vol. Millenium, a different blend formulated to celebrate the millenium of the city of Brussels, is available in a handmade decanter.

Pimm's • British fruit cup. Strictly speaking Pimm's is not a liqueur but it is made with them, together with fruit extracts, on a gin base. Pimm's is a quintessentially English — as opposed to British — drink that comes into its own in leafy gardens in summertime. Wimbledon, Henley Regatta, Royal Ascot,

Oxbridge May Balls — Pimm's is part of them all. It is made for diluting and is an excellent party drink with a bitter-sweet taste. The present product, while it was the original Pimm's, used to be one of a range of six cups whose recipe varied according to the spirit base. The others have been out of production for some time now but some vodka cup is being made once again.

James Pimm served his fruit cups in tankards in his City of London oyster bar in the early 19th century. The product was not bottled until after Pimm's restaurant — and the secret formula — changed hands in 1880. Ingredients for Pimm's have always been bought in varying quantities by the company since the time when someone tried to reconstruct the formula by studying the accounts department's receipts for purchases of raw materials.

Polmos Goldwasser • Polish gold-flake liqueur. Poland was the original producer of *goldwasser* — 'goldwater' (*złota woda* in Polish on the label) — going back to 1598 when it was produced in Danzig, present-day Gdansk. It originally had a medical function, gold having then been regarded as a powerful cure-all. Tiny flakes of real gold are added to the spirit, together with more than a dozen botanicals, including caraway and anise. It is a sweet and pleasantly full-bodied liqueur and this recipe is probably genuinely over 400 years old; 40% vol.

Royal Mint Chocolate • French liqueur from specialist blender and producer Peter Hallgarten. The research took two years and, as Hallgarten himself put it, it was like composing a piece of music.

He had as his goal the after-dinner mint flavour, just as a composer has a musical effect in his mind; however, Hallgarten's 'arrangement' was made up of ingredients and not parts for different musical instruments. Just as with a melody, the sequence of Hallgarten's mixing his ingredients turned out to be very important. Finally, he got what he was looking for and the brand was launched in the 1960s. There is now a whole family of other flavours, referred to by the company as its 'Royal Family'.

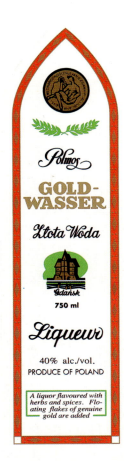

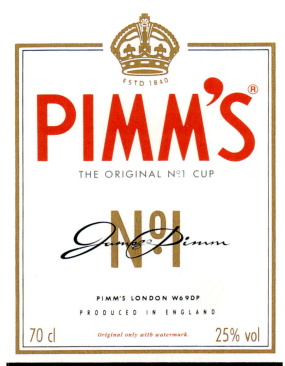

CONSTANTINOPLE – 1880	MELBOURNE – 1909
PEKING – 1889	NEW YORK – 1911
KUALA LUMPUR – 1890	RIO DE JANEIRO – 1913
RANGOON – 1896	CHICAGO – 1920
PARIS – 1897	NEW ORLEANS – 1925
KHARTOUM – 1898	ALGIERS – 1943
ST. PETERSBURG – 1905	CAPETOWN – 1951

240

up its taste and which quickly became successful. He moved to Memphis in 1889, opened a bar on Beale Street and later began bottling his drink in St Louis, at the time the gateway to the West. The drink has a rich and colourful heritage and makes the most of it with its slogan 'the grand old drink of the South'.

The gracious river-bank house pictured on the label is the old Woodland sugar plantation that lay close to where the Missisippi flows into the Gulf of Mexico. The illustration is taken from a contemporary lithograph. Southern Comfort is the fourth-best-selling liqueur in the world (over two million cases a year). It is made under licence in different countries.

$\mathcal{S}$abra • Israeli chocolate orange liqueur, originally made in the 1960s from the sabra cactus that grows in Israel and around the south and eastern Mediterranean. The moving force behind it was Charles Bronfman, co-chairman in the 1960s of the giant Canadian distilling firm, Seagram, after he had visited Israel.

Native-born Israelis are known as sabras because they are said to be like the plant — prickly on the outside but sweet on the inside. The bottle is based on a 2,000-year-old Phoenician wine jug that may be seen in the Israeli Museum. The main style is made with Jaffa oranges and chocolate and is 26% vol. Distillation is carried out at Rehovot amidst the citrus groves where the oranges are grown. There is also a coffee version of 30% vol.

$\mathcal{S}$outhern Comfort • American liqueur with a dominant peach flavour, often assumed to be, or at least made with, bourbon whiskey. While it will have had a local whiskey base to begin with, it is produced today with neutral spirit and a surprisingly complex formula of 100 ingredients. The final liqueur matures for eight months prior to bottling. Southern Comfort's origins lie in the improvements that a young 1860s New Orleans barman called Heron tried to make to the awful whiskey from the barrel that he dispensed. He created a recipe which spruced

The early development of Southern Comfort was closely associated with the great riverboat trade.

Gigantic branding balances any architectural anonymity at the Tia Maria headquarters.

Stag's Breath • Scottish honey and whisky liqueur. Stag's Breath was the name of one of the whiskies 'liberated' by the islanders from the stricken ship in *Whisky Galore*, Sir Compton Mackenzie's rewriting of the *SS Politician* shipwreck story in World War II. The Meikle company in the Highland town of Newtonmore have taken the name for their liqueur made from blended malt whiskies and fermented honeycomb. The result is a light, musky flavour with a dryish finish; 19.8% vol.

Strega • Italian herb liqueur. The liqueur was introduced by the Alberti family in Benevento, a Papal enclave in southern Italy, in 1860, the very year that the town was taken over by Garibaldi and his army. As wine exporters, they saw their business shrink in later years due to a customs war between France and Italy, so they began to promote their little liqueur and by the turn of the century it had become the largest brand of its kind in the world. Made from more than 70 botanicals, the distillates are produced in pot stills and aged in wood after blending. A Benevento folk tale tells of maidens who dress up as witches and mix a magic drink, *Strega* is Italian for 'witch'; 40% vol.

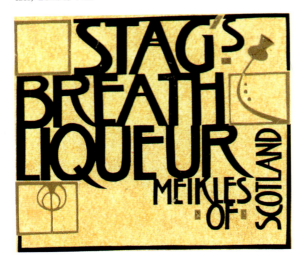

Tia Maria • Coffee liqueur originally from Jamaica. The recipe is said to have belonged to a servant woman (the eponymous Aunt Mary) who left Jamaica just before the British took over the island in 1655. The famous Blue Mountain coffee of Jamaica forms the basis of the formula but there is a lacing of chocolate in the final flavour. The style is lightish and less unctuous than some competing brands.

Vana Talinn • Estonian citrus and rum liqueur. Essential oils of orange and lemon are combined with cinnamon and vanilla infusions in neutral spirit flavoured with rum essence. The flavour is soft and balanced, despite 45% vol alcohol. The liqueur was created in 1960 and is exported to Scandinavia and to Russia.

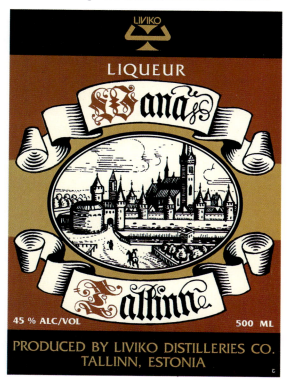

Verpoorten • German advocaat. Verpoorten was founded in 1876, and today lays claim to being the best-selling advocaat in the world. Originally Dutch, the family now has production plants in Holland, Italy, Switzerland and Austria, as well as in Germany. Verpoorten uses 1.3 million fresh eggs every day to make up to 130,000 bottles of advocaat; 20% vol.

Warnink's • Dutch advocaat. Made from egg yolks, sugar and spirit, advocaat (also known as eggnog or eggflip), derives from an alcoholic drink Dutch colonists in South America made from the yellowish pulp of the *abacate* fruit. Back in Holland egg yolks took the place of the *abacate* flesh and the name, having evolved into *avocado* among Portuguese colonists in Brazil, became advocaat in Dutch.

Warnink's was founded in 1616 in Amsterdam and today, as the largest producer of advocaat in the Netherlands, uses upwards of 60 million eggs a year. These are supplied by 300,000 freelance 'employees' on specially contracted chicken farms. In addition to liqueur advocaat, which is drunk from a glass, there is another thick type which is eaten with a spoon. Strictly speaking, the name 'advocaat' should be restricted to traditionally made Dutch products but there are many non-Dutch advocaats on the market.

The company has an Egg-breaking Department with egg-breaking machines which separate 18,000 yolks and whites an hour. There are four production lines, so up to 72,000 yolks an hour go on to be mixed with sugar, brandy and vanilla before being stored in tanks for a period of maturation.

Fact File

NB – **Bold** references indicate separate entries which may also be consulted.

ABV • Alcohol by volume. See **Alcoholic strength.**

Acrospire • The tiny first growth of the new shoot that protrudes from each grain of barley when germination gets under way and starch in the grain turns to sugar.

Ageing • The process of improvement or maturation undergone by some spirits, usually in oak barrels, during which their fieriness recedes and aromas and flavours improve. Most worthwhile ageing takes a number of years and while it is under way the porosity of the cask mellows the distillate by allowing the access of air and moisture, and wood substances like lignin, vanillin and tannin are endowed in it. Where ageing is an intrinsic part of the characteristics of a product, there are usually laws governing the way it is carried out. Where an age is given on the label of, for example, whiskey, brandy, rum *etc*, it must relate to the youngest spirit in the bottle, if it is a blend, and the entire contents, if it is unblended.

Aguardente • Portuguese-language term for spirit ('burning water') with variation in detailed meaning depending on where it is used. In Portugal, it usually indicates a grape brandy; in Brazil the meaning is more general, for instance *aguardente de cana de azúcar* — sugar-cane spirit — *cachaça.*

Aguardiente (de orujo) • The Spanish word *aguardiente* (*cf* **aguardente**, above) on its own means grape brandy or wine distillate; used with *orujo* it means pomace brandy or any grappa-like spirit.

Alambic armagnaçais • Type of continuous still traditionally used in the production of armagnac. The still was invented and developed in the Armagnac region around 1850 by a Monsieur Verdier and it produced a spirit that was fuller bodied, grapier and lower in distillation strength (55% vol compared with 70% vol) than cognac. The still was made compulsory in 1936 and continues to be used for production of the best

Wood ageing makes an intrinsic contribution to many spirits.

armagnacs. Cognac stills (*qv*) are permitted, nonetheless, but the spirit is used for blending in younger, high-turnover armagnacs.

Alambic charentais/cognaçais • Pot still used in the Charente region of south-west France in the production of cognac. Like all pot stills (*qv*), the cognac still involves single-batch production, *ie* it has to be loaded with wine, boiled off and then reloaded for the next distillation run. The alambic charentais was designed in the Middle Ages by the Dutch so that the Charentais wine growers could distil wines into spirits in advance of trading trips from Holland to La Rochelle. See **Pot still**.

Alcoholic strength • The proportion of alcohol to water in a spirit, usually expressed internationally as a percentage of its volume and indicated 'vol' or 'abv', alcohol by volume, *eg* 40% vol, or 40% abv. In making comparisons of strength, it is important not to confuse volume with 'proof' which is also expressed in percentage terms but according to a different scale. (In less scientific times 'proof' of a spirit's strength was shown by its readiness to burn when mixed with a set quantity of gunpowder.) Both the UK and the USA developed their own proof systems which were unaligned with each other but at least the latter's is based on the volume of alcohol and equal to its double; hence 40% vol = 80% US proof, but 70% UK proof. With such a simple calculation the only potential penalty, the US proof system is still widely used within that country, but fortunately the British scale has been dropped completely. Under it a 100% proof spirit actually contained only 57.1% of alcohol by volume; such an abstruse system deserved to disappear.

Alquitara • Term used in Spain to describe both a pot still and the spirit produced in it.

Bagaceira • Portuguese pomace brandy.

Blended whisky • In Scotland, a combination of malt and grain whiskies. Most Scotches, such as Famous Grouse, Johnnie Walker, Cutty Sark *et al*, are blends. In the USA, blended whiskey is a combination of whiskey and neutral spirit.

Attending to an alambic armagnaçais, a special type of continuous still.

Boil pot • A bulge in the neck of a pot still which causes reflux (flowing or falling back) of heavier vapours in distillation and which helps to yield finer distillate.

Boisé • Essences of oak which are added to brandies to enhance their tannin levels and oaky aromas, and often to give an impression of maturity. The term is French but the practice of adding boisé to grape distillates, including cognacs, is regarded as a valid tradition in most brandy-making countries as well as in France. Use of boisé is, however, open to abuse and may be added to confuse consumers into believing that a brandy is older than it really is. Some years ago US import regulators wanted boisé to be listed on cognac labels as an additive and it was only after several appeals by the cognac industry that the idea was dropped. Oak chips added to maturation casks and in-bottle oak novelty cut-outs serve the same ends in less coy ways.

Bonne chauffe • The second and (usually) final distillation in a pot still to make cognac (and other *eau de vie*) spirit. Brandy was not always double-distilled and when the Chevalier de la Croix Maron had the idea in 1538 of distilling cognac spirit for a second time he called the second boil-up the *bonne chauffe* (literally, the 'good heating'). See **Brouillis**.

Bothy • Simple shelter or hut within which a

(usually illicit) still was operated in Scotland. They tended to disappear with the growth of licensed distilleries from the 1820s onwards.

Bouilleur • French term for a distiller. In France a *bouilleur de profession* is a professional distiller. A *bouilleur de cru* is a small farmer or grower who distils his own wines and sells on to a larger operator.

Bourbon cask • A barrel made from American oak first used to mature bourbon whiskey in the USA and then re-used elsewhere (particularly in Scotland and Ireland) to mature other types of whiskey. By law, barrels may be used only once for maturing bourbon whiskey because the vivid influences of new oak are an intrinsic part of the whiskey's character. Other whiskey distillers value the subtler influences of used oak and buy the ex-bourbon barrels for maturing their own whiskeys. These are often passed through several different types of cask, which have been used once, twice or even three times previously, for specific periods in order to achieve fine detail in their ageing. Ex-bourbon casks give clean, natural oaky aromas and flavours, important attributes when it comes to maturing quiet, complex whiskeys. See **Sherry cask**.

Brandewijn • Dutch term for spirit ('burnt wine') and probably the origin of the modern word

brandy (although the Italians point out that *branda* in Old Piedmontese meant aqua vitae).

Brouillis • French term used to indicate the first of the two distillations normally carried out in the production of cognac and any other French pot-still brandy. See **Bonne chauffe**.

Calandre • Type of steam-heated chambered, or *bain-marie*, pot still used in France to produce some marcs and fines. A similar apparatus is used in Italy (called a *bagna-maria*) to produce artisanal grappas.

Cask-strength • The alcoholic strength at which a spirit comes off a still and is put into cask to begin its maturation. Some spirits are bottled and sold at cask-strength but most are reduced with demineralised (distilled) water or weak solutions of the spirit itself to a bottling strength of around 40% vol.

Chai • In France, a ground-level storage building (as opposed to a *cave* which is underground) within which wines or spirits are aged. It is the equivalent of a maturation warehouse in Scotland and the USA, a bodega in Spain and so on.

Chapiteau • The upper part of a pot still through which the vapour passes during distillation to condense. (France).

Chaudière • The lower kettle-like reservoir of a pot still where the wine boils during the process of distillation. (France).

Chauffe-vin • The bulbous copper container situated alongside the kettle in a pot still unit in France. The wine for successive distillation runs to come is stored here and pre-heated by the hot pipe leading from the still through which the spirit vapours pass on their way to condensation. (French, 'wine-heater').

Chiu yeh ching • Popular Chinese summer drink made from **kao liang** sorghum spirit blended with herbs, spices and bamboo leaves. The botanicals are pulverised, mixed and bagged before going on

The type of cask used and the length of time the brandy is left there contribute inimitable differences.

to macerate in the spirit. The bags are squeezed intermittently to extract the flavours and caramelised sugar and syrup are added. The mixture goes through decanting, blending and a marrying period before being filtered and bottled. The final spirit is an attractive transparent green colour and has a tangy, sweetish and refreshing flavour. 45% vol.

Coffey • See **Stills**

Col de cygne • French for 'swan's neck', to describe the curved pipe at the top of a pot still in France which leads the alcoholic vapours boiled off during distillation through the *chauffe-vin* to the condensing worm. See **Serpentin**.

Condenser • Apparatus which transforms the vapours coming off a still into alcoholic spirit. Traditionally vapours were led through a spiral-shaped copper pipe — a worm or, in France, a *serpentin* — immersed in cold water to bring about condensation. Modern condensers use more sophisticated heat-exchange principles.

Congeners • The flavouring elements in a spirit carried over in the process of distillation from the fermented base. The higher the distillation strength of a spirit, the fewer congeners there are, such as in vodka.

Dah chiu • High-strength sweet spirit produced in Szechuan and Kweichow from sorghum and wheat. The two cereals go through three combined non-liquid fermentations, and three distillations, before being mixed with **kao liang** (sorghum) spirit. The combined spirits are matured and the final dah chiu distillate is bottled at 66% vol.

Dechar-rechar • A process of cask-renewal whereby the inner surface of a cask, that no longer imparts aroma or flavour through prolonged exposure to maturing spirit, has the spent top layer of charred wood shaved down to clean wood and is then re-charred in the normal manner of coopering oak. This 'decharring and recharring' gives a new lease of life to barrels which are expensive — £300-plus — to replace if new wood is needed.

The long tradition of monastic distilling continues to thrive.

Distillation • The process of boiling an alcoholic liquid, capturing the vapour given off and condensing them into a new liquid which will have higher alcoholic strength. Wine with an alcoholic strength of 8% vol increases to around 30% vol after one distillation in a pot still, and to around 70% after a second.

In a pot-still distillation the first and final parts of the run — the **heads** and **tails** — are held aside for reasons of quality and purity, and only the **heart**, or middle portion, of the run is collected as good spirit. Pot-still distillation starts at high strength and drops progressively throughout the boiling to almost water if left long enough, and these final 'off-the-still' or **cask-strength** figures are an averaging-out of the accrued quantity of **heart** spirit which is actually collected for maturation. Strengths depend on the efficiency of the still and modern continuous stills can produce alcoholic spirit of 96% purity. The higher the strength of a spirit, the less aroma and flavour it has.

Dram • In Scotland a glass of whisky. Historically in the UK, a measure of whisky in a bar has always been greater in Scotland than in England — a quarter of a gill as against a fifth or even a sixth of a gill under the old imperial system. That differentiation officially disappears with the new metric measurements now in place throughout the UK. Bar owners must henceforth opt for either 25ml or 35ml as a standard house measure — using both is not allowed — for whisky and all other spirits.

Feints • See **Tails**.

Fillings • Nothing to do with teeth, these are newly distilled spirits from individual distilleries which are available on the market for sale to any company. Famous Scotch brands have up to 40 different whiskies in their blends and these are mostly bought at this earliest of stages so that they may be matured according to specific blending requirements and also because this is when they cost least.

Fine • A *fine* is a general term to indicate a good-quality brandy in France; also grape brandy produced under modest regulatory requirements in France *eg* Fine de Bordeaux *etc.* Fine Champagne is a blend of Grande and Petite Champagne cognac (*qv*).

Floor maltings • See **Malting**.

Foreshots • See **Heads**.

Grape brandy • Brandy distilled from grape juice which has been fermented into wine (as opposed to such as **grappa** which is made from **pomace** and/or **lees**). Brandy de Jerez, cognac and armagnac are amongst the best-known grape brandies.

Making the traditional jar that holds Corenwyn.

Grappa • Brandy distilled from the **pomace**, or debris, left over from grape-pressing and/or wine making (as opposed to **grape brandy** made from grape juice fermented into wine). Historically, grappa was exclusively produced in Italy but worldwide interest in the spirit has seen production emerge in other locations, notably California, in the USA.

Grist • In whisky making, the coarse flour ground from the malted barley which is mashed with hot water in order to extract the sugars.

Heads • The first part of a distillation run in a pot still. When the first vapours condense and come over from the still they contain unpleasant and even poisonous by-products so these heads, *ie* from the head, or beginning, of the distillation, are held aside from the main body, or middle cut or **heart**, of wholesome spirit. (The condensate at the end of a run — the **tails** — are also held aside.) Heads are also known as foreshots and, in France, *têtes*.

Heart • The wholesome, by-product-free middle portion of the distillation run from a pot still that is collected for a second distillation or goes into cask to begin maturation. Also called the middle cut, this fraction of the spirit that runs off the still is a matter of selection for the master distiller; it must not begin before he judges, by sight and alcoholic strength, that the good spirit is running through, at which moment he switches the flow into a spirit-receiving container. The flow is subsequently turned away from spirit-receiving when it reaches a specific minimum strength. Both the first and third fractions are added to ensuing distillation runs in order to extract all wholesome distillate. The spirit flow is examined at a **spirit safe** — essentially a control box made of glass and (traditionally brass) metal — through which the feed pipes from the still lead.

Holandas • The principal flavour-rich type of spirit used in the production of Brandy de Jerez. Its name derives from the fact that it was originally produced for visiting Dutch traders — Hollanders — in the Middle Ages.

Infusion • The steeping of aromatising or flavouring materials in alcohol in order to flavour the spirit or to create flavour essences or extracts.

Inventory • A term used to describe the range of different whiskies, ages and styles of maturation (sherrywood, bourbon wood, new wood, seasoned wood *etc*) in a company's warehouses and at its disposal for the maintenance of established blends and, perhaps, the creation of new products.

Kao liang • Strong spirit made in northern China from sorghum. It is matured for a short time and goes through a blending process before bottling. It is also the base-distillate for a number of other flavoured drinks produced in different parts of China. 50% vol.

Kiln • In malt whisk(e)y making, a drying oven for barley that has reached its optimum stage of germination on the way to becoming malt; the heat of the kiln halts the germination. Traditionally the heat source was peat which in Scotland permeated the malt and made the subsequent whisk(e)y smoky in character; in Ireland, although peat was also used as a fuel, the kiln was sealed off from the peat smoke and non-smoky spirit was the result.

Lees • The residue of solids, grapeskins, yeasts *etc* left in the wake of fermentation of a wine. They are often used in the making of **pomace** brandy.

Limousin • A famous forest near Limoges, in France (one of two, the other is **Tronçais**) which yield the oak principally used for the casks in which cognac and many great wines are matured.

Lomond stills • See **Stills**

Low wines • In whisk(e)y production, the first distillate from a pot still. The weak ale called wash goes into the wash still and, once distilled, becomes low wine. This normally goes on to a second distillation in the spirit still to make the final distillate.

Make • The 'make' is the type or 'house style' of whiskey produced at a given distillery.

Compacted lees: the residue left after wine making has been completed.

Malt • Barley whose starch content has been converted to sugar by the onset of germination. The malt is dried, ground into **grist** and mashed with hot water to extract the sugar. See **Mashing**.

Malting • In whisk(e)y making, the conversion of the starches in barley to sugars. Traditionally pre-soaked barley was laid out on an indoor area called a floor maltings where germination — the process that brings about the conversion — began. Temperature was controlled by turning the barley regularly by hand with a flat wooden shovel called a shiel. When the tiny new shoot, the **acrospire**, reached a certain length, the sugars were fully converted and the malt was taken to the **kiln** for drying. The peat fires that dried the malt permeated it with a smokiness that carried right through all the production stages and into the final spirit.

This traditional routine is still carried out at a few distilleries today but most malting is done centrally in large drum machines and a greater or lesser degree of **peat reek** added to order.

Mao tai • Famous strong, sweet, spicy spirit from the Kweichow district of mainland China. Spices are macerated in **kao liang** sorghum spirit, and sugar and syrup are added at a later blending stage. After a period of maturation and/or marrying, the mixture is filtered and bottled. It is rich and aromatic, often served hot. 55% vol.

Marc • French **pomace** brandy. Before distillation, the pomace is sealed into airtight vats for several days to allow build-up of aromas; these add to the final bouquet of the brandy. Marc is distilled in most of the wine-producing areas of France but has only local importance. Perhaps the best-known are those from Burgundy and Champagne where many of the great vineyards produce their own marcs.

Marrying • The practice of leaving distillates which have been recently blended to 'settle' or 'merge' for a period — usually a matter of weeks or months — prior to bottling. It is not an ageing process, rather a homogenisation of previously disparate spirits.

Mashing • In whisky making, the mixing together of sugar-rich **malt grist** with hot water in a large container called a mash tun in order to extract the sugars. Mashing is done several times and results in sugar-rich water called **wort** to which yeasts are added to begin fermentation of the **wash**.

Mei kwei lu • Spicy, sweet liqueur with aroma of roses. 44% vol.

Michiu • Rice liquor, the most popular traditional alcoholic drink in Taiwan. It is made from the local *pon-lai* rice which is fermented into a liquor and then distilled. It is blended with silent spirit made from molasses and bottled at between 20% and 30% vol. Mizhiu tou is the unblended rice distillate; 35% vol.

Middle cut • See **Heart**

Mizuwari • In Japan, a mixture of whisky and water, one of the most popular ways of drinking it.

Ng ka py • Well-flavoured Chinese spirit that is rich in extract and regarded also as a nutritional supplement. As in the preparation of **chiu yeh ching**, herbs and spices are pulverised, blended and then packed in bags prior to maceration in **kao liang** sorghum spirit. Other botanicals are cooked in pressure cookers to produce extracts which are added to the infusion together with caramel, syrup and maltose. After a settling period, ng ka py is bottled. It is fragrant with good body and concentrated flavour; 46% vol.

Nosing • Wines are tasted, spirits are nosed, *ie* sniffed gently; tasting spirits quickly brings on anaesthesia and results in unreliable decisions as to a product's merits. Blenders of whisk(e)y, cognac and other spirits work entirely by nose and drink their products only outside office hours, if at all. Spirit-nosing should be less vigorous than the equivalent activity with wines — your sense of smell is just as vulnerable as your sense of taste — and adding a little water to a distillate helps aromas flourish; the water creates a chemical reaction which releases heat and with it the best fragrances the spirit has to offer.

Oak • The almost-universal type of wood used in the manufacture of casks for maturing wines and some spirits. Not all oaks are the same, some allowing faster ageing due to their having larger pores, some endowing spirits with certain flavour components more than others, and so on. Usually subtle oakiness, with its appealing, vanilla ice-cream fragrance, is seen as a positive attribute, while full-blown woodiness is not, so the art is in the compromise. New oak can swamp a spirit with aroma and taste so it tends to be used a little at a time; on the other hand, all barrels used to mature Kentucky bourbon must, by law, be new so that the oak influences in the whiskey are very much to the fore.

Bourbon producers sell their 'old' barrels on to distillers in Scotland and elsewhere for re-use. Access to casks that have been filled with spirit once or twice previously is important to a distiller because, with their muted influences, he can use them and retain precise control of what happens to his distillate. A cask's capacity to pass on aroma and flavour will depend on how long *in toto* it has previously held spirit and most companies have a computer file on every cask in their possession with a complete history of what it has held to date. After around 30 years most barrels are spent in terms of imparting influence so they are used as simple containers, thrown out or put through **dechar-rechar**. See **Ageing**. (Sawdust from scrapped whiskey barrels imparts a wonderful extra flavour to barbecued steaks!)

Pagoda head · In Scotland, the distinctive pyramidal chimneys with metal terminals which topped the drying kilns of distilleries. An attractive architectural feature that revealed to anyone at a distance that here was a distillery, many have been kept in position even though the kilns that sat below them have long since disappeared, and most new distilleries incorporate false pagoda heads into their designs for ornament.

Peat reek · The degree to which peat smoke permeates the malt used in the production of a given whisk(e)y. A distiller might specify light, medium or heavy to his maltster according to whether his whisk(e)y is subtle or smoky in flavour, and would take into account whether there was peat in the water used to make the whisk(e)y. Peat reek usually ranges from five to 60 parts per million.

Pomace · The debris of grapeskins, stalks and pips left behind after the pressing of the grapes during wine making. Also, for the purpose of making grappa and other pomace brandies, the lees remaining after fermentation in wine making.

Proof · See **Alcoholic strength**.

Prohibition · At 5:30pm precisely on the 23rd of December 1933 one of the most detested pieces of legislation in American history, the 18th Amendment, was finally laid to rest. Its abolition returned the US to a normal way of westernised life: people could drink alcohol without fear of persecution. That had not been the case throughout the country since a minute after midnight January 17th 1920. It was then that the Volstead Act became law. Andrew J. Volstead was representative for Minnesota and a devout 'dry'. The flames of the temperance movement had been sweeping across the country for some time, fanned by religious zealots who regarded any form of liquor as temptation from the devil. Before 1920 some states had already outlawed alcohol; Volstead put in motion the tool to make it national.

Tending to the wash in a whiskey distillery.

In retrospect, such a move begs belief. The outlawing of legalised drinking gave the green light to hoodlums looking for a new racket to cash in on: liquor became a license to distil money. Whiskey was smuggled in from Canada, Scotland and Ireland; rum from the Caribbean, but neither in enough quantities to satisfy a parched nation. Gangs began making their own, sometimes with fatal consequences for the desperate imbiber. Meanwhile gangsters fought to gain control of the speakeasies and bootlegging became its own industry as people began to forget what the real stuff tasted like. Some distilleries were later allowed to distil bourbon to keep enough in stock for doctors to prescribe. But the effects of prohibition were felt long after its ending: many Irish distillers went out of business, as did those in Kentucky. The industry was never quite the same again.

Rancio · Characteristic of very old brandy, an aroma or taste of ultra-mellow, almost over-ripe maturity; the beginnings of decay, but attractively so.

Rectification · The refining or distilling of alcohol to a very high strength and hence great purity.

Sake · Japanese rice wine. It is only very occasionally distilled.

Saladin box • In Scotch whisky production, a semi-mechanised malting system used for several decades in the mid-20th century whereby chain-driven turners travelled up and down long open concrete troughs, or boxes, turning the barley inside them. M. Saladin was the French inventor.

Self whisk(e)y • The product of a single distillery bottled and sold as a stand-alone whisk(e)y rather than, or in addition to, being used solely in blending.

Serpentin • French rendering of **Worm**.

Sherry cask • Oak cask used for maturing whisk(e)y that has previously been used in Jerez, Spain, for fermenting and/or maturing oloroso sherry. Such casks endow sweetness, richness, flavour and body to the whisk(e)y spirit.

Shiel • In Scotch whisky production, a flat wooden shovel or paddle used to turn germinating barley in a floor maltings.

Shochu • Japanese white spirit distilled from a number of different materials. Shochu is thought to have originated in the 15th century on Okinawa in the Ryukyu Islands, which at the time were not part of Japan. Once it had reached Kyushu, the southernmost island of the main Japanese archipelago, it was, as a by-product of sake production, a purely local spirit, but since the 1960s, its popularity has spread throughout Japan. Kyushu is still the main production area and Okinawa shochu is called awamori, or millet brandy.

There are two types of shochu: *otsu* is made in pot stills from barley, rye, buckwheat, corn, sweet potato, rice and even straight sugar, and carries the flavours of these; *ko* is made in continuous stills from molasses and carries no obvious taste. It is clean and dry in style. Both types use malted rice for fermentation.

Shochu is drunk on its own, or with water, cold or hot (50/50 is called *gogowari*), or on the rocks, or with a mixer. *Chuhai* is short for 'shochu highball' and is mixed with soda, flavoured syrup, ice and a slice of lime. Strength is mostly around the 25% vol mark but they go up to 40% vol.

Silent • Silent spirit is distillate that is neutral, that is it is highly rectified and has little or no aroma or flavour of the fermented source from which it derives.

The silent season at a distillery was originally the period in the summer when production stopped due to lack of water. Today it is a convenient time for staff to take holidays and for repairs and maintenance work to be carried out. A silent distillery is one that has been closed, possibly for good. Such distilleries' production plant is either dismantled or 'mothballed' pending possible subsequent reopening, but their warehousing function of storing and maturing casks of spirit usually remains intact.

Single malt • A pot still whisk(e)y made from malted barley by an individual distillery. As with a single-vineyard wine, a malt from a single distillery is unique and particular to the stills, raw materials and geography which produced it. A vatted malt is a blend of two or more malt whiskeys.

Singleton • Alternative name for a single malt whisk(e)y.

Spirit safe • The traditional control box made of glass and brass used by a distiller to guide the separate fractions of spirit coming off a pot still into the appropriate containers. In Scotch whisky making the spirit safe is locked by the excise authorities and there is no physical access to the spirit passing through it and the distiller must work by sight alone; in gin making the top may be freely lifted so that the distiller may nose the spirit.

Stills • A simple still can be any kettle or pan where an alcoholic liquid may be boiled and its vapours condensed and collected. In distilling spirits the traditional vessel is the pot still which remains the best for retaining aroma and flavour. The pot still has to be loaded and distilled a batch at a time and usually spirit it produces must be distilled twice, so it is time-consuming and labour-intensive. A variant of the pot still is the Lomond still, of which a few remain in Scottish distilleries. These have stubby, cylindrical necks and produce heavier spirit than the customary swan-neck variety.

Pot stills are usually worked in pairs so that first and second distillations may be carried out at the same time, if need be. Where stills are paired in this way, first distillations take place in the low wines, or wash still and the second in the spirit still. Since distillation reduces volume by 90%, wash stills are usually much bigger than spirit stills.

In 1828 Robert Stein, of the Haig whisky family, invented a still that produced spirit continuously and Aeneas Coffey's version of it, developed two years later, became the basis of a revolution in the production of cheap, plentiful, good-quality spirit. Continuous stills are also known as Coffey or patent stills.

Straight · Straight whiskey, as in the USA, indicates one which has not had neutral spirit added to it before bottling. Whiskey mixed with neutral spirit is described as a blend. A straight brandy produced in California will have had no flavouring enhancers such as prune juice or local sherry-style wine added to it.

Tails · The third and final fraction of the distillation run from a pot still. This is the tail-end of the run (hence the French term 'queues') and, like the **heads**, is held aside from inclusion in the **heart**, or middle cut, of wholesome spirit. Tails, or feints, are held back because the strength is weak and oils in the spirit vaporise and taint it.

Tronçais · One of the two great French forests (the other is **Limousin**) which yield oak for casks in which wines and cognac are aged.

Uisge beatha · 'Water of life' or 'aqua vitae' in Scots Gaelic. The word 'whisky' is derived from the first part (or the Irish Gaelic equivalent, *uisce*).

Testing grain alcohol in the high-tech environment at Bols.

Van der Hum · South African liqueur made from native bitter oranges called naartjies. The drink was very popular with the Dutch settlers in South Africa, particularly since the Cape brandy they produced was so dreadful, but the name of the distiller who first made it was, unkindly, quickly forgotten. Hence they would ask for some 'What's-his-name's brandy', the uncertainty rendered in Afrikaans as Van der Hum. The name is generic and a number of different brands are produced.

Vatted malt · See **Single malt**.

Vinacce · Italian word for **pomace** used in the production of **grappa** (singular *vinaccia*).

Warehouses · In Scotland, the buildings where casks of whisky spirit are matured. The traditional type had beaten-earth floors which held moisture, humidifying the air during extended dry spells, and absorbing dampness in very wet weather.

Wash • In whiskey-making, the weak ale produced by fermentation of the **wort** and which is distilled in the wash still.

Weinbrand • The official descriptive term for grape brandy in Germany. *Deutscher weinbrand* means it has been made in Germany and *alter* or *uralt* (old) used in conjunction means it has been aged in wood for a minimum of one year.

Whiskey • Until the invention of the continuous still, there was never a doubt about the validity of whiskey. It was always the product of copper stills, but depending on the country in which it was made, from a grain mash consisting of malted and/or unmalted barley, rye, wheat or maize. Whichever, the spirit was quite heavy and pungent. The continuous still produced an altogether lighter spirit. And because it was continuous it was a more efficient and, therefore, cheaper method of distillation. By distilling more efficiently, much of the character of the spirit was lost. Yet a new breed of whiskey merchant, the blender, spotted possible advantages in this. By mixing a straight whiskey with that from a continuous still, a more uniform, softer taste could be created at a reduced price. Not only did they achieve this with Scotch but also Irish, though Dublin companies such as Jameson and Powers were so incensed by this affront to their national drink that they jointly published a book, "Truths about Whiskey", condemning the practice.

In truth, anyone asking for a whiskey in a British pub had little control on what they were getting, much to the resentment of the pot still distillers. Despite the open hostility between the two camps, it was an altogether more unlikely source, the officials of Islington Borough Council who, in November 1905, decided to bring the matter to a head. They issued twelve summonses against whiskey sellers in their area, all purveyors of products 'not of the nature, substance and quality demanded' under Section Six of the Sale of Food and Drugs Act, 1875. Two test cases against a

publican and off-licensee were successful: they were both found guilty and fined, despite the fact the Off-licenses Association had teamed up with the now wealthy grain distillers to fight the case.

However, the final word on the matter was said in 1909. A year later a Royal Commission on Whiskey had begun to look into the 'What is Whiskey?' question. Their findings, after lengthy and scientifically detailed hearings, was that spirit produced from continuous 'patent' stills had as much right to be regarded as whiskey as that made from traditional pot stills.

Whiskey Rebellion • Wherever whiskey was made, as a natural sustenance to a demanding way of life, tax would surely follow. It happened to the Irish and the Scots; and in 1791 it happened to the Americans. A great many of those Americans were the same Irish and Scots who had fled Britain and its taxes on their precious 'water of life'.
At the time America was still a fledgling country, fresh from its ousting of the British. Irish and Scottish settlers had moved into western Pennsylvania and those with the skill and apparatus to distil found this a very useful way of supplementing their income. So when it was decreed that farmers must pay either an annual fee for the right to distil or a sum for each gallon they produced there was an uproar.

The revolt began with meetings and petitions, and though the government tinkered with the new law to try to quell the bad feeling, it was already too late. Over 50 writs had been issued, each one capable of ruining the farmer concerned. By 1794 skirmishes had started between the Whiskey Boys and government soldiers; there were deaths and buildings were torched. Leaders of the rebellion aimed for independence from the United States and formed an army which marched on Pittsburgh in a display of solidarity. However, the 6,000 rebels began to disperse when George Washington sent in around twice that number to restore order and round up the ringleaders. Apart from a couple more deaths it was a relatively quiet yet conclusive exercise, and although two men were tried and sentenced to death, they were later freed.

Whisky Crash • The 1890's witnessed unprecedented boom years in the Scotch whisky industry. Wherever you looked in Scotland, Speyside in particular, new distilleries were being built and a generation of Whisky Barons — men who were making a fortune blending and marketing their own-brand whiskies — were in their prime. Whisky had become big business. The highway, for some, to vast wealth and a lofty social position. But like all bubbles, it is only a matter of time before the burst. With extensive overproduction of malt and grain whisky it was always likely to be sooner rather than later. Finally it was the collapse of the Pattison Empire which not only hastened the industry's decline, but soiled its reputation in the process.

In 1887 two brothers, Robert and Walter Pattison, formed the blending company Pattison, Elder and Co. Its success was swift and the brothers not only bought expensive houses in keeping with their newly-found status, they also moved the company into premises opulent even by distillers' standards. By 1894 there were grave doubts about Pattison's true financial position, but it was a further five years before those fears were realised.

When the company was floated, its worth was significantly over-valued by the brothers with the aid of a cooked balance sheet. Their fraudulent behaviour carried on for three more years before the company was forced into liquidation in 1899 with debts of £500,000 and assets valued at very much less. The brothers were gaoled for their activities but their personal ignominy was nothing compared to the devastation within the industry.

Pattison had operated a complex network of credit from distiller to distiller, broker to broker who were now short of cash. Worse still, banks took a dim view of an industry where such fraud could flourish. Consequently where loans and overdrafts were once freely given, many were now called in, forcing the closure of several distilleries. It was many years before confidence seeped back into the Scotch whisky industry. Even today caution prevails.

Whisky or Whiskey? — By convention, the 'ky' spelling refers to Scotch, Canadian and Japanese whisky/whiskies, and everything else is 'key/keys'. Individual brand-owners often opt for the form that is not typical in their local industry, such as Maker's Mark bourbon which uses '-ky'.

Worm • The spiral-shaped copper cooling pipe traditionally used to condense pot-still distillation vapours. It sat in a tub of cold water.

Wort • In whiskey-making, the sugar-rich water yielded by **mashing**. Yeast is added to the wort and it ferments to produce the weak ale called **wash**, which goes on to be distilled.

Vieilles faibles • A very weak solution of brandy — usually cognac — which is used to bring down the alcohol level of an eau-de-vie to bottling strength. It should be made from the same brandy it is reducing and, if done properly, the process is carried out over a period of years; often as many as five or six.

Traditionally designed gas-fired pot stills for Hennessy cognac.

Index of Brand Names

256

Luksusowa vodka Poland 162
Lungarotti grappa Italy 112
Lysholm Linie akvavit Norway 215

Macallan whisky Scotland 43
Macduff whisky Scotland 44
Macieira brandy Brazil 147
Mackinlay whisky Scotland 44
Mainstay cane spirit South Africa 204
Maker's Mark bourbon USA 64
Mandarine Napoléon liqueur Belgium 240
Maqintosh whisky India 81
Mariachi tequila Mexico 210
Mariacron brandy Germany 107
Marolo grappa Italy 112
Marquis de Caussade armagnac France 99
Marquis de Montesquiou armagnac France 99
Marquis de Puységur armagnac France 100
Martel brandy Brazil 141
Martell cognac France 93
Martignac brandy Slovakia 149
Mascaro brandy Spain 120
Paul Masson brandy USA 125
McDowell's whisky India 81
Melcher's Rat brandy Germany 107
Mellow-Wood brandy South Africa 132
Men's Club whisky India 81
Metaxa brandy Greece 148
Metaxa ouzo Greece 223
Meukow cognac France 94
Meyboom genever Belgium 187
Midleton whiskey Ireland 57
Glen Millar whisky Scotland 55
Miltonduff whisky Scotland 44
Monopolowa vodka Poland 162
Mons Ruber brandy South Africa 132
de Montal armagnac France 100
Mount Gay rum Barbados 199
Moskovskaya vodka Russia 156

Nardini grappa Italy 113
Natu Nobilis whisky Brazil 80
Nemunas gin Lithuania 188
Nikka whisky Japan 75
Nonino grappa Italy 113
Notaris genever Holland 178
Noyac brandy Armenia 143

Oban whisky Scotland 44
Okhotnichya vodka Russia 156
Old whisky Japan 76
Old Cask rum Trinidad 200
Old Charter bourbon USA 64
Old Château brandy South Africa 133
Old Crow bourbon USA 65

Old Elgin whisky Scotland 44
Old Fitzgerald bourbon USA 65
Old Forester bourbon USA 65
Old Oak rum Trinidad 200
Old Parr whisky Scotland 44
Old Smuggler whisky Scotland 45
Olmeca tequila Mexico 210
Olof Bergh brandy South Africa 130
Original Bushmills whiskey Ireland 55, 57
Oro Pilla brandy Italy 109
Osborne brandy Spain 119
Otard cognac France 94
Oude Meester brandy South Africa 133
Ouzo 12 ouzo Greece 223

Paarl Rock brandy South Africa 134
Paddy whiskey Ireland 57
Pampero rum Venezuela 203
Passport whisky Scotland 45
Pastis 51 anise France 220
Don Pedro brandy Mexico 141
Peket De Houyeu genever Belgium 187
James E. Pepper bourbon USA 65
Pepe Lopez tequila Mexico 212
Père François calvados France 102
Père Magloire calvados France 102
Perfect vodka Poland 163
Pernod anise France 220
Pertsovka vodka Russia 156
Pieprzówka vodka Poland 163
Pig's Nose whisky Scotland 45
Pimm's liqueur United Kingdom 240
Pinch whisky Scotland 45
Pirassununga white spirit Brazil 205
Player Special whisky Scotland 46
Plymouth gin England 185
Poit Dubh whisky Scotland 45
Polignac cognac France 95
Polish Pure Spirit vodka Poland 163
Polmos Goldwasser liqueur Poland 240
Polmos Winiak Luksusowy brandy Poland 149
Polonaise vodka Russia 163
Posolskaya vodka Russia 157
Power whiskey Ireland 58
Presidente brandy Mexico 141
Pride of Strathspey whisky Scotland 46
Prima vodka Poland 163
Prince of Wales whisky Wales 85
Pshenichnaya vodka Russia 157
Punt e Mes bitters Italy 228
Pure Malt Black whisky Japan 76
Pure Malt Red whisky Japan 77
Pure Malt White whisky Japan 77
Pusser's rum British Virgin Islands 200
Ramazzotti bitters Italy 228
Ramazzotti sambuca Italy 222

Raynal/Three Barrels brandy France 104
Real Mackenzie whisky Scotland 46
Rebeka vodka Poland 163
Rebel Yell bourbon USA 66
Rémy Martin cognac France 95
Renault cognac France 96
Reserve whisky Japan 77
Ricard pastis France 221
Richelieu brandy South Africa 134
Riga Balsam/Melnais Balzams bitters Latvia 229
Rives Pitman gin Spain 189
RMS brandy USA 125
Robin cognac France 96
Romana sambuca Italy 222
Romano Levi grappa Italy 112
Ronsard brandy France 104
Royal whisky Japan 77
Royal Citation whisky Scotland 46
Royal Dark genever Holland 179
Royal Lochnagar whisky Scotland 46
Royal Mint Chocolate liqueur France 240
Royal Oak brandy South Africa 134
Royal Oak rum Trinidad 200
Royal Salute whisky Scotland 46
Ruche brandy France 104
Russkaya vodka Russian 157
Rye Base whisky Japan 78
Ryn brandy South Africa 134

S.S.Politician whisky Scotland 48
Sabra liqueur Israel 241
Sans Rival ouzo Greece 223
St Agnes brandy Australia 137
St George Spirit grappa USA 126
St Nicolaus brandy Poland 149
Samalens armagnac France 100
Sanchez Romate brandy Spain 119
São Francisco white spirit Brazil 205
Sauza tequila Mexico 212
Scapa whisky Scotland 47
Seagram's gin USA 189
Seagram's VO whisky Canada 72
Select vodka Poland 163
Sempé armagnac France 100
Sheep Dip whisky Scotland 47
Sibirskaya vodka Siberia 169
Sierra tequila Mexico 213
Singleton whisky Scotland 47
Slovignac brandy Czech 148
Smeets genever Belgium 187
Smirnoff vodka United Kingdom 166
Somerset Royal brandy England 145
Soplica vodka Poland 163
Southern Comfort liqueur USA 241
Speyburn whisky Scotland 47
Speyside whisky Scotland 47

General Index

Acknowledgments

The publishers would like to thank the following for their generous help with this book.

Absolut
Allied
Heather Angel 218
Angove's
Asbach
Aveleda
Bénédictine
Berger
Rick Bolen 124, 247
Bols
Bombay Spirits Company
Bonny Doon 126/Shmuel Thaler
Borco
Brown-Forman International Ltd
Bulmer Ltd
Michael Busselle 13 (top), 88, 99, 249
Buton
Calvados Boulard
Camel
Campari
Campbell
Camus
Cephas 82/Colin Culbert; 12,
    101Top/Daniel Czap; 61/John Heinrich;
    146/John Millwood; 88, 96 (both), 114,
    139, 146/Mick Rock; 188/Roy Stedall;
    105; 147/Helen Stylianou; 203/Graham
    Wicks
Ceretto
Chartreuse
Château de Laubade
Clear Creek
Cognac Information Center
Courvoisier
Danish Distillers
Danish Tourist Board/Ole Akhoj 214
Delon
Domecq
Drambuie
Patrick Eagar/Jan Traylen 144
Eckes AG
Filliers
Finlandia
Derek Forss 57

Fourcroy
Fratelli Branca
Galliano
Germain-Robin
Gibson International
Matthew Gloag
Godot Frères
Gonzalez Byass
Hardley, Dennis 16, 18, 19, 20, 23, 48
Heaven Hill
Henchell & Sohnlein
Hennessy
Herbertsons
Herradura
Heublein USA
Hiram Walker
Hooghoudt
Hutchison Library 130, 142, 165, 191,
    193, 195, 205, 206
Images 54, 59, 70 (top), 80, 135, 136,
    140, 141, 150, 151, 159, 176, 180,
    186, 190, 229
Japan National Tourist Office 73
KWV
Kirin-Seagram
Laird
Lang Bros.
Martin Leckie 22
Macallan
Maker's Mark
Mansell Collection 24, 154, 192 (top),
    181, 194, 198, 201, 221, 227
Marnier Lapostelle
Martell
Metaxa
Metzendorff
Mons Ruber
Nardini, Dita Bortolo
Nature Photographers' Ltd/Robin Bush
    174
Peter Newark 66, 72, 192 (bottom), 264
Nikka
Noyac
Nonino

Osborne
Pernod-Ricard
Polmos
Ronald Grant Archive 22, 39
Russia & Republics Photolibrary/Mark
    Wadlo 152, 155, 169, 170
St George Spirits
Sanchez Romate
Sauza
Seagram
Spectrum 101 (bottom), 122, 123, 153,
    157, 160, 167, 202, 216, 217, 231,
    232
Spink & Son Ltd 20 (top)
Stock
Suntory
Suze
Swedish Travel &Tourism/Ake Mokvist
    171
Torres
Underberg
United Distillers
UTO
Valdespino
Wenneker
World Pictures 128